C. MARVIN PATE

THE
END
OF THE
AGE
HAS
COME

THE THEOLOGY
OF PAUL

ZondervanPublishingHouse
Grand Rapids, Michigan

A Division of HarperCollins*Publishers*

The End of the Age Has Come
Copyright ©1995 by C. Marvin Pate

Requests for information should be addressed to:
  Zondervan Publishing House
  Grand Rapids, Michigan 49530

Library of Congress Cataloging in Publication Data
Pate, C. Marvin, 1952–
    The end of the age has come : the theology of Paul / C. Marvin Pate
      p. cm.
    Includes bibliographical references and index
    ISBN 0-310-38301-3 (softcover : alk. paper)
    1. Bible. N.T. Epistles of Paul—Criticism, interpretation, etc. 2.
Eschatology—History of doctrines—Early church, ca. 30–600. I. Title.
    BS2655.E7P38 1995
    225.9′2—dc20   94-33069
                                                                 CIP

Edited by Verlyn D. Verbrugge

Printed in the United States of America

94 95 96 97 98 99 /❖ DH / 10 9 8 7 6 5 4 3 2 1

CONTENTS

ABBREVIATIONS

I. PERIODICALS AND REFERENCE WORKS

CBQ	*Catholic Biblical Quarterly.*
ExpT	*Expository Times.*
FRLANT	Forschungen zur Religion und Literatur des Alten und Neuen Testaments.
HDS	Harvard Dissertation Series.
HR	*History of Religions.*
HTR	*Harvard Theological Review.*
JAAR	*Journal of the American Academy of Religion.*
JBL	*Journal of Biblical Literature.*
JES	*Journal of Ecumenical Studies.*
JETS	*Journal of the Evangelical Theological Society.*
JSNT	*Journal for the Study of the New Testament.*
JSNT Supp.Ser.	Journal for the Study of the New Testament Supplement Series.
JSOT	*Journal for the Study of the Old Testament.*
JTS	*Journal of Theological Studies*
KNT	Kommentar zum neuen Testament.
NIDNTT	*The New International Dictionary of New Testament Theology.*
NTS	*New Testament Studies.*
SB	H. L. Strack and P. Billerbeck, *Kommentar zum Neuen Testament aus Talmud und Midrash, I–IV.*
SBLDS	Society of Biblical Literature Dissertation Series.
SBLMS	Society of Biblical Literature Monograph Series.
SBT	Studies in Biblical Theology.
SJT	*Scottish Journal of Theology.*
SNTSMS	Society for New Testament Studies Monograph Series.
SPCK	Society for the Promotion of Christian Knowledge.
Supp.Nov.T	Supplements to Novum Testamentum.
TDNT	*Theological Dictionary of the New Testament.*
TJ	*Trinity Journal.*
WUNT	Wissenschaftliche Untersuchungen zum Neuen Testament.

| WZKM | *Wiener Zeitschrift für die Kunde des Morgenlandes.* |
| ZThK | *Zeitschrift für Theologie und Kirche.* |

II. COMMENTARIES

FBBS	Facet Books Biblical Studies.
HNTC	Harper New Testament Commentary.
ICC	International Critical Commentary.
NIGNTC	The New International Greek New Testament Commentary.
TNICNT	The New International Commentary on the New Testament.
WBC	Word Biblical Commentary.

III. BIBLICAL LITERATURE

[O.T.]	Isa.	Acts
Gen.	Jer.	Rom.
Ex.	Lam.	1 Cor.
Lev.	Ezek.	2 Cor.
Num.	Dan.	Gal.
Deut.	Hos.	Eph.
Josh.	Joel	Phil.
Judg.	Amos	Col.
Ruth	Obad.	1 Thess.
1 Sam.	Jonah	2 Thess.
2 Sam.	Mic.	1 Tim.
1 Kings	Nah.	2 Tim.
2 Kings	Hab.	Titus
1 Chron.	Zeph.	Philem.
2 Chron.	Hag.	Heb.
Ezra	Zech.	James
Neh.	Mal.	1 Peter
Est.		2 Peter
Job	[N.T.]	1 John
Ps. (Pss.)	Matt.	2 John
Prov.	Mark	3 John
Eccl.	Luke	Jude
Song	John	Rev.

IV. EXTRA-CANONICAL LITERATURE

Apocrypha and Pseudepigrapha

2 Bar.	2 Baruch
Jub.	Book of Jubilees
T.Ab.	Testament of Abraham
T.Isa.	Testament of Issachar
T.Dan	Testament of Dan
T.Zeb.	Testament of Zebulon
T.Ben.	Testament of Benjamin
T.Reub.	Testament of Reuben
T.Jud.	Testament of Judah
T.Levi	Testament of Levi
Sib.Oracles	Sibylline Oracles
Apoc.Mos.	Apocalypse of Moses
Pss.Sol.	Psalms of Solomon
Wisd.Sol.	Wisdom of Solomon
As.Moses	Assumption of Moses
Apoc.Elijah	Apocalypse of Elijah
Ecclus.	Ecclesiasticus

Qumran

CD	Cairo Damascus Document
4Q	Flor.Florilegium
1QH	Thanksgiving Hymns
1QM	War Scroll
1QpHab.	Pesher on Habakkuk
1QS	Manual of Discipline
1QSb	Appendix to 1QS

Midrashim

Gen.R.	Genesis Rabbah
Exod.R.	Exodus Rabbah
Num.R.	Numbers Rabbah
Sif.Deut.	Sifre Deuteronomy
SongR.	Song of Solomon Rabbah

Talmud

b.Menahoth	Babylonian Menahoth
b.Sanh.	Babylonian Sanhedrin
b.Shab.	Babylonian Shabbath
b.Sotah	Babylonian Sotah
p.Berakoth	Palestinian Berakoth
Pirke Ab.	Pirke Aboth

New Testament Apocrypha

Ep.Barn.	Epistle of Barnabus
Gos.Eg.	Gospel of the Egyptians
Gos.Phil.	Gospel of Philip

Aramaic Targumim

Targum Isa.	Targum Isaiah

Josephus

Ant.	Antiquity of the Jews

ACKNOWLEDGMENTS

Writing and publishing a book is a process that involves numerous people. It is therefore with sincere appreciation that I make mention of some of those who collaborated with me in this project. First, I should like to thank the staff of Zondervan Publishing House/HarperCollins Publishers for accepting this manuscript and then preparing it for publication. In this regards, special thanks goes to Dr. Verlyn D. Verbrugge, not only for his editing skills, but also for his theological insights that were so helpful to me along the way. Next, I wish to express my heartfelt gratitude to my typist, Mrs. Cathy Wegner. Her indefatigable effort and her expertise were indispensable to the task. Also to my research assistants and good friends, Mr. Bill Search and Mr. Ryan Hannah, I offer my enduring thanks for their attendance to the details of the bibliography, confirming the references, and a myriad of other matters related to the book. Furthermore, I would be remiss not to call attention to my students' perceptive comments and provocative questions, which have served as a catalyst for the work. Finally, I am so very grateful for my godly, loving wife Sheryl and our delightful and dear daughter Heather Lee. Hopefully, the latter will one day grow up to love the writings of the apostle Paul as much as her father has grown to love them.

—C. Marvin Pate

I

PAUL: THE MAN, HIS MESSAGE, AND HIS LETTERS

INTRODUCTION

The apostle Paul, like the message of the cross he preached, was something of a paradox, a study in contrasts. His own testimony is eloquent witness in this regard. He was a Jewish rabbi transformed into a Christian theologian (Phil. 3:5–11); a persecutor of the church turned apologist for the gospel (1 Cor. 15:9–11); simultaneously sinner and saint (Rom. 7:13–25; 2 Tim. 1:12–16); a citizen of two kingdoms—Christ's (Col. 1:13; 2 Tim. 4:18) and Caesar's (Acts 22:28; Rom. 13:1–7). Paul says that he can live with or without the amenities of life (Phil. 4:11–12). He claims that he is exclusively focused on Christ (Phil. 3:13–14), while being an astute observer of his day (2 Tim. 4:3–4).

Stark contrast apparently even extended to Paul's appearance for, according to the vivid picture of him reported in the apocryphal *Acts of Paul and Thecla*, the apostle was, "a man of little stature, thin haired upon the head, crooked in the legs, of good state of body, with eyebrows joining, and nose somewhat hooked, full of grace, for sometimes he appeared like a man, and sometimes he had the face of an angel" (cf. 1 Cor. 2:3–4; 2 Cor. 10:10). Perhaps the most profound antinomy characterizing Paul's message was his resolute conviction that the end of time had arrived *within* human history, in the climactic events of Christ's death and resurrection. He writes in 1 Corinthians 10:11 that, in light of this, Christians are the ones "upon whom the ends of the ages have come" (pers. tr.). This assertion is pregnant with meaning, the truth of which forms the basis for the following study and calls for some introductory remarks.

Our point of departure for grasping Paul, arguably the most important figure in Christianity (except of course, for Jesus) is to appreciate the force that drove him. The Old Testament, and the Judaism that resulted from it, viewed the structure of reality as comprised of two basic periods—this age and the age to come (Isa. 40; Dan. 2, 7, 12; Joel 2; Zech. 9–14; *1 QH* 3; *1 QS* 4; *4 Ezra* 4, 7; *2 Bar.* 44; etc.).[1] The former of these was identified with the present time, which has been given over to sin and suffering because of the fall of Adam and Eve; but it will one glorious day be replaced by the latter, with its inbreaking of the kingdom of God and attendant righteousness and peace. These two eras were thought to be consecutive in nature, with the arrival of the Messiah effecting the eschatological, or end-time, shift of the two ages.[2] Gordon Fee captures the New Testament's modification of the preceding Jewish twofold delineation:

> The absolutely essential framework of the self-understanding of primitive Christianity . . . is an eschatological one. Christians had come to believe that, in the event of Christ, the new (coming) age had dawned, and that, especially through Christ's death and resurrection and the subsequent gift of the Spirit, God had set the future in motion, to be consummated by yet another coming (*Parousia*) of Christ. Theirs was therefore an essentially eschatological existence. They lived "between the times" of the beginning and the consummation of the end. Already God had secured their . . . salvation; already they were the people of the future, living the life of the future in the present age—and enjoying its benefits. But they still awaited the glorious consummation of this salvation. Thus

---

[1]For a convenient survey of the Old Testament's and Judaism's perceptions of the two-age structure, see French L. Arrington, *Paul's Aeon Theology in 1 Corinthians* (Washington, D.C.: University Press of America, 1978), 66–112.

[2]Not all Jewish apocalyptic works in the Second Commonwealth period envisioned the age to come as associated with a Messiah; see, for example, *Jub.* 31:18. For further discussion of this issue as well as other matters on this issue, consult the standard treatment of Jewish apocalypticism by D. S. Russel, *The Method and Message of Jewish Apocalyptic* (Philadelphia: Westminster, 1964).

they lived in an essential tension between the "already" and the "not-yet."[3]

As we will repeatedly observe during the course of this work, such an eschatological view of Christian existence is thoroughgoing in Paul, especially the "already/not yet" paradox. In order to set the stage for the discussions that follow, the present chapter situates Paul in the context of his day by orienting the reader to the contours of Paul's world, exploring different proposals claiming to be the key to his thought, and identifying the *corpus*, or body, of his writings.

A. THE MAN: THE CONTOURS OF PAUL'S WORLD

Paul did not live in a vacuum; certain influences unavoidably shaped his life and thought. Three such dynamics will be surveyed here: Greco-Roman society, Judaism, and Christianity. These movements may be viewed as concentric circles. The Greek and Roman setting of the first century provided the outer sphere of influence—the cultural and political context. The Jewish world, the matrix from which early Christianity emerged, supplied Paul his formative environment, while his Damascus Road conversion initiated the core of his Christian experience.[4]

1. Greco-Roman Influence

The secular setting of Paul's day involved the interfacing of two powerful forces—Greek culture and Roman government. Thanks to Alexander the Great and his Hellenizing policy,[5] Greek culture dominated the world from 331 to 63 B.C.E.[6] Its chief

---

[3]Gordon D. Fee, *1 and 2 Timothy, Titus* (Peabody, Mass.: Hendrickson, 1988), 19.

[4]A thorough treatment of the background of early Christianity can be found in Everett Ferguson's, *Backgrounds of Early Christianity* (Grand Rapids: Eerdmans, 1987). The classic investigation of the mutual relationship existing between Hellenism and Judaism in the period of our interest is Martin Hengel's *Hellenism and Judaism*, 2 vols. (Philadelphia: Fortress, 1974).

[5]This policy is well described by Ferguson, *Backgrounds of Early Christianity*, 6–9.

[6]In deference to Judaism, New Testament scholars today use the abbreviations B.C.E. (Before the Common Era) and C.E. (Common Era), terms approximating the time periods once labeled B.C. and A.D.

contributions to society included: the establishment of a common language; the assimilation of rhetoric and the pursuit of philosophical questions raised by Socrates, Plato, Aristotle, etc.; adherence to a pantheon of deities; and an emphasis on the city, or *polis*, as the integrative center of the population. In one way or another, these elements impacted Paul.

The merger of Greek with other languages that it encountered created a common (*koinê*) trade dialect for the ancient world (ca. 300 B.C.E. to 300 C.E.). Though Paul's mother tongue as a Jew was Hebrew (more technically Aramaic, a cognate language of Hebrew), he also spoke and wrote fluently in Greek. The latter afforded at least two advantages over Semitic speech. First, as the *lingua franca* of the day, *koinê* Greek made world evangelization possible. Second, because of its grammatical precision, the Greek language was well suited for theological expression. Precedence for doing so could be found in the Septuagint, the Greek translation of the Hebrew Old Testament (ca. 250 B.C.E.) and the Bible Paul most often used.[7]

Greek literary style and philosophical speculation also influenced Paul. For example, the apostle used such rhetorical features as the diatribe (a Cynic-Stoic mode of argumentation; see Rom. 2:1–20; 3:1–9; 1 Cor. 9);[8] the fool's speech (a sarcastic and ironic method of exposing the weaknesses of one's critics, whose origin is attributed to Socrates; see 2 Cor. 10–13);[9] the tribulation lists (patterned after the suffering wise sage of Hellenism; see,

---

[7]This was called the Septuagint (abbreviated LXX), because according to the tradition of the *Letter of Aristeas*, a Jewish pseudepigraphical writing from about the second century B.C.E., it was written by seventy scribes. The Septuagint was the Bible of the dispersed Jews outside Palestine.

[8]The classic, though somewhat dated, analysis of Paul's reliance on the diatribe is that by Rudolf Bultmann, *Der Stil der paulinischen Predigt und die Kynisch-stoische Diatribe* (FRLANT, 13, Göttingen: Vandenhoeck & Ruprecht, 1910). A more recent study has been done by Stanley K. Stowers, *The Diatribe and Paul's Letter to the Romans* (SBLDS 57; Chico, Calif.: Scholars Press, 1981).

[9]One of the first to call attention to Paul's use of this form of argumentation in 2 Corinthians 10–13 was H. D. Betz, *Der Apostel Paulus und die sokratische Tradition. Beiträge zur Historischen Theologie* (Tübingen: J. C. B. Mohr [Paul Siebeck], 1972).

for example, 1 Cor. 4:9–13; 2 Cor. 4:7–12; 6:3–10);[10] not to mention the Greek epistolary genre that forms the very structure of Paul's letters.[11] That the apostle was conversant with Greek philosophy is evident in some of the terminology he employs ("freedom" [Gal. 5:1, 13]; "conscience" [Rom. 2:15; 1 Cor. 8:7, 10, 12; 10:25–29; 2 Cor. 5:11]; "all that you need" [2 Cor. 9:8]; etc.);[12] the leading thinkers he quotes (1 Cor. 15:32–33; Titus 1:12; cf. Acts 17:24); the conceptual heritage he shares (note, for example, the possible influence of the Platonic contrast of spirit and matter [2 Cor. 5:1–10];[13] the Stoic idea of the divine reason permeating the cosmos [1 Cor. 8:6; etc.];[14] and the Hellenistic household code of ethics reflected in Eph. 5:18–6:9 and Col. 3:18–4:1).[15]

Paul's encounter with Greco-Roman religious beliefs manifests itself in various ways. He gives advice on whether or not Christians should eat meat sacrificed to the pagan deities (1 Cor. 8; 10). He forbids the church from adopting the promiscuous tendencies of the cultic centers of the day (1 Cor. 6:12–20; 14:1–35; 1 Tim. 2:11–15; etc.). He counters Caesar worship with the admonition to believers to be loyal to Christ (Rom. 10:9; Titus 2:11–13;

---

[10]See John T. Fitzgerald, *Cracks in an Earthen Vessel. An Examination of the Catalogues of Hardships in the Corinthians Correspondence* (SBLDS 99; Atlanta: Scholars Press, 1988).

[11]The influence of Greek letter writing on Paul's correspondences is explored by, among others: Adolf Deissmann, "Prolegomena to the Biblical Letters and Epistles," in *Bible Studies* (Edinburgh: T & T Clark, 1901), 1–59; John Lee White, *The Form and Function of the Body of the Greek Letter* (SBLDS 2; Missoula, Mont.: Scholars Press, 1972); David E. Aune, *The New Testament in Its Literary Environment* (Philadelphia: Westminster, 1987), chaps. 5–6.

[12]Conveniently documented by Joseph Fitzmyer, *Pauline Theology: A Brief Sketch*, 2d ed. (Englewood Cliffs, N.J.: Prentice Hall, 1989), 15.

[13]The influence of Platonic philosophy on Paul's writings is a much debated subject. I am inclined to see its impact more on the periphery, rather than at the heart, of his thought; see my work on 2 Corinthians 4:16–5:10, one of the most celebrated Pauline passages reputedly evincing the Platonic dualistic contrast of body and soul, *Adam Christology as the Exegetical and Theological Substructure of 2 Corinthians 4:7–5:21* (Lanham, Md.: University Press of America, 1991).

[14]See Ferguson's fine description of the Stoicism current during Paul's day (*Backgrounds of Early Christianity*, 281–94).

[15]These household ethics are called the *Haustafel* (house-table). For a useful digest of their origin and early Christian adaptation, see Peter O'Brien's discussion in *Colossians, Philemon* (WBC 44; Waco, Tex.: Word, 1982), 214–19.

etc.). On a more positive note, some have thought that Paul formulated his faith in Christ against the backdrop of the Mystery Religions (note, for example, the possible contact of such with Paul's imagery of baptism and the Lord's Supper).[16]

Finally, the importance and influence of city life bequeathed to the first century C.E. by ancient Greece appears in the apostle's literature. For example, he uses Greek commercial language (e.g., "charge" in Philem. 18), he refers to the Hellenistic slave trade that infested the cities (Rom. 7:14; 1 Cor. 7:22), and he alludes to the Greek games (1 Cor. 9:24–27; Phil. 2:16). Above all, Paul's missionary travels to the major population centers of the day set the tone for the expansion of the church.

The pervasiveness of Hellenistic culture in Paul's time was coupled with the formidable presence of the Roman government. Three significant factors associated with the empire served to promote the advancement of Christianity: *pax Romana*, Roman legal jurisprudence, and freedom of travel and trade. These considerations undoubtedly suggested to Paul the idea that Roman rule was ultimately under the auspices of God (Rom. 13:1–7).

With Caesar Augustus (31 B.C.E.–14 C.E.), Rome's military might cast its shadow across the then-known world and, with it, a new sense of peace. Civil wars were ended; the threats of piracy on the seas and brigandage on land were quelled; order was established in the provinces.[17] Such a stable condition was conducive to propagating the gospel. The fullness of time had indeed come (Gal. 4:4).

The fame of ancient Roman law is well known. Its legislation was specific, its process was fair, and its jurisdiction transcended local authority (cf. Acts 18:12–16; 19:40; 21:31; 25:16; etc.).[18] Paul especially benefited from Roman law. Born a Roman

---

[16]This view is not nearly as fashionable today as it once was; see notes 48–50 of this chapter.

[17]Augustus' accomplishments were even praised by Jews; note the accolades heaped on him by Philo, the Jewish philosopher of the first century C.E. (*Embassy to Gaius*, 145–54).

[18]The definitive work on Roman law during the nascent stage of Christianity is by Adrian N. Sherwin-White, *Roman Society and Roman Law in the New Testament* (New York: Oxford University Press, 1963). For an excellent introduction to the topic, see John J. O'Rourke's article, "Roman Law and the Early

citizen, he could not be condemned or punished without due process (Acts 16:35–39), nor could he be scourged or crucified (Acts 22:25–29); he could appeal his case to the emperor in the event of injustice at the local level (Acts 25:10–12), and he was exempt from the poll tax. These privileges did not belong to the non-citizen, and Paul used them to his advantage in preaching the gospel.

Epictetus said of Rome, "Caesar has obtained for us a profound peace. There are neither wars nor battles, nor great robberies nor piracies, but we may travel at all hours, and sail from east to west" (*Discourses* 3.13.9). This statement bespeaks of the freedom of travel and flourishing trade that accompanied Roman rule. Sturdy roads, safe ships, common coinage, effective communication, and the interchange of goods combined to produce a bustling, unified world with a cosmopolitan spirit. All of this paved the way for Paul's missionary enterprise.

2. Jewish Upbringing

Paul was born a Jew, as his name "Saul" indicates (see Acts 7:58; 8:1, 3; etc.).[19] Moreover, in Philippians 3:5 (cf. 2 Cor. 11:28), Paul proudly identifies himself as "a Hebrew of Hebrews" (probably with reference to his ability to speak the Palestinian language). Three aspects of his Jewish upbringing call for comment: his geographical orientation, sociological status, and theological training.

Paul's early geographical orientation was twofold—he was born in Tarsus, the capital of the Roman province of Cilicia in

Church" in *The Catacombs and the Colosseum. The Roman Empire as the Setting of Primitive Christianity*, eds. Stephen Benko and John J. O'Rourke (Valley Forge, Pa.: Judson, 1971), 165–86.

[19]Acts 13:9 says that Saul was simultaneously called Paul, thus dispelling the common misconception that the apostle's name was changed from Saul to Paul at his conversion. It was normal in antiquity for Jews to have both Semitic and Roman names. A Roman name consisted of three parts: a first name (*praenomen*), a family name (*nomen*), and a surname (*cognomen*). Concerning the apostle, we only know the last of these—*Paulos*. See the discussions by Joseph A. Fitzmyer, *Paul and His Theology. A Brief Sketch*, 2–3 and D. A. Carson, Douglas J. Moo, and Leon Morris, *An Introduction to the New Testament* (Grand Rapids: Zondervan, 1992), 216.

Asia Minor (Acts 21:39; 22:3),[20] but raised in Jerusalem. As such, Paul was a dispersion Jew,[21] which accounts for his exposure to Hellenism. It is possible, though debatable, that Paul's later livelihood as a leather maker (tentmaker?, see Acts 18:3; 1 Cor. 4:12) may have received its impetus from the fact that Tarsians traded in leather goods and *cilicium* (derived from the name Cilicia), a cloth woven from the hair of the black goats that populated the slopes of the Taurus mountains. "The black tents of Tarsus were used by caravans, nomads, and armies all over Asia Minor and Syria."[22]

How Paul's family came to reside in Tarsus is a matter of speculation. Long ago, Sir William Ramsay proposed the theory that Paul's ancestry formed part of the colony of Jews that the Syrian ruler Antiochus Epiphanes transplanted from Palestine to Tarsus, in 171/170 B.C.E. These families became influential and powerful in the governing of that city and continued to be so during Roman times. If so, Paul's family would have been in Tarsus for four generations when he was born.[23] Be that as it may, Paul's parentage in Tarsus was noteworthy in that he was born a Jewish Roman citizen.

Even though Paul's family lived in Tarsus, it traced its origin to the tribe of Benjamin (Rom. 11:1; Phil. 3:6), a tribe that was

---

[20]On the advisability of using Acts, a secondary witness to Paul, see the defense of Lucan historical reliability by I. Howard Marshall, *Luke: Historian and Theologian* (Exeter: Paternoster, 1970).

[21]From the Babylonian captivity of Jerusalem (586 B.C.E.) on, most Jews lived outside of Israel and were called *Diaspora* Jews.

[22]John Polluck, *The Apostle* (Wheaton, Ill.: Victor, 1972), 5. This view has been criticized by Theodore Zahn (*Die Apostelgeschichte des Lukas* [KNT 5; Leipzig and Erlangen: Deichert, 1921], 633–34), who observes that: (1) *cilicium* was used for other things and only seldom for tents; (2) Paul's connection with Cilicia, Tarsus, and its production of *cilicium* becomes irrelevant if he moved to Jerusalem as a boy (Acts 22:3); (3) a Pharisee like Paul would not have chosen tentmaking because it was a despised trade. Ronald Hock approvingly develops Zahn's argument (*The Social Context of Paul's Ministry. Tentmaking and Apostleship* [Philadelphia: Fortress, 1980]).

[23]Sir William Ramsay, *St. Paul the Traveller and the Roman Citizen* (Grand Rapids: Baker, 1972), 32; *The Cities of St. Paul* (Grand Rapids: Baker, 1949), 169–86.

native to Palestine and a connection it preserved.[24] VanUnnik convincingly shows that Paul returned to his Palestinian roots as a youth, to be trained in Jerusalem. He argues that Acts 22:3 means that Paul was born in Tarsus but "brought up in Jerusalem" and educated in the latter by the well-known Pharisee, Gamaliel.[25] This suggests that the Palestinian influence on Paul during his formative years was substantial.[26]

Two pieces of data help to locate Paul on the sociological rung of Roman society, which had five levels or classes: senatorial aristocracy, equestrian (or knight) order, plebeians, freedmen, and slaves.[27] First, Paul was most likely from the plebeian or "middle" class, the hallmark of which was free-born citizenship, but a group not normally known for its economic stability. Second, if Ramsay's theory about Paul's parents being descendants of one of the original families of Tarsus is true, it would imply that he came from the upper echelon of the plebeian class. This suggestion is strengthened by the fact that Paul was independently employed as an artisan.

Paul's theological training was that of a Pharisee, an orthodox Jewish group of the first century (Phil. 3:5–6; see also Acts

---

[24]Eckhard J. Schnabel provides an interesting discussion of Paul's family history, as well as his socio-economic status (*Law and Wisdom from Ben Sira to Paul* [WUNT 16; Tübingen: J. C. B. Mohr (Paul Siebeck), 1985], 227–32).

[25]W. C. VanUnnik, *Tarsus or Jerusalem: The City of Paul's Youth* (London: Epworth, 1962).

[26]We should note Hengel's thesis that during the first century C.E. there was mutual interpenetration between Hellenism and Judaism (*Judaism and Hellenism*). If, as seems likely, Paul did grow up and receive his education in Jerusalem in a Pharisaic setting, his exposure to Greek thought and literature, as well as to the LXX, can be traced to the following sources (see Schnabel, *Law and Wisdom*, 230–31): (1) the school of Gamaliel, in which rudiments of Greek learning were probably passed on; (2) the period between Paul's return from Damascus after his conversion and the beginning of his ministry in Antioch, which is linked with Tarsus (cf. Acts 9:30; 11:25); (3) Paul's missionary career to the Gentiles, starting with the provinces of Syria and Cilicia, which confronted him with the Hellenistic world.

[27]One of the seminal studies on the socioeconomic status of early Christianity is by John G. Gager, "Religion and Social Class in the Early Roman Empire," in *The Catacombs and the Colosseum*, ed. Stephen Benko et al. (Valley Forge, Pa.: Judson, 1971), 99–120. Gager's research has sparked renewed interest in the subject.

23:6; 26:5). He studied under one of the leading Pharisaic scholars of the period, Gamaliel the Elder (Acts 22:3), who was a member of the Sanhedrin, the ruling religious body of Judaism (Acts 5:34). It is possible that, according to Acts 26:10, Paul was also a member of that elite company. He was zealous in striving to keep the written Old Testament Law (some 613 commandments) as well as the scribal oral traditions (perhaps as many as 6,000!). These rules were designed to be a protective fence around the Torah (Law) by reducing life to a system of rules that covered every conceivable circumstance. Furthermore, Saul the rabbi was well versed in rabbinic Old Testament interpretive techniques (e.g., see Rom. 5:12–21; 2 Cor. 3:1–4:6). Indeed, it is probable that he was in line to become one of the leading Torah teachers of his generation. So committed was he to his ancestral religion that he felt personally obligated to purge Judaism of its newest rival faith—Christianity (Acts 9:1; 1 Cor. 15:9–12).

3. Christian Experience

Christianity played the most significant role of all in Paul's life, forming the inner core of his being. Two foundational experiences of his Christian spirituality forever changed his direction: his conversion to Jesus as Messiah and his call to be an apostle to the Gentiles. Both of these are best understood from an eschatological perspective.

Paul probably never met the historical Jesus, but he did encounter the risen Christ on the road to Damascus (1 Cor. 9:1; 15:8; cf. Acts 9:17; 22:6–11; 26:16). One of the key characteristics of that appearance was "glory" or splendorous light (Acts 9:3; 22:6; 26:13; cf. 1 Cor. 15:8 with 15:20–49; see also 2 Cor. 4:6). Glory was a familiar concept to Judaism because it was used to describe the future resurrection body that awaited believers in heaven at the end of time (see Dan. 12:2–3; 1 Enoch 62:15–16; 2 Bar. 51:3–11; 4 Ezra 7:88; etc.). Jesus' resurrection body itself exuded the glory of God (Luke 24:26; Phil. 3:21; Rev. 1:14–15), thus signifying to Paul that the general resurrection that Judaism expected to occur at the end of the age had broken into present history through Christ. This revelation of the risen Savior to Paul had a soul-stirring effect on the very center of his thought. The experience made him realize that the crucified Jesus was none other than the resurrected Messiah, thus turning his life around.[28] The end of the age had dawned in Jesus, God's anointed one.[29] Joseph Fitzmeyer's comments are apropos on this point. Speaking of Paul's conversion, he writes:

> The experience on the road to Damascus taught him that the Messianic age had already begun. This introduced a new perspective into his view of salvation history. The eschaton, so avidly awaited before, had already begun—although a definitive stage was yet to be realized. . . . The Messiah had not yet come in glory. Paul realized that he (with all Christians) found himself in a double situation: one in which he looked back to the death and resurrection of Jesus as the inauguration of the new age, and another in which he still looked forward to his coming in glory, his parousia.[30]

Paul's other fundamental Christian experience was his commission to be the apostle to the Gentiles (Acts 26:11–18; Rom. 1.5, 1 Cor. 15:8–10; Eph. 3:1–13; Col. 1:24–26). Though not often acknowledged today, Paul's apostleship conveys eschatological meaning, as Johannes Munck pointed out some time ago in his influential book, *Paul and the Salvation of Mankind.* He argues that, on the basis of Acts 9; 22; 26, and Galatians 1, Paul viewed his apostolic call as placing him and the world on the edge of the full arrival of the eschaton. As the missionary to the Gentiles, he was responsible for fulfilling the divinely appointed requirement that Israel be saved before the end. In the eschatological, or apocalyptic, scheme of things, the Gentiles had to be converted before that could happen (2 Thess. 2:6; cf. Mark 13:10/Matt. 24:14), and

---

[28]Seyoon Kim has recently championed the view that the Damascus Road conversion is the key to Paul's thought (*The Origin of Paul's Gospel* [WUNT II, 10; Tübingen: J. C. B. Mohr (Paul Siebeck) 1981]), though not all scholars agree with the author's somewhat uncritical employment of the Acts material.

[29]J. Christiaan Beker masterfully demonstrates the end-time connotation of Christ's resurrection for Paul (*Paul the Apostle: The Triumph of God in Life and Thought* [Philadelphia: Fortress, 1980]).

[30]Joseph A. Fitzmyer, "Pauline Theology," in *The Jerome Biblical Commentary*, eds. Raymond E. Brown, Joseph A. Fitzmyer, Roland E. Murphy (Englewood Cliffs, N.J.: Prentice-Hall, 1963), 2:800–27; 804; reprinted as *Pauline Theology: A Brief Sketch* (Englewood Cliffs, N.J.: Prentice-Hall, 1967).

Paul himself was the agent of such evangelization (he is the "restrainer" of 2 Thess. 2:7).[31] Munck concludes from this that:

> Paul, as the apostle to the Gentiles, becomes the central figure in the story of salvation. . . . The fullness of the Gentiles [Rom 11:25] which is Paul's aim, is the decisive turning-point in redemption history. With that there begins the salvation of Israel and the coming of Antichrist, and through it the coming of Christ for judgment and salvation, and so the end of the world.[32]

While one need not subscribe to all the aforementioned points (especially equating Paul with the restrainer in 2 Thess. 2:7 who holds back evil), there is merit in Munck's main argument, that Paul perceived his ministry to the Gentiles as a means for hastening the return of Christ. Eschatology, therefore, was a constituent part of Paul's Christian experience. However, as the next section highlights, other alternatives have been put forth as the key that unlocks the apostle's thought.

B. THE MESSAGE: THE QUEST FOR THE CENTER OF PAUL'S THOUGHT

Paul's thought is so rich and complex that it raises the question: Where does one find the main entrance into the edifice of his theology?[33] This issue is complicated by two considerations. Since the apostle's letters are occasional in nature (i.e., were written to churches or individuals for specific reasons), can we distill from them an overarching concept? Furthermore, what is the extent of Paul's writings anyway? Many scholars in the past said that out of the thirteen epistles attributed to him, only seven are genuinely Pauline. The decision one reaches with regard to this particular problem greatly affects one's view of Paul's thought as

---

[31]Johannes Munck, *Paul and the Salvation of Mankind*, trans. F. C. Clarke (Richmond, Va.: John Knox, 1959).

[32]Ibid., 49.

[33]The literature on the research of the center of Paul's thought is voluminous. A helpful summary and bibliography can be found in Herman Ridderbos', *Paul: An Outline of His Theology*, trans. John Richard DeWitt (Grand Rapids: Eerdmans, 1975), 13–43.

a whole (for more on this last consideration, see the third section of this chapter). Despite the difficulties associated with the quest to grasp the main message of Paul, there does seem to be something of a consensus emerging among modern interpreters concerning the core of his thought. This is vital because, without an integrating idea to bind together his letters, the data found therein will be left unrelated and therefore, for all practical purposes, unclear. In order to gain a sense of the issue and its solution, we will briefly track the four major interpretations of Pauline theology.

1. Justification by Faith

With the Protestant Reformers Martin Luther and John Calvin, the principle of justification by faith was established for many years to come as the key to understanding Paul. Their emphasis on "salvation through grace by faith alone apart from works" became the "canon within the canon,"[34] and the theme of the righteousness of God being imputed (or credited) to the believing sinner became the watchword of the movement. Perhaps the best way to appreciate this approach is to quote Luther's commentary on Romans 1:17, an exposition that powerfully encapsulates the idea of the gift status of God's righteousness that burst on the Reformer's consciousness:

> For, however irreproachably I lived as a monk, I felt myself before God to be a sinner with a most unquiet conscience, nor could I be confident that I had pleased him with my satisfaction. I did not love, nay, rather I hated this righteous God who punished sinners. . . . At last, God being merciful . . . I began to understand the justice of God as that by which the righteous man lives by the gift of God, namely by faith. . . . This straightway made me feel as though reborn and as though I had entered through open gates into Paradise itself. . . . And now, as much as I had hated the word "justice of God" before, so much the more sweetly I extolled this word to myself.[35]

---

[34]The words "canon within the canon" are idiomatic, referring to the central core within the Scripture, i.e., its major message, which varies from reader to reader.

[35]Found in the translation series, *Luther's Works*, vol. 34, ed. Lewis W. Spitz (Philadelphia: Muhlenberg, 1960), 336–37.

Influential and venerable as this viewpoint proved to be, however, the nineteenth and twentieth centuries witnessed a turning away from it, for at least three reasons: (1) The topic of justification by faith, as important as it was to Paul, is only developed at length in two of his letters—Galatians and Romans. Interpreters of Paul reasoned that such a theme seems to be restricted to those two letters because the apostle was having to refute the Judaizers, who taught that salvation comes by faith plus works. Given the accuracy of this interpretation of the situation behind Galatians and Romans, the elevating of justification by faith to the place of supremacy in Paul's thought seemed ill-advised. (2) Luther's extremely negative perspective on the role of the Old Testament Law in Galatians and Romans was shown to be at odds with the apostle's more positive statements about the Law in the same letters (Rom. 2:12–16; 8:4; 13:8–10; Gal. 5:14; 6:2). (3) Stress on the need for faith in order to be justified before God tended to overemphasize the role of the individual in Paul's writings, resulting in the neglect of his teachings on the corporate entities of the church and creation.[36]

2. The Tübingen School of Interpretation

In the nineteenth century the university of Tübingen in Germany led the way in articulating liberal theology, including a radical reinterpretation of Paul. The foremost proponent of this approach was F. C. Baur, whose hallmark was the application of the philosophy of Hegel to Pauline literature. In particular, the Hegelian dialectic—which viewed all historical development as a series of thesis (advance), antithesis (reaction), and synthesis (a new thesis)—was used to explain the theology behind Paul's thought as well as gauge the authenticity of his letters.[37]

---

[36]These criticisms received their basic formulation in Albert Schweitzer's works, especially, *The Mysticism of Paul the Apostle*, trans. William Montgomery (New York: Henry Holt, 1931).

[37]The principal writings of Baur in which he sets forth his ideas about Paul are: *Paul, the Apostle of Jesus Christ. His Life and Work, His Epistles and His Doctrine* (London: Williams and Norgate, 1873); and *The Church History of the First Three Centuries*, 3d ed. (London: Williams and Norgate, 1878–79).

Concerning the Hegelian dialectic, using 1 Corinthians 1:12 as his hermeneutical key, Baur asserted that the party strife in the Corinthian church could be reduced to two factions—Paul and Hellenistic Christianity (the thesis of grace) versus Peter and Jewish Christianity (the antithesis of grace plus law). To Baur, the inherent opposition between these two groups was widespread in the early church and formed the underpinning of Paul's thinking. Only under the threat of the second century heresy, Gnosticism (more on this teaching shortly), was "catholic" unity (synthesis) achieved.

Concerning the authenticity of Paul's letters, Baur's usage of Hegel resulted in accepting only four of the purported Pauline letters as genuinely written by him: Romans, Galatians, 1 and 2 Corinthians.[38] He identified only these as authentic because the opposition between law and grace is clearly visible therein, while in the other letters ascribed to Paul there is already evidence of a syncretistic union between the two.

The popularity of the Tübingen School's approach, though enormous during the nineteenth century, all but vanished in the twentieth century. A number of searching criticisms rendered it untenable. (1) Scholars recognized the movement for what it was—the imposing of Hegelian philosophy onto the New Testament. (2) Baur's reconstruction of Pauline Christianity, like the theme of justification by faith before it, could not account for the positive role of the Law in Romans and Galatians. (3) The compatibility of Peter and Paul as portrayed in Acts, though alleged by Baur to be a late second-century fabrication giving the impression that the two pillars of the faith enjoyed a harmonious relationship in the early church, has been upheld. Furthermore, no informed theologian today dates Acts later than the first century C.E. (4) An increasing number of scholars are arguing for Pauline authorship of the "questionable" letters, a subject to which we will return later.[39]

---

[38]Called the *Hauptbriefe* (the major letters).

[39]For a summary of the criticisms registered against Baur's approach, see Ridderbos, *Paul*, 16–17; E. Earle Ellis, *Paul and His Recent Interpreters* (Grand Rapids: Eerdmans, 1961), 18–20; and Stephen Neill, *The Interpretation of the New Testament 1861–1901* (London: Oxford University Press, 1964), 27.

3. The History of Religions Approach

For the first half of the twentieth century, the History of Religions School of thought (*religionsgeschichtliche*) dominated the scholarly understanding of Paul. In contrast to the interpretations of the Tübingen School and liberal theology that basically rooted the apostle in Greek philosophy (especially the Platonic dualism of flesh and spirit), this powerful movement turned to popular Hellenistic religion, particularly the syncretism that resulted from the intermingling of eastern and western spirituality in the first century B.C.E., as the key to Paul's theology. Four highly significant individuals espousing this perspective call for comment here: Adolf Deissmann, Richard Reitzenstein, Wilhelm Bousset, and Rudolf Bultmann.

a. Adolf Deissmann and Christ Mysticism

In his widely read publications, Adolf Deissmann proposed that the words "in Christ," occurring approximately 164 times in Paul's letters, constituted a formula that expressed the heart of the apostle's message—Christ mysticism.[40] For him, this phrase signified mystical union with Christ, which was initiated at conversion (for Paul himself, on the road to Damascus) and was effected by the indwelling of the Holy Spirit. Such a religious dimension was to be experienced by the Christian, not expounded by the theologian! In fact, being literally placed into Christ by the Spirit defies explanation. Under the influence of the Greek notion that the believer through worship could be caught up into the divine, Deissmann interpreted Paul to say that the Christian was absorbed into Christ, "a light ethereal form of existence."[41]

Deissmann's proposal has not gone unscathed. Three caveats have been leveled against his treatment of Paul: (1) Grammatically, his claim that the phrase "in Christ" is a formula for Paul, has proved to be simplistic. (2) Theologically, the

---

[40]This perspective is succinctly described in Adolf Deissmann's work, *Paul: A Study in Social and Religious History*, trans. William E. Wilson (Magnolia, Mass.: Peter Smith, 1972), 137–42.

[41]Ibid., 142.

supreme importance he attached to Paul's mystic experience with Christ on the Damascus Road, though vital, is not the only factor to be reckoned with in the Pauline understanding of Christianity. (3) Psychologically, Deissmann's assertion that Paul's Christ mysticism did not deny him (Paul) his personality nevertheless came dangerously close to denying Christ's his![42]

b. Richard Reitzenstein and Wilhelm Bousset and the Mystery Religions

A second emphasis within the History of Religions approach to Paul was the concerted attempts by Richard Reitzenstein and Wilhelm Bousset to ground the apostle's thinking in the Mystery Religions of his day. These authors claimed that such wide-ranging religions as the Eleusinian mysteries and the cults of Isis and Osiris, Adonis, Attis, Mithras, etc., shared at least two commonalities. (1) they focused on the dying/rising again of their respective hero/heroine or gods/goddesses, (2) worshipers entered into mystical union with these gods by participating in the cults' sacraments (baptism, cultic meal, etc.).[43] Bousset tended to emphasize the former's supposed connection to the Pauline proclamation of the resurrection of Jesus, especially as the church gathered to worship Christ as risen Lord.[44] Reitzenstein tended to emphasize the latter as the foundation for Paul's teaching on baptism and the Lord's Supper.[45]

---

[42]The quip is from Ernst Best (*One Body in Christ* [London: SPCK, 1958], 9), whose work remains one of the finest critiques of the mystical approach to Paul and provides an excellent presentation of the idea that the body of Christ is best understood in terms of Hebrew corporate personality.

[43]For recent descriptions of the individual Mystery Religions, the following two authors should be consulted: David Seeley, *The Noble Death, Graeco-Roman Martyrology and Paul's Concept of Salvation* (JSNT Supp.Ser. 28; Sheffield: Sheffield Press, 1990), 67–82; and A. J. M. Wedderburn, *Baptism and Resurrection. Studies in Pauline Theology Against Its Graeco–Roman Background* (WUNT 44; Tübingen: J. C. B. Mohr [Paul Siebeck], 1987). A somewhat dated, but still useful, investigation of the issue is the one by Gunther Wagner, *Pauline Baptism and the Pagan Mysteries*, trans. J. P. Smith (Edinburgh and London: Oliver & Boyd, 1967). See also Ferguson, *Backgrounds of Early Christianity*, 197–240.

[44]Wilhelm Bousset, *Kyrios Christos*, trans. John E. Steely (Nashville: Abingdon, 1970).

[45]Richard Reitzenstein, *Hellenistic Mystery Religions*, trans. John E. Steely (Pittsburgh: Pickwick, 1978).

Various weaknesses pinpointed in the Mystery Religions approach have rendered it largely unsuccessful: (1) H. A. A. Kennedy[46] and J. G. Machen[47] subjected the proposed parallels between Paul and the Mysteries to a thorough critique and concluded that the Old Testament was the real source of the apostle's thought. (2) Wesley Carr has provided damaging evidence showing that the Mystery Religions were not all that influential until the third and fourth centuries C.E., long after the time of Paul.[48] (3) David Seeley[49] and A. J. M. Wedderburn[50] have recently effectively refuted the assumption that the Mystery Religions ever taught an actual resurrection of the deity. (4) Substantial differences between Paul's understanding of Christ and the Mystery Religions have also been identified: the Mystery deities' deaths were not vicarious; they died unwillingly rather than obediently; they were not historical personages; and they did not possess an apocalyptic framework.[51]

c. Rudolf Bultmann and Gnosticism

The Mystery Religions' parallels paled; nevertheless, the conviction of the overall History of Religions approach remained strong, namely, that Paul's thought was substantially impacted by Hellenism. In particular, Rudolf Bultmann sought the inspiration for Paul's theology in Gnosticism,[52] especially its redeemer myth. According to this tradition, the original, primal man was a macrocosmic, or universal, figure who was composed of light. Unfortunately, this man fell into sin, the consequence of which

---

[46]H. A. A. Kennedy, *St. Paul and the Mystery Religions* (London: Hodder and Stoughton, 1913).

[47]J. G. Machen, *The Origin of Paul's Religion* (Grand Rapids: Eerdmans, 1947).

[48]A. Wesley Carr, *Angels and Principalities. The Background, Meaning, and Development of the Pauline Phrase Hai Archai Kai Hai Exousai* (SNTSMS 42; Cambridge: Cambridge University Press, 1981), chap. 1.

[49]Seeley, *The Noble Death*, 67–82.

[50]Wedderburn, *Baptism and Resurrection*.

[51]Seeley, *The Noble Death*, 81–82.

[52]His pertinent works include: *Primitive Christianity in Contemporary Setting*, trans. R. H. Fuller (New York: World, 1956); "The New Testament and Mythology" in *Kerygma and Myth: A Theological Debate*, ed. H. E. Bartsch, trans. R. H. Fuller (New York: Harper & Row, 1961), 1–44; *Theology of the New Testament*, vol. 1, trans. Kendrick Grobel (New York: Charles Scribner's Sons, 1951), part II.

was that his body disintegrated into myriads of particles of light, which were then seeded in the souls of humans in this dark world. The plight of humanity, therefore, is the need for individuals to remember the heavenly origin of their souls. God solved this problem by sending his Son, Jesus Christ the Redeemer, whose task was to bring this knowledge (*gnosis*) to people. On recollecting their true nature, those souls are led back to their heavenly home, no longer encumbered by their sinful bodies.

According to Bultmann, this redeemer myth of Gnosticism formed the substructure of Paul's thinking.[53] This interpretation was popular among New Testament theologians through the middle of this century, but it has basically been discarded today, for the following reasons: (1) To posit such an influence on Paul, Bultmann had to argue that Gnosticism preceded Christianity (rather than the reverse), a contention no longer acceptable to many scholars. (2) The unified and pervasive redeemer myth that Bultmann relied on so heavily in his understanding of Paul has been shown to be a mosaic of divergent, and even contradictory, traditions from later Gnostic and Hermetic literature, which was then extrapolated back into the New Testament. (3) Bultmann's demythologizing of Paul (which reduced myth to its essential truth) has been exposed for what it is—an anachronistic foisting of modern-day existential philosophy onto the apostle.[54]

d. Jewish Apocalypticism

The word *apocalypticism* has as its root "apocalypse," which means "revelation" or "uncovering," with reference to the future. Thus apocalypticism, like the term, *eschatology*, has to do with the events at the end of time. Jewish apocalypticism was a strong force at the time of Paul, almost at fever pitch. Many Jews firmly believed that the age to come, or the kingdom of God, was

---

[53]Two other currents of thought factored heavily into Bultmann's reconstruction of Pauline theology—Jewish apocalypticism and Heiddeger's existentialism; see his article, "The New Testament and Mythology."

[54]French L. Arrington gives a perceptive analysis of Bultmann's existentialist approach to demythologizing Pauline categories (*Paul's Aeon Theology in 1 Corinthians*, 31–42), while Edwin Yamauchi provides a devastating critique of the theory of a pre-Christian Gnosticism (*Pre-Christian Gnosticism* [Grand Rapids: Eerdmans, 1973]).

poised to descend to earth from heaven. Judaism expected certain events to precede the coming of the kingdom of God, or God's rule on earth, especially the Great Tribulation (a time of unparalleled suffering, which God's faithful would endure at the hands of their enemies immediately before the arrival of the Messiah and the kingdom)[55] and religious apostasy (a large-scale turning away from God in the face of persecution).[56] The Messiah, or God's Anointed One, would then come to earth to establish the kingdom of God or the age to come.[57] At that time, a resurrection of the righteous dead,[58] a judgment of the wicked,[59] and cosmic renewal or a new creation[60] would also occur. The controlling factor behind all these events was the belief that this age would give way to the age to come.[61]

At this point a distinction between Jewish apocalypticism and Christian eschatology surfaces: Early Christians believed that the age to come had already dawned in the life, death, and resurrection of Jesus. That is, apocalyptic end-time events had occurred within, but without replacing, human history. So, in effect, Christian eschatology refers to the overlapping of the two ages in Christ, which is a significant modification of a purely future-oriented apocalypticism. It is this concept that lies behind Ernst Käsemann's famous statement that "apocalyptic is the

---

[55]Often called the "messianic woes," because it was thought that Israel's suffering, like birth pangs, would give birth to the Messiah (cf. Dan. 12:1; 1 Enoch 80:4–5; Jub. 23:11; 4 Ezra 7:37).

[56]See, for example, 1 Enoch 91:7; Jub. 23:14–23; 4 Ezra 5:1, 2.

[57]Not all Jewish apocalyptic authors expected a Messiah to come (see note 2).

[58]Dan. 12:2–3; 1 Enoch 51:1–2; 4 Ezra 7:32; 2 Bar. 21:23.

[59]Dan. 2, 7; 12:2; 4 Ezra 7:113; 2 Bar. 85:12.

[60]Isa. 65:17–25; 1 Enoch 45:4; 72:1; Jub. 1:23; 4 Ezra 7:75; 2 Bar. 32:6.

[61]Two matters not yet mentioned relative to apocalypticism need to be sketched out at this juncture—the origin of Jewish apocalypticism and the relationship between the genre and the motifs of apocalypticism. Concerning the former, four suggestions have been made: Old Testament prophecy, the Wisdom Movement, Hellenistic-Oriental syncretism, and Canaanite religion. Of these four possibilities, we lean toward the first as the most likely option. Arrington includes a good discussion of this issue, along with a helpful bibliography, in his Paul's Aeon Theology in 1 Corinthians, 5–6. Regarding the latter concern, it needs to be kept in mind that, although an author's writings may not take the form of an official apocalypse (similar, for example, to that of Daniel or Revelation), it may

mother of all Christian theology."[62] So it is with Paul. The ensuing discussion overviews the inestimable significance of Jewish apocalyptic background, now modified by the Christ event, for understanding the apostle. Three individuals call for consideration: Albert Schweitzer and futurist eschatology; C. H. Dodd and realized eschatology; Oscar Cullmann and inaugurated eschatology.

i. Albert Schweitzer and Futurist Eschatology

Albert Schweitzer set the stage for twentieth-century dialogue relative to Pauline theology by calling attention to the apocalyptic nature of the apostle's message. According to him, Judaism, not Hellenism, was the soil out of which Paul's thought grew. To quote him, "From his first letter to his last Paul's thought is uniformly dominated by the expectation of the immediate return of Jesus, of judgment and the messianic glory."[63] Schweitzer considered Paul's teaching to rest on Jesus' proclamation that the kingdom of God was at hand. While for Jesus this

still be indebted to apocalyptic motifs. Thus, with the exception of 1 Corinthians 15; 1 Thessalonians 4:13–18; 2 Thessalonians 2, though Paul's letters do not conform to the form and style of the apocalyptic genre, they are greatly determined by the fundamental motif of apocalypticism—the two-age structure.

[62]"Die apokalyptik ist . . . die mutter aller christlichen Theologie gewesen," in "Die anfänge christlicher Theologie," *ZThK* 57 (1960): 162–85; esp. 180. For identification of the basic components of apocalypticism, the classic texts should be consulted, including Philip Vielhauer, *Geschichte der urchristlicher Literatur: Einleitung in das Neue Testament, die Apokryphen und die apostolischer Väter* (Berlin/New York: Walter de Gruyter, 1975); E. Hennecke, "Introduction to Apocalypses and Related Subjects" in *New Testament Apocrypha*, ed. W. Schneemelcher, 2d vol. (Philadelphia: Westminster, 1963–65), 2:581–607; Klaus Koch, *The Rediscovery of Apocalyptic. A Polemical Work on a Neglected Area of Biblical Studies and Its Damaging Effects on Theology and Philosophy. Studies in Biblical Theology* (London: SCM, 1972). One of the more recent attempts to root Paul's understanding of the death/resurrection of Jesus, as outlined in 1 Corinthians 15, in apocalypticism is Beker's *Paul the Apostle*. Beker reduces apocalypticism to three basic ingredients: (1) historical dualism; (2) universal cosmic expectation; and (3) the imminent end of the world. According to him, these three foundational motifs are present in Paul, though in a modified form because of the Christ event (145–46). To our way of thinking, the term "eschatology" reflects Paul's Christian modification of Jewish apocalypticism, though we practically equate the two in this work.

[63]Albert Schweitzer, *The Mysticism of Paul the Apostle*, trans. William Montgomery (New York: Henry Holt, 1931), 52.

kingdom was still future, Paul faced a new situation: If Christ's resurrection was the beginning of the age to come, why had the other events associated with the end of history (the Great Tribulation, resurrection of righteous believers, judgment of the wicked, etc.) not also happened?

Schweitzer's proposed solution to this quandary was Christ-mysticism. Like Deissmann before him, minus the supposed Hellenistic influence, Schweitzer argued that the Pauline formula "in Christ" signifies that the kingdom of God or age to come has begun—but for Christians only, because, through union with the Spirit, they have died and been raised with Christ. Schweitzer writes, "Through Christ we are removed out of this world and transferred into the state of existence proper to the Kingdom of God, notwithstanding the fact that it has not yet appeared."[64] In other words, Paul's Christ-mysticism was a makeshift attempt to explain how it was that, despite Jesus' resurrection, the kingdom of God had not yet appeared on earth. Or, as Ellis puts it, "Schweitzer argued that Paul's *en Christo* concept arose from the failure of the Kingdom of God, i.e., the end of the world, to arise at Christ's death and resurrection."[65]

ii. C. H. Dodd and Realized Eschatology

Against Schweitzer, C. H. Dodd contended that through Christ's death and resurrection, the age to come did arrive; eschatology was now realized as much as it ever would be, and that within history.[66] Dodd exclaims, "It is in the epistles of Paul, therefore, that full justice is done for the first time to the principle of 'realized eschatology' which is vital to the whole *kêrygma* [Christian preaching].[67] That supernatural order of life which the apocalypticists had predicted in terms of pure fantasy is now described as an actual fact of experience."[68]

---

[64]Ibid., 380.

[65]Ellis, *Paul and His Recent Interpreters*, 32.

[66]C. H. Dodd, *The Apostolic Preaching and Its Developments* (New York: Harper & Row, 1964); this proceeds from his foundational work, *The Parables of the Kingdom* (London: Nisbet, 1935).

[67]The bracketed words are my own insertion for clarification.

[68]Dodd, *The Apostolic Preaching*, 65.

For Dodd, the new age is already fully here by virtue of Christ's death and resurrection, the proof of which is the indwelling Holy Spirit in the lives of believers. In fact, so powerfully present is the kingdom of God on earth that the expectation, or even the need, of the return of Christ (the Second Advent), recedes into the background for Paul. "If the Advent is deferred to an indefinite future, then the present gains in significance. And . . . side by side with the diminishing emphasis on the imminence of the Advent goes a growing emphasis on the eternal life here and now in communion with Christ."[69]

iii. Oscar Cullmann and Inaugurated Eschatology

Oscar Cullmann's classic work, *Christ and Time*,[70] paved the way for the application of "inaugurated" eschatology to the thought world of the New Testament and Paul. His thesis was that *both* elements—the age to come as present (Dodd) and future (Schweitzer)—are at work in Paul. The age to come has "already" dawned in the first coming of Christ but has "not yet" been completed; the latter awaits the second coming of Christ (the *Parousia*). Using a now famous illustration, Cullmann likened the first coming of Christ, especially his death and resurrection, to D-Day, the beginning of the end of World War II, while comparing the *Parousia* to V-Day, the end of the conflict.

A particular concern of Cullmann's was to contrast the New Testament's linear view of time (which is founded on the Old Testament's understanding of history as having beginning and ending points) with the Greek cyclical perspective (history is an endless circle without start or finish and, hence, without meaning). For Cullmann, the death and resurrection of Christ, and the subsequent sending of the Spirit, attest to God's salvation *in* history. The consummation of redemption, however, awaits Christ's return. Cullmann's work has served as a rallying point for many

---

[69]Dodd, "The Mind of Paul II," *New Testament Studies* (Manchester: The University Press, 1953), 112–13. In this evaluation, Dodd reverts back to a Platonic reading of Paul's temporal categories (83–128).

[70]Oscar Cullmann, *Christ and Time. The Primitive Christian Conception of Time and History*, trans. Floyd V. Filson (Philadelphia: Westminster, 1950); cf. also Gerhardus Vos, *The Pauline Eschatology* (Grand Rapids: Eerdmans, 1952).

interpreters of Paul, including the important studies by W. Kümmel,[71] E. Käsemann,[72] H. Ridderbos,[73] and C. Beker.[74] This present work continues in that same vein and is concerned to confirm that the "already/not yet" eschatological tension constitutes the heart of Paul's message. We will pursue this theme after having addressed the extent of Paul's writings, the final section of this introductory chapter.

C. HIS LETTERS: THE EXTENT OF PAUL'S WRITINGS

Any introduction to Paul the apostle must necessarily deal with the subject of Paul the letter-writer. What is the extent of Paul's writings? That is, how many epistles[75] did the apostle write? The answer one gives to this question significantly determines how one understands Paul. If he indeed wrote thirteen

---

[71]W. G. Kümmel, *Promise and Fulfillment. The Eschatological Message of Jesus* (Naperville, Ill.: A. R. Allenson, 1957), 141–55.

[72]Ernst Käsemann, "Die Anfänge christlicher Theologie"; reprinted as "On the Subject of Primitive Christian Apocalyptic" in *New Testament Questions of Today*, trans. W. J. Montague (Philadelphia: Fortress, 1969), 108–37; see also "Justification and Salvation History in the Epistle to the Romans" in *Perspectives on Paul*, trans. M. Kohl (Philadelphia: Fortress, 1971), 60–78. In these and other writings, Käsemann reasserts justification by faith to be the key to interpreting Paul, but with an apocalyptic orientation to it. In a sense, one can perceive Käsemann as responding to the three criticisms of the older view of justification by faith: (1) For Käsemann, justification by faith is the substructure of Paul's thought and should not be restricted to Galatians and Romans. It is God's end-time gift of salvation to the believer now, within history, that informs all Paul's letters. (2) Käsemann attributes a more positive role to the Law in the Christian life than Luther did, by emphasizing the gift status of justification and the divine *power* for holy living accompanying that gift, thereby fulfilling the Law. (3) In reaction to the criticism that the theme of justification by faith degenerates into individualism, Käsemann stresses that the believer is part of the obedient people of God, God's new creation, the church.

[73]Herman Ridderbos, *Paul*.

[74]Beker, *Paul. The Triumph of God*; cf. note 62.

[75]We have been using the terms "letter" and "epistle" interchangeably. The older classification by Adolf Deissmann, in which he sharply distinguished "epistles" (carefully composed public pieces of literature) from "letters" (unskilled, private communications) is no longer followed by scholars. Paul's writings, and basically the New Testament as a whole, seem to fall somewhere between the preceding two stereotypes.

epistles, as the traditional view maintains, then we have a large body of material from which to interpret Paul. However, if he only authored seven epistles, as the pseudonymous view claims, then the collection for grasping the message of the apostle is considerably reduced. This difficulty will be explored here under three headings: the traditional view, the pseudonymous view, and the latest research appealed to by the traditional approach.

1. The Traditional View Regarding Paul's Epistles

Until the mid-nineteenth century, the majority of Pauline scholars assumed that Paul authored thirteen letters. The names of those letters, their historical framework, and approximate dates are provided below in chart form. Also included is a column which correlates Paul's literature with the narrative material of Acts,[76] insofar as it is applicable.

Historical Framework	Date	Name	Acts
Conversion of Paul	33 C.E.	—	Chap. 9 (cf. 22, 26)
Famine Relief Visit to Jerusalem by Paul	46	—	11:27–30
Paul's First Missionary Journey	47–48	—	13:1–14:28
Apostolic Council	49	Galatians	15:1–35
Paul's Second Missionary Journey	50–51	1 & 2 Thessalonians	15:36–18:22
Paul's Third Missionary Journey	56–57	1 & 2 Corinthians, Romans	18:23–21:14
Paul's First Imprisonment at Rome	61–62	Colossians, Ephesians, Philemon, Philippians	28:11–31
Paul's Release from Prison and Further Missionary Activity	63–64	—	—
Paul's Second Imprisonment at Rome and Martyrdom	64	1 & 2 Timothy, Titus	—

---

[76]The point of departure for establishing the chronology of Paul's writings and linking it to Acts is the Gallio inscription discovered in Delphi, Greece. It dates Gallio's proconsulate in Achaia to 52 C.E. (cf. Acts 18:12). A concise explanation of the inscription is provided by Fitzmyer, *Paul,* 6–7.

2. The Pseudonymous View

From the time of the Tübingen School on, the tide of scholarly opinion dramatically changed so that it was popular to claim Pauline authorship for no more than seven epistles, written (generally) in this order: Galatians, 1 Thessalonians, 1 and 2 Corinthians, Romans, Philippians, and Philemon. The remaining letters purporting to be by Paul were classified as deutero-(secondarily) Pauline, written by a later, close associate of the apostle (Colossians, Ephesians, 2 Thessalonians) and pseudo-(false) Pauline, composed by a later individual who, though not having contact with Paul, admired his theology (the Pastoral Epistles). Five basic criteria supposedly supported this new arrangement of the material: vocabulary, style of writing, theology, history, and the practice of pseudonymity.[77]

(1) Regarding vocabulary, many interpreters of Paul concluded that the presence of *hapax legomena* (words that occur nowhere else in the New Testament) in the disputable Pauline correspondences render them inauthentic. For example, 2 Thessalonians has 40 unique words and expressions; Colossians has 38; the Pastoral Epistles have 175. (2) Differences in style are said to exist between the debatable and genuine Pauline letters. Second Thessalonians' lack of chiasms (ABB'A' order), parallelism, and antithetical formulations discredit it. Colossians' abundance of synonymous expressions and its liturgical style raise doubts about its credibility. The Pastorals' omission of 112 particles, prepositions, and pronouns found in the other letters of Paul make Pauline authorship of them highly unlikely, etc. (3) The contested Pauline literature seemingly manifests different theological perspectives than that of the uncontested writings. For example, 2 Thessalonians presents certain signs that must occur before the *Parousia*, whereas 1 Thessalonians does not; Colossians views the body of Christ as universal but Romans and 1 Corinthians portray it as local; Ephesians defines Paul's

---

[77]Full treatment of these matters can be found in the standard works by those like Donald Guthrie, *New Testament Introduction* (Downers Grove, Ill.: InterVarsity, 1970) and W. G. Kümmel, *Introduction to the New Testament* (Nashville: Abingdon, 1975).

word "mystery" as the union of Jew and Gentile in Christ, while Colossians restricts the term to Christ; the Pastoral Epistles do not touch on justification by faith, the keynote of the apostle's legitimate writings. (4) The historical problem pertains primarily to the Pastorals and the lack of documentation for a second Roman imprisonment of Paul, a hypothesis that those letters appear to require in order to be genuinely Pauline. (5) Those who advocated non-Pauline authorship of the disputable letters appealed to the apparent widespread acceptable practice of pseudonymity (writing a document in the name of someone else) in antiquity (e.g., 1 Enoch, 4 Ezra, Acts of Paul) in order to extricate the authors from any charge of ethical impropriety.

3. Recent Research Supporting the Traditional View

More recent research, however, seems to be tilting the scales back toward the traditional perspective. A group of scholars are effectively presenting counterarguments to the aforementioned criteria. For convenience sake, we will combine the vocabulary and stylistic issues. (1) Preformed materials help account for differences in vocabulary and style—i.e., hymns, creeds, etc., written by others that Paul incorporated into his letters.[78] (2) Paul undoubtedly took over his critics' terminology and used it polemically in his writings.[79] (3) Paul's versatility as a writer should figure into the analysis of his compositions. H. J. Cadbury's query about Ephesians is germane to this point: "Which is more likely—that an imitator of Paul in the first century composed a writing ninety or ninety-five percent in accordance with Paul's style or that Paul himself wrote a letter diverging five or ten percent from his usual style?"[80] (4) Paul's use of amanuenses (i.e., secretaries; see Rom. 16:22; cf. also 2 Thess. 3:17; Gal. 6:11, where Paul signs his signature to the letter his secretary composed) explains many divergences in

---

[78]To name only a few, Rom. 1:3–4; Phil. 2:5–11; Col. 1:15–20; 1 Tim. 3:16.

[79]Fee nicely illustrates this practice of Paul in the Pastoral Epistles (1 and 2 Timothy, Titus, 14–17).

[80]H. J. Cadbury, "The Dilemma of Ephesians," NTS 5 (1958–59): 101.

vocabulary and style.[81] (5) Paul's remarks that others participated with him in writing his materials (coauthorship) are increasingly being recognized by scholars as a viable explanation for changes in vocabulary and style (see 1 Cor. 1:1; 2 Cor. 1:1; Phil. 1:1; Col. 1:1; 1 Thess. 1:1; 2 Thess. 1:1).[82] (6) More and more, computer analysis points toward Paul as the author of those letters bearing his name.[83]

Regarding the apparent contradictions in the theological perspectives of the disputable Pauline material, the traditional school of thought offers at least three replies: (1) Different life settings of the churches called for different approaches on the part of Paul. Thus in Colossians, the metaphor of the body of Christ as universal can be understood as Paul's attempt to buttress the confidence of that church in the Lycus Valley, which suffered from feelings of inferiority in the face of heresy and criticism.

(2) A general continuity runs throughout Pauline literature. Thus, for example, the eschatological tension of the "already/not yet" aspect of the Christ-event explains the relationship between 1 and 2 Thessalonians: 1 Thessalonians, in its emphasis on the imminence of Christ's second coming, features the "already" side, whereas 2 Thessalonians, with its positing of certain signs heralding the *Parousia*, stresses the "not yet" side. Current research is demonstrating that this eschatological tension is commonplace even in the contested Pauline epistles.

---

[81]E. Randolph Richard's recent work confirms the importance of the secretary for explaining divergences in vocabulary and style in the Pauline literature (*The Secretary in the Letters of Paul* [WUNT 2, 42; Tübingen: J. C. B. Mohr (Paul Siebeck), 1991]).

[82]Ably demonstrated by VanRoon, *The Authenticity of Ephesians* (Supp.Nov.T, 39; Leiden: E. J. Brill, 1974), and, more recently, by Michael Prior, *Paul the Letter-Writer and the Second Letter to Timothy* (JSNT Supp.Ser., 23; Sheffield: JSOT, 1989).

[83]Kenneth J. Neumann's *The Authenticity of the Pauline Epistles in the Light of Stylostatistical Analysis* (SBLDS 120; Atlanta: Scholars Press, 1990) is destined to become the classic computer analysis of the Pauline literature relative to their authenticity. His conclusion is provocative: "Through the present investigation Pauline studies are given new information which may result in better understanding of the Pauline corpus, notably the disputed letters, and which give more serious consideration to the position that the apostle is the author of the letters whose origin has been so much debated," 226.

(3) The pseudonymous view seemed predisposed to reading contradictions into the theology of the debated Pauline literature. For example, to say that Ephesians' description of the term "mystery" (the union of Jew and Gentile) is at odds with Colossians' definition of the term (the "mystery" is Christ) overlooks Ephesians 2:20, a verse that identifies Christ as the cornerstone of the church and occurs in the context of Paul's discussion about the union of Jew and Gentile in it. The supposed neglect in the Pastorals to speak of the Pauline doctrine of justification by faith fails to take into account verses like 1 Timothy 1:15 (Christ came to save sinners); 1 Timothy 3:13 (the importance of faith in Christ); 2 Timothy 1:9 (the necessity of grace for salvation); and Titus 3:5 (mercy, not works, is the basis for salvation). One cannot help but think that the presumed theological inconsistencies in the questionable Pauline literature were born out of contemporary theory that was projected back into the apostle's writings. Thus the tendency to pit the Pastorals' apparent emphasis on works against the "true" Pauline doctrine of justification by faith smacks of Hegelian philosophy, not careful exegesis. Or, to assert that the Pastorals' complex church organizational structure is a significant advancement beyond Paul's charismatic, spontaneous understanding of church governance sounds more like Weberian sociology than historical description.[84]

Concerning the problem of the difficulty of meshing the historical situation alluded to in the Pastorals (i.e., a second Roman imprisonment) with Acts and the other Pauline letters, the traditional approach provides three rejoinders. (1) Acts leaves open the possibility of Paul's release from prison (see 25:25; 26:32; 28:16, 30). The impression one gets from these references is that Paul's crime was not thought to be all that serious, hence the degree of freedom allotted to him while under house arrest. (2) So little is known about Paul's activity during his years of ministry (e.g., when did the apostle experience the events of 2 Cor. 11:23–27?) that it would be presumptuous to preclude the possibility of a second Roman imprisonment.

---

[84]For a more specific investigation of the application of the sociology of religion to Paul, especially Max Weber's construct of the routinization of the charisma, consult C. Marvin Pate, *The Glory of Adam and the Afflictions of the Righteous: Pauline Suffering in Context* (New York: Edwin Mellen, 1993), 59–63.

(3) Defenders of the verisimilitude of the Pastorals turn the tables on the pseudonymous viewpoint by asking the question, "What other reason, other than historical fact, accounts for the personal reminiscences found in the Pastoral epistles (1 Tim. 1:3; 3:14–15; 2 Tim. 1:16–17; 4:13; Titus 3:13)?" To posit a second-century author creating a *hypothetical* situation by mimicking incidents from the undisputed Pauline writings, thereby giving the impression that he was Paul, requires as much theorizing as a second Roman imprisonment!

Finally, in response to the highly touted argument that the genre of pseudonymity was a commonly accepted practice in the early church, the following facts need to be kept in mind. (1) While in antiquity pseudonymity was common in some genres (e.g., history and apocalypticism), it was not prevalent in others, notably the epistle format. In actuality, only two ancient pseudonymous Jewish letters are known today—the *Epistle of Jeremy* and the *Letter of Aristeas*, neither of which is truly a letter. (2) The early church criticized pseudepigraphic letters. Paul himself warns the Thessalonians about letters falsely written in his name (2 Thess. 2:2; cf. 3:17; Rev. 22:12, 19). Such repudiation of pseudonymous letters continued into the second century. Thus Tertullian approved of defrocking a church presbyter in Asia Minor because he composed the apocryphal *Acts of Paul* (*On Baptism*, 17).[85] (3) As M. R. James notes, only six pseudonymous Christian epistles are extant, none of which date to New Testament times.[86] (4) The scathing criticism against deception that one finds in the Pastorals (1 Tim. 2:7; 4:1; 2 Tim. 3:13; Titus 1:10; 3:3) would not bode well for the integrity of a pseudonymous author thereof!

CONCLUSION

This preliminary investigation has been necessary both to situate Paul in the context of his day and to establish the parameters of his writings, from which vantage point we can best ascer-

---

[85]Carson, Moo, and Morris (*An Introduction to the New Testament*, 367–71) provide more examples of early Christianity's disapproval of pseudonymous writings, as well as an excellent overview of the issue.

[86]M. R. James, *The Apocryphal New Testament* (Oxford: Clarendon, 1926), 476.

tain the center of his thought. The thesis broached here is eschatological in nature—the overlapping of the two ages (the "already/not yet" tension produced by the Christ-event) is the key to interpreting the apostle. We now proceed to apply this concept to Paul's major categories of thought: theology, Christology, soteriology, anthropology, pneumatology, ecclesiology, society, and eschatology.[87] Each chapter devoted to these respective topics contains an explanation of the doctrine and an exposition of pertinent scriptural passages.

---

[87]Some may wish to take exception to designing a book on Paul around the categories listed here. This approach to Paul, so it is argued, fails to realize that the apostle's thought cannot be grasped in terms of systematic doctrines or dogmas. His writings were more expressions of his experience, personal reflection, and polemical battles than a compendium of beliefs. There is a measure of truth in this evaluation, but three criticisms can be offered. (1) This perspective on Paul naively assumes that systematic theology (doctrinal categories) and biblical theology (exegesis of the text) are enemies when, in reality, they are friends. (2) The preceding evaluation is often in tandem with the older view that accepted only seven letters as genuinely Pauline. But such an approach, besides greatly restricting the data from which to interpret Paul, no longer enamors a good many scholars, for reasons we have already documented. (3) The criticism of using terms like "doctrine" or "categories" when discussing Paul's thought smacks more of modern-day deconstructionism literary theory than solid historical hermeneutics. Though he does not use the word deconstructionism, Ernst Käsemann correctly complains about the results of applying that idea and methodology to Paul, "The inclination of earlier times to view Paul as the first Christian dogmatist has swung to the other extreme. He is conceded the honour of being the most important reflective theologian in the New Testament; but it would be generally denied today that he developed a system . . . or possesses a firm methodology. . . . Both these opinions may be correct. But that does not mean that the dominating centre of Paul's theology must be denied as well. Although he composed no *Summa Theologica*, it would probably be going too far to set in its place a collection of interrelated ideas about the encounter between God and man, with at most a general thesis about 'judgment and grace.' . . . Such statements are so general that they no longer allow the specific character of Pauline theology to emerge, a character which simply cannot be overlooked and which distinguishes him from all other New Testament writers." See Ernst Käsemann, "The Spirit and the Letter," in *Perspectives on Paul*, trans. Margaret Kohl (Philadelphia: Fortress, 1971), 138–66; esp. 138.

II

PAULINE THEOLOGY:
THE TRIUMPH OF GOD
IN THE WORLD

INTRODUCTION

We properly begin to identify the influence of the two-age structure on Paul's thought by examining an all but forgotten category in the apostle's writings—God! N. H. Dahl makes a provocative statement concerning this neglected "factor" in New Testament theology:

> For more than a generation the majority of New Testament scholars have not only eliminated direct references to God from their works, but also neglected detailed comprehensive investigation of statements about God. Whereas a number of major works and monographs deal with Christology, . . . it is hard to find any comprehensive or penetrating study of the theme "God in the New Testament."[1]

J. Christiaan Beker has attempted to address this omission relative to Paul—hence the title of his work, *Paul the Apostle: The Triumph of God in Life and Thought*. In that study, the author argues that the key to recovering "God" in the apostle's writings is to recognize the centrality of apocalypticism. Some sample statements by Beker illustrate the point:

---

[1]Nils Alstrup, "The Neglected Factor in New Testament Theology," *Reflection* 73, 1 (1975): 5.

Paul is an apocalyptic theologian with a theocentric outlook. The Christ-event is the turning point in time that announces the end of time. . . .[2]

Paul's apocalyptic emphasis on Christ as inaugurating
the triumph of God's reign at the end of time and on the resurrection of Christ as "the first in a series to come" is dis-
placed by . . . speculations about the relation of the "persons
of the Trinity" and about the . . . unity of God. . . .[3]

Paul's apocalyptic theocentrism, then, is not to be contrasted with his Christo-centric thinking, for the final hour of
the glory of Christ and his Parousia will coincide with the
glory of God, that is, with the actualization of the redemption
of God's created order in his kingdom.[4]

Thus an important clue for interpreting Paul is to ascertain
the relationship that exists in his letters between God and the
two-age structure of reality; that is, to study the concept of "salvation in history." If one culls together Paul's "aeon" terminology and traces its impact on him, the following temporal frame
of reference surfaces: God's kingdom or reign (the age to come)
has begun in Christ, but it exists in the midst of this present
world (this age). In effect, Christ's death and resurrection initiated the temporary messianic kingdom, the consummation of
which will occur at the Second Coming. In other words, the
Christ-event has produced an overlapping of the two ages.[5] The

---

[2]J. Christiaan Beker, *Paul the Apostle: The Triumph of God in Life and Thought*
(Philadelphia: Fortress, 1980), 362.

[3]Ibid., 357.

[4]Ibid., 363.

[5]The Hebrew terminology for this idiom that emerged in both apocalyptic and
rabbinic literature for the two ages is *olam hazzeh* ("this age") and *olam habbah*
("the coming age"). The corresponding Greek terms are *ho aiôn* and *ho aiôn
mellôn*. The explicit aeon vocabulary occurs in Paul in Gal. 1:4; 1 Cor. 1:20; 2:6, 8;
3:18; 10:11; 2 Cor. 4:4; Rom. 12:1–2; Eph. 1:21. However, the concept is broader
than the term itself. Thus this age is often interchangeable with the word "world"
(*kosmos*) (e.g., 1 Cor. 3:19; 7:29–31; Gal. 4:3; 6:14; Eph. 2:2; Col. 2:8). Also, even
though apart from Eph. 1:21 Paul does not specifically label the future era as the
"age to come," he does frequently mention the eschatological kingdom of God
(1 Cor. 6:9; 15:50; Gal. 5:21; Eph. 5:5; 1 Thess. 2:12; 2 Tim. 4:1, 18), a semantic
equivalent. See Hermann Sasse's informative article on the subject, "αἰών,"
Theological Dictionary of the New Testament, ed. Gerhard Kittel, trans. Geoffrey W.
Bromiley (Grand Rapids: Eerdmans, 1964–74), 1:197–209.

tension that results from the coexistence of these two realities affects four basic areas or spheres: the anti-God forces, humans, creation, and Christ himself.

A. THE ANTI-GOD FORCES

Jewish apocalyptic literature assigned a significant role to anti-God forces, including Satan(s) (Zech. 3:1 [cf. 1 Chron. 21:1; Job 1–2]; 1 Enoch 37–71; T.Dan. 3:6; 5:6), Belial (Sib.Oracles III:63–92; T.Isa. 6:1; 1 QS 1), fallen angels or evil spirits (Dan. 10:13; Zech. 3:1–2; 1 Enoch 6:26; 7:4–6; Jub. 2, 4–5, 15), the Devil (Apoc.Mos. 20:1–3), the two sea monsters, Leviathan and Behemoth (1 Enoch 60:7–10; 4 Ezra 6:49–52), and the man of lawlessness (Antichrist, Dan. 9:27; 11:31; 12:11). These malevolent figures personify the notion that the angels to whom God had given authority over the nations and the universe rebelled against him and took power into their own hands. Summarizing the intent of these cosmic culprits, Russell writes, "Thus those 'tendencies toward evil' which appear in the biblical references to 'the Satan' and his legions are presented as archenemies of God, bent on controlling and so ultimately destroying not only the human race but even the cosmos itself."[6]

Paul, too, operated from an apocalyptic-demonic understanding of the world order.[7] He believed that the present age lay in the clutches of these evil forces, but that the death and resurrection of Christ spelled their defeat. In effect, the cross marked the turning point of the two ages, when the age to come began the process of replacing this evil age. Inherent to this paradigmatic shift is the eschatological tension of the "already" and the

---

[6]D. S. Russell, The Method and Message of Jewish Apocalyptic (Philadelphia: Westminster, 1964), 238.

[7]Paul's demonic vocabulary includes the following: rulers and principalities (Rom. 8:38; Col. 1:16; 2:15; Eph. 3:10; 6:12), power or powers (Rom. 8:38; 1 Cor. 15:24; Eph. 1:21), lordship (Eph. 1:21; Col. 1:16), Devil (Eph. 4:27; 6:11; 1 Tim. 3:7), Satan (1 Cor. 5:5; 2 Cor. 11:14), Belial (2 Cor. 6:15), and elements of the world (Gal. 4:3; Col. 2:8, 20). For helpful discussions of this terminology, see G. H. C. Macgregor, "Principalities and Powers: The Cosmic Background of Saint Paul's Thought," NTS 1 (1954): 17–28; and Wesley Carr, Angels and Principalities. The Background, Meaning and Development of the Pauline Phrase Hai Archai Kai Hai Exousiai (SNTSM 42; Cambridge: Cambridge University Press, 1981).

"not yet": already the anti-God forces have been dealt a death blow at the cross but not until the *Parousia* will they be forever banished. This tension resulting from the overlapping of the two ages is essential to understanding the major Pauline passages on the subject of the anti-God figures: 1 Corinthians 2:6–10; 2 Corinthians 4:3–6; Colossians 2:15 (cf. 8, 20); and Ephesians 6:10–13. According to these texts, Paul believed that God's kingdom had already begun to triumph over his enemies on earth.

1. 1 Corinthians 2:6–10

First Corinthians 2:6–10 reflects the view that the cross effected the shift of the two ages, with devastating repercussions for the enemies of God.[8] This idea is developed in the passage in terms of three eschatological tensions:

(1) The mystery of the divine plan is hidden to the rulers of this age, but is revealed to the righteous by the Spirit. A familiar Jewish apocalyptic theme undergirds this contrast—the things to be revealed in the last days are present in heaven and are the privy information of the apocalyptic seer.[9] For Paul, the mystery[10]

---

[8]Those identifying these rulers as demonic forces include C. K. Barrett, *Commentary on the First Epistle to the Corinthians* (HNTC; New York: Harper & Row, 1968), 69–70, and Judith L. Kovacs, "The Archons, the Spirit and the Death of Christ," *Apocalyptic and the New Testament. Essays in Honor of J. Louis Martyn*, eds. Joel Marcus and Marion Soards (JSNT Supp.Ser. 24; Sheffield: JSOT, 1989), 217–36. Those opting for the political interpretation only include Wesley Carr, *Angels and Principalities*, and Gordon Fee, *The First Epistle to the Corinthians* (NICNT; Grand Rapids: Eerdmans, 1987), 103–4. Those combining the two previous views (demonic influence lies behind the governmental rulers) include Oscar Cullmann, *Christ and Time* (Philadelphia: Westminster, 1956), 80–82, and G. H. C. MacGregor, "Principalities and Powers." Of the three views, the second view seems to have the least to commend itself. In particular, Martinus C. de Boer is unimpressed with Carr's thesis that the idea of suprahuman powers is not present in Paul's thought. He rejects that posture for three reasons: (a) Carr omits any discussion of the figure of Satan in Paul's letters (which is amply attested therein: Rom. 16:20; 1 Cor. 5:5; 7:5; 2 Cor. 4:4; 11:14; 12:7; 1 Thess. 2:18); (b) he fails to perceive that death for Paul is a personified, cosmic ruler (see especially Rom. 5:12–6:23); (c) as a last resort to evade the evidence, Carr deems Ephesians 6:12 to be a later interpolation dating to the second century C.E.! ("The Defeat of Death: Apocalyptic Eschatology in 1 Corinthians 15 and Romans 5" [Ph.D. Dissertation, Union Theological Seminary, 1983], 23–24).

[9]See Dan. 2:28; *1 QH* 1:21; 2:13; 4:27–29; *1 Enoch* 104:11–13; *4 Ezra* 14:26.

[10]The word *mystêrion* ("mystery") appears in Pauline literature 21 times, two of which (Rom. 16:25–27; Col. 1:26–27) have the closest links with 1 Cor. 2:6–10.

of God's salvation accompanying the age to come is experienced by Christians now because they possess the gift of the end time par excellence, the Spirit.[11] The rulers and citizens of this age, however, are ignorant of God's intent. Thus the revealed/hidden motif of the divine mystery is rooted in the notion of the overlapping of the two ages: the divine plan is already comprehended by Christians in the Spirit, but not yet made manifest to others on the earth.

(2) The anti-God forces unwittingly crucified the Lord of glory, thereby sealing their own doom. The persecution/glory motif informing this statement stems from the Jewish apocalyptic belief that the people of God would undergo unparalleled suffering at the hands of God's enemies immediately prior to the coming of the kingdom of God on earth. Such affliction was expected to signal the end of this evil age and the beginning of the glory of the age to come. At that time, the anti-God forces would be defeated (see Ezek. 38–39; Dan. 12:1–3; Ps. Sol. 17:44; 1 Enoch 80:4; 4 Ezra 5:4–5; 2 Bar. 70:2). For Paul, the wisdom reserved for the righteous is that the humiliated one is indeed the apocalyptic redeemer and that the crucifixion was by divine design. In essence, God's enemies are pawns in his hands.

Paul's message here closely resembles the *Ascension of Isaiah* 10, which states that the heavenly Christ was not recognized by the demonic powers as he descended to earth veiled in human flesh. Not understanding God's mystery, these principalities and powers killed Jesus on the cross, only to discover that they had crucified the heavenly Lord. In Paul's thinking, the cross therefore effected the beginning of the end of these demonic denizens.

(3) At the cross, though the evil powers were dispossessed, they were not destroyed. This tension is evident in the phrase, "the rulers of this age ... are coming to nothing" (v. 6), especially in the participle *katargoumenon*. The term means "to abolish; to

---

The classic treatment of the Jewish, as opposed to Hellenistic, background of the term *mystery* is by Raymond Brown, *The Semitic Background of the Term "Mystery" in the New Testament* (FBBS 21; Philadelphia: Fortress, 1968).

[11]That the Spirit was thought to be the sign that the New Age had arrived is evident from Isa. 21:15; 34:16–44:3; Ezek. 11:19; 36:26, 27; 37:4–14; Joel 2:28–32; T.Ben. 9:2–4; T.Jud. 24:2–3; 1 Enoch 49:3; 1 QS 3.

bring to nothing," signifying that the age to come has arrived. Nevertheless, the present tense of this word indicates that the victory over the anti-God forces is still in process. In particular, death, the most feared of enemies, still persists (1 Cor. 15:26).

2. 2 Corinthians 4:3–6

Though the apostle does not explicitly refer to the cross in 2 Corinthians 4:3–6, it is implied in verse 5 ("servants for Jesus' sake") and in verses 10–11 (the "death of Jesus"). Paul's flow of thought here suggests that the cross has initiated the defeat of the "god of this age" (v. 4). He uses two primeval or creation metaphors to describe the eschatological tension that has resulted from the Christ event: darkness/light and first Adam/second Adam.

(1) In verses 4 and 6, Paul uses Genesis 1 and its imagery of darkness and light in both ethical and eschatological ways. This age (*aiônos*, v. 4) and its unbelievers are under the sway of Satan's spiritual darkness ("the god of this age," v. 4; cf. 2 Cor. 11:3, 14), the hallmark of the old creation. However, with the death and resurrection of Christ, the light of the glory of God characteristic of the age to come has burst onto the hearts of believers (v. 6; cf. 3:16–18; 4:4–6). This is nothing less than the start of a new creation (cf. 5:17).

(2) Though not as pronounced as the first metaphor, Paul also draws on the contrast between the first and second (or last) Adam in verses 4 and 6. The clue to the presence of Paul's Adam theology lies in the words "image" and "glory," the combination of which in Pauline literature always signifies the Adam theme.[12] This, too, possesses ethical and eschatological import. The serpent's temptation in the Garden of Eden precipitated Adam's fall, thereby making him the father of this sinful age (cf. Rom. 5:12–21). Yet Jesus Christ, the last (*eschatos*, 1 Cor. 15:45) Adam, has inaugurated the coming age and a new humanity. The presence of the new creation and the new humanity on earth is proof that the god of this world is fighting a losing battle.

---

[12]See Rom. 1:23; 8:29; 1 Cor. 11:7; 15:43–49; 2 Cor. 4:4, 6; Col 3:4–10. For further discussion, see Pate, *Adam Christology as the Exegetical and Theological Substructure of 2 Corinthians 4:7–5:21* (Lanham, Md.: University Press of America, 1991), 82–85.

3. Colossians 2:15; cf. 8, 20

The classic Pauline text on the defeat of the anti-God rulers and authorities is Colossians 2:15 which, along with 2:8, 20 and the references to the "elements of the universe," illustrate that the cross of Christ is bringing about the demise of the evil powers, though their ultimate destruction is yet future. Thus verse 15 portrays the already side of the victory over the wicked principalities while verses 8 and 20 ("the elements of the world") present the not yet aspect (i.e., the demonic figures are still forces with which to be reckoned). Paul's line of thinking here can best be unpacked by (1) focusing on the three verbs in verse 15 that depict Christ's victory over the supernatural forces, and (2) by noting the relationship between the "elements of the world" and the "Colossian heresy" as well as the strong temptation that the two posed for that church in the Lycus Valley.

(1) Three graphic verbs are used in Colossians 2:15 to depict Christ's victory over the angelic powers: "stripped," "disgraced," and "triumphed over" (pers. tr. based on the Greek text). These militant actions of Christ were accomplished because of the cross (v. 14).

(a) Christ "stripped" the rulers and authorities. The meaning of the verb *apekdysamenos* has occasioned much discussion, with three possibilities surfacing. The Greek Church Fathers took the verb to be in the middle, or reflexive, voice, thus translating it: Christ "stripped off himself" the hostile forces that had clung to him on the cross like an alien garment. The Latin Fathers took the verb to be active in voice but intransitive (though they understood the object to be Christ's death). The resulting translation is: Christ "stripped himself" of his flesh through death on the cross, since the flesh was the means by which the evil powers could exercise their tyranny over humans. Most interpreters today, however, believe the verb is active in voice and transitive: Christ "stripped the rulers and authorities" of their power by virtue of his death on the cross and subsequent resurrection.[13]

---

[13]An excellent analysis of this exegetical difficulty is provided by Peter T. O'Brien, *Colossians, Philemon* (WBC 44; Waco, Tex.: Word, 1982), 126–28. This view takes the word as a deponent verb, middle in form but active in meaning.

(b) Christ publicly "disgraced" (*edeigmatisen*) the rulers and authorities. Having divested them of their authority, he exposed to the universe their helplessness. Gustaf Aulén captures Paul's sentiments powerfully in his book, *Christus Victor*, when he asserts that at the cross, in the nadir of his exposure and weakness, Christ showed the acme of his glory and power by subjugating his cosmic enemies.[14]

(c) Christ "triumphed [*thriambeusas*] over them." This verb calls to mind the ancient Roman triumphal procession, in which the victorious general and his army, preceded by the captives of war, marched tumultuously through the streets of Rome to celebrate their military accomplishment. Clarke's description of that ancient custom accentuates the magnificence of Christ's victory:

> He was carried in a magnificent chariot, adorned with ivory and plates of gold, and usually drawn by two white horses. Musicians led up the procession, and played triumphal pieces in praise of the general; and these were followed by young men, who led the victims which were to be sacrificed on the occasion, with their horns gilded, and their heads and necks adorned with ribbons and garlands. Next followed carts loaded with the spoils taken from the enemy, with their horses and chariots. These were followed by the kings, princes, or generals taken in the war, loaded with chains. Immediately after these came the triumphal chariot, before which, as it passed, the people strewed flowers and shouted, "Io, triumphe!" The triumphal chariot was followed by the senate; and the procession was closed by the priests and the attendants, with the different sacrificial utensils, and a white ox, which was to be the chief victim. They then passed through the triumphal arch, along the via sarca to the capitol, where the victims were slain. During this time all the temples were opened, and every altar smoked with offerings and incense.[15]

---

[14]Gustaf Aulén, *Christus Victor: A Historical Study of the Three Main Types of the Idea of the Atonement*, trans. A. G. Hebert (New York: Macmillan, 1969), 86.

[15]Adam Clarke, *Commentary on the Whole Bible* (Grand Rapids: Baker, 1967), 1058. Two of the best primary descriptions of this event are by Josephus (*Jewish War* 7:4–6) and Dio Cassius (*Roman History* 6). *Thriambeuô* refers to the celebration of victory, not to the battle itself.

(2) However, that these spiritual powers have not yet been annihilated is clear from Colossians 2:8, 20 (cf. Gal. 4:3), for there Paul challenges the Colossian Christians not to permit themselves to be reenslaved to the "principles of this world." Undoubtedly the "principles of the world,"[16] the "rulers and authorities" (1:16; 2:15), and the "worship of the angels" (2:18) are parallel expressions forming a part of the heresy infiltrating the churches in the Lycus Valley in ancient Asia Minor.

Though the specific nature of that doctrine has been greatly debated,[17] there is an emerging consensus today that Paul is refuting a type of Jewish *merkabah* (throne) mysticism.[18] This aberrant teaching emphasized ascetic-mystic visionary experiences of the throne of God, patterned somewhat after Ezekiel 1:15–26. In order to achieve this "beatific vision," the worshiper was required to observe scrupulously the Old Testament law, especially rituals of purification. Furthermore, the seeker engaged in a period of asceticism (estimated to be twelve or forty days). Then the heavenly mystic ascent was attempted, all the while showing deference to the angels who led the mystic along the journey. The path to the abode of God led through some seven heavens, each controlled by an archon or angel. Within the seventh heaven, the mystic had to pass through seven halls or palaces (*hekalot*), each . one of which was guarded by an angelic gatekeeper. Only after

---

[16]The phrase "principles [*stoicheia*] of the world" occurs three times in Paul's letters (Gal. 4:3; Col. 2:8, 20). Its meaning is contested, with three major possibilities: (1) principles such as an alphabet, elementary religious beliefs, or mathematical propositions; (2) the four elements of the universe as enumerated in ancient Greek philosophy (earth, water, air, and fire); (3) angelic beings that control the earth and astronomical bodies. O'Brien (*Colossians*, 129–32) provides a helpful overview of the issues involved and makes a convincing case for the third view.

[17]Four of the dominant interpretations of the Colossian heresy are: Judaizers, Gnosticism, Mystery Religions, and Jewish *merkabah* (throne visions) mysticism. The scholarly opinion today is leaning toward the last of these options; see O'Brien, *Colossians*, xxx–xli; F. F. Bruce, *The Epistles to the Colossians, to Philemon and to the Ephesians* (Grand Rapids: Eerdmans, 1984), 17–26; F. O. Francis, "Humility and Angelic Worship in Col. 2:18," *Conflict at Colossae*, eds. F. O. Francis and Wayne Meeks (SBLMS 4; Missoula, Mont.: Scholars Press, 1975), 163–95.

[18]The following description is adapted from Bruce's discussion in *The Epistles to the Colossians*, 17–26.

negotiating this heavenly maze could the worshiper view the glorious divine throne and participate with the angels in the worship of God. This emphasis on angels in *merkabah* mysticism, however, too easily moved from worshiping *with* angels to actually worshiping the angels. Also, it was inevitable that the seven heavens or the seven palaces would be correlated with the seven planetary spheres ruled by their respective lords, so popular in ancient astrology.

The similarities between *merkabah* mysticism and the Colossian heresy are striking: mysticism (Col. 2:2–3, 18c), legalism (2:13–14, 16–17), asceticism (2:18a, 21–23), angelology (1:16–18; 2:8, 18b, 20), and the glorious throne of God (3:1–4). Paul appears to be challenging the Colossians not to grovel before these weak and beggarly foes who supposedly control the heavenly spheres. Rather, they need to reaffirm the defeat of the supernatural powers by continually submitting themselves to the lordship of Christ. Such an admonition assumes the "not yet" aspect of Paul's perspective on the Christian life.

4. Ephesians 6:10–13; cf. 1:19b–23

Our final passage on the overthrow of the inimical spiritual powers is Ephesians 6:10–13.[19] Once again, the eschatological tension produced by the Christ-event colors the apostle's thinking. Comparing Ephesians 1:20; 2:5; 2:16; 5:2 and 5:25 reveals the cross and resurrection of Christ as the turning point of the two ages. Ephesians 1:20–21 is especially clear, referring to the death and resurrection of Christ and his subsequent enthronement "far above all rule and authority and power and dominion, . . . not

---

[19]Two others passages call for brief remarks relative to the subject of anti-God forces in Paul's letters: 2 Thessalonians 2:3–12 and Ephesians 4:8–10. The former is Paul's portrait of the coming man of lawlessness, the Antichrist. Because he believes this person is still to come and therefore not yet a force for the people of God to reckon with, we will not examine this text. However, it should be noted that the already/not yet tension is at work regarding the man of lawlessness, albeit in negative fashion: the mystery of lawlessness is *already* at work in the world (v. 7) but, until the divine restrainer is removed from the scene, the Antichrist has *not yet* been revealed (vv. 7b–12). Regarding Ephesians 4:8–10, a passage often associated with the idea of Christ's "harrowing of hell," two facts

only in the present age, but also in the one to come." Christians, too, are a part of this victory. They "once walked according to the course of this age, according to the prince of the power of the air" (2:2), but now they have been "raised up and seated in the heavenlies in Christ Jesus, in order that in the ages to come he might show the incomparable riches of his grace . . ." (2:6–7).[20]

However, Ephesians 6:10–13 prevents the readers from becoming overconfident because of their position in Christ, for even in the heavenly sphere a spiritual battle rages with the anti-God forces. Nevertheless, believers can be assured of victory if they avail themselves of the divine resources, the armor of God (6:14–18). Thus the already/not yet eschatological paradox is also at work in Ephesians. In what follows, we will elaborate on this thesis by comparing Ephesians 1:20–23 with 6:10–13, two closely related texts. The former accentuates the already aspect of the Christian's triumph over the spiritual enemy while the latter stresses the not yet side. In this regard, at least three points of contact between the two passages can be detected, as the chart and explanation below indicate:

Eph. 1:20–23: Already	Eph. 6:10–13: Not Yet
(1) Seated in the heavenlies (1:20; cf. 2:6).	(1) Conflict in the heavenlies (v. 12).
(2) Defeat of the spiritual rulers and powers (v. 21a).	(2) The threat of the rulers and powers (v. 12).
(3) The age to come has dawned in the resurrection of Christ (v. 21b).	(3) This evil age is in effect until the return of Christ (v. 13).

---

disallow this text from being included in the anti-God forces category in Pauline literature: (1) v. 9b, "He also descended into the lower parts of the earth" (pers. tr. based on the Greek text) is best taken as a genitive of apposition. Thus the last phrase should be translated, "He also descended into the lower parts, that is, the earth." On this reading, it is not hell that Christ descends to between his death and resurrection, but rather the earth that he descends to at his incarnation. (2) The words in v. 8, "He led captives in his train," refer to Christians who once were held captive to sin but have now been delivered and been given spiritual gifts (vv. 9–11), rather than to the demonic hosts who have been enchained by the victorious Christ. While the latter concept is present elsewhere in Paul, as we have seen, it is not operative in Ephesians 4:8–10.

[20]These three translations are based on the Greek text, rendered by the author.

(1) The phrase "seated us with him in the heavenly realms in Christ Jesus" (2:6; cf. 1:20) denotes realized eschatology. By virtue of Christ's death on the cross and triumphant resurrection, Christians have been raised to "the heavenly realms," a term possessing both spatial and spiritual shades of meaning. *Epouraniois* refers to heaven as distinct from earth, and more specifically to the abode of God ("[God] seated him [Christ] at his right hand in the heavenly realms," v. 20). The word also conveys a spiritual nuance by signifying the divine blessings that God has lavished upon believers. However, in this same heavenly sphere Christians presently engage the rulers of darkness in combat (6:12). F. F. Bruce expresses the idea well: "The heavenly realm may be envisaged as comprising a succession of levels, with the throne of God on the highest of these and the hostile forces occupying the lowest . . . the domain of the air (Eph. 2:2) ruled by the spirit which now operates in the disobedient."[21] In other words, as Andrew Lincoln has demonstrated, heaven itself, until the return of Christ, is still under the rubric of this age.[22]

(2) According to Ephesians 1:21a, at his ascension Christ was enthroned over all rulers, authorities, and powers. While this spiritual hierarchy is not restricted to evil forces, it certainly includes them (Eph. 6:12; cf. 1 Cor. 2:6–8; Col. 2:15). Taken together, then, 1:21 and 6:12 signal that Satan and his cohorts are already defeated but not yet vanquished. The notion that Satan has access to the abode of God is not unlike Job 1:6–12 and Rev. 12:7–9, two passages describing the spiritual warfare in heaven between God and his foes. Undoubtedly inherent to all of this is the Jewish apocalyptic belief that the tribulations God's people encounter on earth are the counterpart to the heavenly battle between good and wicked spiritual powers,[23] both of which are being simultaneously waged.[24]

---

[21]Bruce, *The Epistles to the Ephesians*, 406.

[22]Andrew Lincoln, *Paradise Now and Not Yet* (SNTSMS 43; Cambridge: Cambridge University Press, 1981), 173.

[23]The threat that faced the recipients of the letter of Ephesians has been variously identified: e.g., magic, associated with the cult of Artemis, which was so popular in Ephesus; astrology; demonology; psychological inferiority in the face of the imposing Roman empire.

[24]Job 1–2; Daniel 10:10–14.

(3) In Ephesians 1:21b the language of the two-age structure is explicit: "not only in the present age but also in the one to come." The occurrence of these terms in their specific context suggests that Paul believes the death and resurrection of Christ has resulted in the inbreaking of the age to come into this present age, a significant consequence of which is the subjugation of all heavenly powers under the lordship of Jesus (vv. 21–22). However, that the age to come has not yet fully replaced this evil age is clear from 6:13: "Therefore put on the full armor of God, so that when the day of evil comes, you may be able to stand your ground" (cf. 5:16). Although the term "age" is not used here, it is undoubtedly the same time frame as "the present evil age [*aiônos*]" in Galatians 1:4,[25] a period under the control of the forces of evil. Yet Christians who avail themselves of the panoply of God can resist the pressure and stand firm (Eph. 6:14–18). With the return of Christ, all such hostile personages will be disposed of (1:10).

B. HUMANS

Paul's view of humanity and the world illustrates his basic eschatological outlook. Rather than espousing cosmological dualism (the pitting of earth against heaven) or anthropological dualism (the body and soul are diametrically opposed to each other)—both of which view matter as intrinsically evil and, therefore, in contrast to the spiritual—Paul's basic structure of thinking is rooted in eschatological dualism. He is conscious of standing in an interval between two ages—this age and the age to come.

The redemptive work of God is progressing toward the full realization of the kingdom of God in the age to come and includes all creation. Until then, the world remains in the grip of this present evil age. But through Christ, the blessings of the new age have reached back into time to the new humanity, i.e., to those who are in him. On this reading of Paul, earth and heaven,

---

[25]As we have previously noted, the concept of the two ages is broader than the terminology itself.

body and soul are all good, because God created them. What is bad in the scheme of things is sin's takeover of the world, which has adversely affected humanity.[26]

Paul frequently refers to the process of the divine triumph over humanity, but two passages in particular encapsulate his thinking on this point: Romans 1:18–32 and 12:1–2. Though usually treated separately, juxtaposing these texts powerfully illustrates God's creation of a new order within this present world. This becomes clear in chart form; we will elaborate on its antitheses.[27]

Rom. 1:18–32: Old Humanity	Rom. 12:1–2: New Humanity
(1) Worship of creature (vv. 18b–20, 25, 28a).	(1) Worship of Creator (v. 1c).
(2) Perverted lifestyle (vv. 24, 26–27, 28b–32).	(2) Holy lifestyle (v. 1b).
(3) Conformed to this age (vv. 21–23).	(3) Not conformed to this age (v. 2).
(4) Under the wrath of God (v. 18).	(4) Under the mercy of God (v. 1a).

(1) According to Romans 1:18b–20, 25, 28a, one of the fundamental sins[28] of humanity is its refusal to worship God as Creator. All humans have access to the truth of God's power and deity through observing creation, and thus they are without excuse for substituting the worship of idols for the worship of God. They have exchanged the truth about God for a lie, and worshiped and served the creature rather than the Creator (v. 25). Such idolatry is not restricted to Gentiles but has infested Jews as well (2:1). In sharp relief to this picture of idolatry, however, is

---

[26]This paragraph is indebted to George Ladd's discussion in *A Theology of the New Testament* (Grand Rapids: Eerdmans, 1974), 396–97.

[27]One is justified in placing these two texts adjacent to each other for at least three reasons: (1) Literarily, both introduce the two major parts of the epistle: 1:18–32 begins Part I (2:1–11:36), while 12:1–2 begins Part II (12:3–16:27). Thus, it stands to reason that the two introductions are related to one another. (2) As we will see, there are verbal and conceptual connections between the two texts that indicate mutual dependence: worship, two-age structure, lifestyle, etc. (3) Adam theology, as argued below, informs both passages. For a similar pairing of the old and new humanities in Paul's letters, see Ephesians 4:17–32 and Colossians 3:5–13 (cf. Gal. 5:16–26).

[28]For an informative survey of Paul's vocabulary for sin and related concepts, see Ladd, *A Theology of the New Testament*, 405–07.

Paul's exhortation in 12:1c for Christians to dedicate themselves to the service and worship of God, which, in light of their salvation from sin, is only reasonable.

(2) What Paul means by "worship" is specified in 12:1b: "Offer your bodies as living sacrifices, holy and pleasing to God." Perhaps the most apt term encompassing "living," "holy," and "pleasing" is "righteousness" (*dikaiosynê*), the foundational concept of the book of Romans. If so, a further penetrating difference surfaces between the old humanity (1:18–32) and the new humanity (12:1–2): The one possesses the righteousness of God while the other does not. Of the old humanity outside Christ, God's wrath is pronounced against it for displaying "godlessness and wickedness" (1:18). The tragic consequence of refusing to worship God and emulating his holy nature is a perverted lifestyle (vv. 24, 26–27, 28b–33). The list of vices provided by Paul is a sad commentary on what happens when the creature revolts against the Creator. Human dignity degenerates into animal-like behavior.

By contrast, the new humanity (12:1b) espouses honorable and obedient character, because it has received God's righteousness by faith in Christ (see 3:21–11:36). Here Ernst Käsemann's provocative argument that righteousness is apocalyptic in orientation is helpful in plumbing the depths of Paul's thought. When the apostle implores Christians to commit their bodies to God for the purpose of holiness and worship, he has the deep conviction that the church is the divine beachhead for redeeming the world. Christian existence involves a change of lordship, and visible expression of God's reign on earth can be sought in the *bodily* obedience of Christians carried out in daily service to their Lord.[29] God's righteousness, therefore, is both gift and power, because it makes his cause to triumph in a world that has fallen away from him but, as creation, still belongs to him.[30] Thus the individual's justification by faith must be seen in the wider context of God's will to save the entire cosmos.[31]

---

[29]Käsemann, "The Righteousness of God in Paul," *New Testament Questions of Today*, trans. W. J. Montague (Philadelphia: Fortress, 1969), 176.

[30]Ibid., 180.

[31]Ibid., 182.

If Käsemann is correct in his assessment that Paul's concept of God's righteousness is derived from Jewish apocalypticism, then the urgency of the apostle's appeal for Christian commitment takes on deeper significance—the church is none other than the kingdom of God manifested within human history. Christians, as a redeemed society, constitute a new world order of obedience.

(3) The eschatological scope of the new humanity continues with Paul's admonition not to be conformed to this age (*aiône*), but to be transformed by the renewing of the mind (12:2). This antithesis correlates with disassociating oneself from this present evil age and becoming aligned with the age to come. One should note the verbal link between 12:2 and 1:28—mind (*noos*), which highlights the contrasting humanities. The people of this age are characterized as having depraved minds (1:28), while the minds of the people of the age to come are renewed (12:2). In other words, the old humanity is conformed to this age (1:18–32); the new humanity is being transformed to the age to come (12:1–2).

One can probe even deeper into the meaning of these two passages by examining the Adam theology that forms its substructure. It was typical of Jewish apocalyptic literature at about this time to relate the figure of Adam to the two ages. The first Adam, because of the Fall, was thought to be the founder of this age while the Messiah of God, the New Adam, was expected to initiate the age to come.[32] Viewing Romans 1:18–32 and 12:1–2 through this Adamic lens reveals two more significant differences between the old humanity (which is still in the first Adam)

---

[32]There seem to be two traditions in Judaism roughly contemporaneous with Paul concerning the relationship between Adam and Messiah. (1) Because Adam was expected to be restored to his original glory which he lost in the Garden, he was identified with the future Messiah. When Adam's glory returns, humanity and creation will be renewed (*Apoc.Mos.* 13:3; 37:5; 39:2; cf. *1 Enoch* 46; *4 Ezra* 13). Murmelstein was one of the first scholars to identify this belief in some circles of Judaism. He argued that the idea of Adam himself as the coming redeemer was suppressed in these texts and in others, in response to the Christian doctrine of the second Adam and his correspondence with the first Adam (B. Murmelstein, "Adam, ein Beitrag zur Messiaslehre," *WZKM* 35 [1928]: 242–75; 36 [1929]: 51–86; *contra* Robin Scroggs, *The Last Adam* [Philadelphia: Fortress, 1966], x–xv; and Kim, *The Origin of Paul's Gospel* [WUNT 2, 10: Tübingen: J. C. B. Mohr (Paul

and the new humanity (which is in Christ, the last Adam): (a) the image of God is marred in the one, but renewed in the other; (b) the one lives a life of foolishness and evil while the other lives by the good will of God.

(a) Romans 1:23 presents humanity's estrangement from God in terms reminiscent of Adam's fall. "Image" (*eikonos*), "likeness" or "form" (*homoiômati*), and "glory" (*doxa*) undoubtedly allude to Adam's (and Eve's) creation in the image of God and their concomitant endowment with the glory of God, both of which were altered in some way by the entrance of sin into the Garden of Eden (see Gen. 1–3; Ps. 8:4–8; cf. *Wis.Sol.* 2:23–24; *Jub.* 3:28–32; *4 Ezra* 4:30; *2 Bar.* 54:17–19).[33] The language of creation is also echoed in the words "man and birds and animals and reptiles," in that Romans 1:23 reverses the creation order of Genesis 1:21–28. With the advent of sin, creation has, in effect, reverted back to a chaotic state. The unfortunate result of Adam's sin is that human beings, like Adam before them, do not acknowledge their creaturely dependence on God (cf. Rom. 1:24–31 with Gen. 3).[34]

In marked contrast, however, is the process of the renewal of the image of God that is at work in the new humanity (12:2). We have already observed that this verse, by using the word "mind," recalls by way of contrast Romans 1:18–32—especially verse 28 and the old humanity's depraved mindset. This connection is heightened by the term "renew" (*anakainôsei*) in 12:2, which also has an Adamic connotation. This word is used three other times by Paul, and each time in relation to the new humanity: 2 Corinthians 4:16; Colossians 3:10; and Titus 3:5. The Adamic hue is especially significant to the interpretation of 2 Corinthians 4:16 and Colossians 3:10. The description of the decaying of the outer man and the renewing of the inner man in

---

Siebeck)], 180–86). (2) The more dominant tradition is that Messiah would be a separate figure from Adam, who would correct Adam's sin by inaugurating the age to come (*T.Levi* 18:10–18; *Gen.R.* 12:6; *Num.R.* 13:12; *Ex.R.* 30:3; *Gen.R.* 24:4; *1 Enoch* 90:37–38).

[33]For further details and documentation of the pervasive belief in Judaism and Christianity that Adam and Eve were endowed with the glory of God, see Pate, *Adam Christology*, chap. 2.

[34]Morna Hooker should be credited as one of the first scholars to detect Adam theology in Romans 1:18–32, in her "Adam in Romans 1," *NTS* 6 (1960): 297–306.

the former passage is best understood against the backdrop of the restoration of the marred image of God in the heart of the believer by Christ, the last Adam. Similarly, Colossians 3:10 admonishes the believer to "put on the new self, which is being renewed . . . in the image of its Creator." That is, the image of God depreciated by Adam's sin is being restored to the believer through Christ.[35] Romans 12:1–2 continues this line of thinking by challenging Christians to extricate themselves from this age and associate themselves with the new nature of the last Adam by renewing their minds. This is nothing less than the restoration in them of the image of God.

(b) The old humanity lives a life of foolishness and evil while the new humanity lives by the good will of God. The Adamic background sheds new light on the phrase, "Then you will be able to test and approve what God's will is, his good, pleasing and perfect will" (12:2). The denial of the good will of God was precisely the underlying problem of the choice of the primeval couple in their disobeying the commandment of God in the Garden (Gen. 3). Believing themselves to know what was best for them, they obeyed the voice of the serpent by eating of the Tree of Knowledge of Good and Evil. The consequence of that fateful decision was foolishness and evil for the human race (cf. Rom. 1:18–32 with Gen. 3:5). But for those who obey God by renewing their minds in Christ, there is the promise of experiencing the divine plan for their lives (Rom. 12:2).

The opposing philosophies of living a life of futility and foolishness (Rom. 1:21–22) and of walking according to the perfect will of God (Rom. 12:2) is striking. Ephesians 5:15–17, a passage also devoted to the categorization of the old and new humanities (see 4:17–5:21), depicts the same contrast—Christians are not to walk foolishly, but must make the most of this evil age by doing the will of God.

(4) Those outside Christ have incurred the wrath of God (Rom. 1:18) while those in Christ are indebted to his mercy (12:1a). Both situations reflect realized eschatology. The most vivid term Paul uses to describe those who are involved with

---

[35]For further discussion on this matter, see Pate, *Adam Christology*, 109–10.

this present evil age is "wrath" (Rom. 1:18; cf. Rom. 2:5; Eph. 2:3; 1 Thess. 1:10). In Jewish apocalypticism divine anger toward sin was expected to fall on unbelievers at the end of history (Isa. 24; Joel 3; Dan. 12:1–2; *1 Enoch* 91:12–13; *2 Enoch* 65:6; *1 QS* 3:4). *Fourth Ezra* 7:113 expresses it well, "But the day of judgment shall be the end of this age and the beginning of the eternal age that is to come." Yet, in Paul's view, with the first coming of Christ, that final denouement has broken into this present age on those who reject God's righteousness (cf. the present tense in Rom. 1:18). Such is the condition of this age and those who find themselves in it. But those who have received God's righteousness in Christ by faith are under God's mercy. Justification by faith is nothing less than sinners being declared righteous before God *now*, in anticipation of the Great Assize (see Rom. 3:21–8:39; especially 5:1–2; 8:1).

These four contrasts in Romans 1:18–32 and 12:1–2 between the old and new humanities, then, are eschatological in nature in that they correlate with this age and the age to come. But it must be stressed that, for Paul, the Christ event has resulted in an overlapping of the two ages. The age to come has moved into the present, so that the believer currently exists at the turning point of the ages. This accounts for the tension and ambiguity that Christians presently experience. The believer belongs to the new age but is not isolated from this evil age. The presence of the evil anti-God forces in this world give rise to the struggle between the flesh and the Spirit within the believer. Although the flesh is not evil in itself, when allowed to be controlled by sin it becomes an ally of the wicked powers of this age, defeated though they are (see Rom. 6–8). This is why Paul's challenges in Romans 12:1–2 are expressed in the present tense: "offer" (v. 1); "do not conform" (v. 2a); "be transformed" (v. 2b). Indeed, this dialectical relationship between the already and the not yet will govern the Christian life until the *Parousia* (see Rom. 7:14–25; 13:11–14).

C. CREATION

For Paul, redemption includes creation. His frame of reference here is Genesis 1, with its repeated declaration that God's creation is good (see 2 Tim. 4:4; cf. 1 Cor. 8:6). However pervasive and perverse sin is in the world, it is still an alien force not inherent to the cosmos (see Gen. 3). Therefore, along with the Judaism of his day, Paul believed that God would someday reclaim his world by recreating out of it a new heaven and a new earth (see Isa. 65:17–25). But in the death and resurrection of Christ (2 Cor. 5:17; Gal. 6:15), Paul held that the new creation has already dawned, though the full revelation of the kingdom of God is not yet completed. Thus the eschatological tension resulting from the overlapping of the two ages impacts his understanding of creation itself. Nowhere is this clearer than in Romans 8:19–22. The divine triumph over the cosmos is developed there in three time frames: this age (v. 20); the age to come (vv. 19, 21); and the overlapping of the two (v. 22).

1. This Age (Rom. 8:20)

That the juxtaposition of the two ages is in view in Romans 8:19–22 is evident in the thematic statement of verse 18, "I consider that our present sufferings are not worth comparing with the glory that will be revealed in us." The phrases "present sufferings" and "glory that will be revealed" correspond to this age and the age to come, respectively. According to verse 20, creation[36] exists now under the burden of this age; most agree that the words "the creation was subjected to frustration, not by its own choice, but by the will of the one who subjected it" refer to Genesis 3:17–19 as the cause of such a condition. In that passage, the earth was cursed by God[37] because of Adam's sin: "cursed is the ground because of you." The net result of the divine judgment is that the destinies of creation and humankind are thereafter interlocked.

---

[36]*ktiseôs* has been variously interpreted as the whole creation, including humanity (both believing and nonbelieving) and the angels; humanity only; angels only; and subhuman nature only. Most interpreters today rightly understand the last alternative to be the most accurate. C. E. B. Cranfield provides both a good survey of the options as well as a convincing case for this last choice (*The Epistle to the Romans*, Vol. 1 [ICC; Edinburgh: T. & T. Clark, 1975], 411–12).

[37]Undoubtedly the implied subject of *hypotaxanta* ("the one who subjected it") in Romans 8:20 is God.

2. The Age to Come (Rom. 8:19, 21)

Paul attributes human-like qualities to creation when he asserts, "The creation waits in eager expectation for the sons of God to be revealed" (v. 19; see a similar description in v. 21). The longing of the cosmos for the final glorification of the people of God and the simultaneous restoration of the earth is a dominant refrain in Jewish apocalypticism and is succinctly summarized in the expression, *Urzeit-Endzeit* (original time-end time). That is, the end of time, or the age to come, will recapitulate the paradisiacal setting of the beginning of time (see: Isa. 11:6–8; 65:17–25; Ezek. 34:25–27; *Jub.* 1:29; *1 Enoch* 45:4–5; *2 Bar.* 32:6; 49; 73:5–7; *4 Ezra* 6:16; 7:25, 119–126).

The hopes for effecting this shift of the two ages were often pinned on the coming Messiah. A famous rabbinic quote (*Gen.R.* 12:6) epitomizes in negative fashion both Judaism's desire for the renewal of creation and the recovery for humanity of Adam's lost glory when it states that the first man lost "his lustre, his immortality, his height, the fruit of the earth, the fruit of trees, and the illuminaries. . . . Though these things were created in their fullness, yet when Adam sinned they were spoiled, and they will not again return to their perfection until the son of Perez [the Messiah] comes."

3. The Overlapping of the Two Ages (Rom. 8:22)

A third time frame operative in Romans 8:19–22 is the overlapping of the two ages. The upshot of this perspective is that the new creation has already begun in the Christian but has not yet been finished on the earth (cf. 2 Cor. 5:17; Gal. 6:15). There are three indicators to this effect in the passage:

(1) In the cryptic description of creation "wait[ing] in eager expectation for the sons of God to be revealed" (v. 19) is an eschatological tension, produced because the earth is between the first coming of Christ ("up to the present time," v. 22) and his second coming, which will return the glory of God to both the world and his people (cf. Col. 3:4). The first of these events began the process of restoring creation and creature to the purpose for which they were made—to display the divine glory; the second will consummate that process. Using the language of personification, Paul

exclaims that the cosmos itself knows that the divine program of redemption is already underway, hence its straining forward (*apokaradokia*, v. 19) to see the culmination of that day.

(2) It would be easy to overlook the significance of the words, "in hope that the creation itself will be liberated from its bondage to decay and brought into the glorious freedom of the children of God" (vv. 20–21). Paul's understanding of "hope" is thoroughly rooted in eschatology; it is the comforting assurance that results from the knowledge that the age to come, having broken into this age, is soon to appear fully. As such it is dependent on faith (e.g., Rom. 8:24–25; 5:5; 12:12; Col. 1:27). In other words, according to Romans 8:20, Paul believes that the presence of the age to come within the believer raises the hope of creation for its own deliverance.

(3) Romans 8:22, at first glance, is enigmatic: "we know that the whole creation has been groaning as in the pains of childbirth right up to the present time." However, the Jewish apocalyptic background of Paul's thought elucidates the meaning of the verse. The metaphor of birth pangs used here is common in Jewish apocalypticism to denote the messianic woes, the trials and tumults of the end time that will increase in frequency and intensity immediately prior to the appearance of the Messiah (often associated with the day of the Lord; see Dan. 12:1; Joel 1; Amos 5:16–17; Zeph. 1:14–16; *Jub.* 23:11; 2 *Bar.* 55:6; 4 *Ezra* 7:37). In fact, the Greek word used for the messianic woes or birth pangs—*hôdines*—is precisely the term used in Romans 8:22 of creation. Moreover, the other word in verse 22—"groan" (*stenazei*)—undoubtedly calls to mind the LXX translation of Genesis 3:15–16, where Eve is given a twofold word from God. God promises that Eve will give birth to a future deliverer, but he warns of the intense pain that will henceforth accompany childbirth (*stenazei*). Most likely this metaphor of birth pangs, with its mixed message of suffering and joy, is the source for the later idea of the messianic woes.[38]

Prominent in the concept of the messianic woes is the expectation that creation will undergo cosmic upheaval right before

---

[38]I have worked this out in more detail in *Adam Christology*, 117–18.

the arrival of the age to come. The signs of the end include earth-quakes, famines, eclipses of the sun and the moon, falling stars, etc. (Isa. 24:17–23; Joel 2:1–2; Zeph. 1:14–16; *1 Enoch* 80:4–5; *4 Ezra* 5:4–5; *Sib.Oracles* 3:77–92; *As.Mos.* 10:3–5; *1 QH* 5; cf. Matt. 24:29; Mark 13:24; Luke 21:11). These portents on earth and in heaven were thought to be cosmic convulsive-like labor pains that would precede the birth of a new heaven and earth. Paul draws on this imagery in Romans 8:22—except that for the apostle, with the death and resurrection of Jesus the Messiah, the labor pangs have *already* begun. In effect, the earth is analogous to the womb, while the cosmic waves of upheaval are comparable to labor pangs. The closer the birth of the new creation gets, the more intense and frequent are the catastrophic signs in the old creation.

It is probable that Paul, like other New Testament authors, believed that, since the coming of Christ signaled the arrival of the last days, the messianic woes must have been set in motion at the event of the cross.[39] This period was expected to run its course and be replaced with the kingdom of God at the *Parousia* (Matt. 24; Mark 13; Luke 21; 2 Peter 3:3–14; Rev. 6–19). Thus, Paul likely believed that the natural disasters his generation encoun-tered would shortly give place to cosmic disturbances, and that these would, in turn, herald the return of Christ (cf. Rom. 8:22 with Mark 13:19). The apostle may even have interpreted the ex-tensive famine in his day to be one of those signs of the end times (cf. Rom. 15:26 with Acts 11:27–30).[40] In other words, the idea of creation's groaning in the pains of childbirth is full of meaning—it is proof that the age to come has already broken into this age, creating an eschatological tension present in the cosmos.

---

[39]See Schweitzer, *The Mysticism of Paul*, trans. William Montgomery (New York: Henry Holt, 1931), 144; French Arrington, *Paul's Aeon Terminology in 1 Corinthians* (Washington, D.C.: University Press of America, 1978), 119–24; Beker, *Paul the Apostle*, 146; more on the subject in chap. 9 of this work.

[40]I have not seen this suggestion proposed by others, but it fits nicely with the idea that Paul viewed his ministry to the Gentiles as eschatological in nature.

D. CHRIST

It undoubtedly comes as a surprise to many interpreters of Paul that, according to him, the role of Christ in the triumph of God in the world, as crucial as it is, nevertheless is provisional. For the apostle, Christology is subordinate to theology. Beker puts it well:

> Paul is an apocalyptic theologian with a theocentric outlook. The Christ-event is the turning point in time that announces the end of time. Indeed, Christ has become "Lord" since his exaltation and is now God's appointed world ruler who bears the divine name (Phil. 2:10), but—as Paul adds—"to the *glory* of God the Father." All that Christ does is for the sake of the final eschatological glory of God. . . . Christ remains the subordinate son, the agent of God's redemptive purpose. . . .[41]

The classic Pauline text that emphasizes the subordinate role of Christ in the triumph of God over the world is 1 Corinthians 15:20–28, which applies the already/not yet eschatological tension to the Son himself. The apostle makes two points there: (1) the messianic kingdom has already been inaugurated (vv. 20–25); (2) the rule of God has not yet been consummated (vv. 26–28).

1. The Messianic Kingdom Has Already Been Inaugurated (1 Cor. 15:20–25)

Albert Schweitzer placed Pauline scholars in his debt with his remarkable demonstration that 1 Corinthians 15:20–28 is based on the Jewish apocalyptic idea of a temporary (*interregnum*) messianic kingdom, which itself will be replaced by the eternal kingdom of God.[42] The impetus for this concept is perhaps Ezekiel 33–48. There the prophet looks forward to the establishment of a believing remnant (chs. 33–37). However, the spiritual renewal of God's people is not an end in itself; God's ultimate purpose is to create a new Jerusalem (chs. 40–48), which

---

[41]Beker, *Paul the Apostle*, 362–63.

[42]See Schweitzer, *The Mysticism of Paul*, 67–68. The most recent treatment of this idea is the one by L. Joseph Kreitzer, *Jesus and God in Paul's Eschatology* (JSNT Supp. Ser. 19; Sheffield: JSOT, 1987), especially chap. 3.

will appear on earth after the anti-God forces have been defeated (chs. 38–39).[43] Thus, the idea of a temporary messianic kingdom is adumbrated in the Old Testament, but it receives its fullest expression in 2 Bar. 29:3 and 4 Ezra 7:26–31 (cf. Rev. 20). Moreover, it surfaces in those rabbinic writings that distinguish between the temporary "days of the Messiah" and the eternal "age to come."[44] In this composite literature, therefore, the following order of events emerges: this age, the transitional messianic kingdom, and the world (or age) to come. This eschatological schema undergirds 1 Corinthians 15:20–25, except that, for Paul, the messianic kingdom is no longer future—it has already been inaugurated in the person of Jesus. Two blessings resulting from the arrival of the messianic kingdom are highlighted in verses 20–25: (a) the restoration of the eternal life Adam lost, by the resurrection of Christ (vv. 20–22); and (b) Christ's retrieval of Adam's lost dominion (vv. 23–25).

a. The Restoration of the Eternal Life Adam Lost, by the Resurrection of Christ (1 Cor. 15:20–22)

In a reference to the Adam story of Genesis 2–3, Paul lays the blame for the entrance of death into the human race at the feet of Adam, but believes that Jesus Christ, through his own death and subsequent resurrection, has restored eternal life to all whose faith is in him, "For since death came through a man, the resurrection of the dead comes also through a man. As in Adam all die, so in Christ all will be made alive" (vv. 21–22). Paul portrays Adam and Christ as the two representative people with whom the destiny of humankind interfaces. Christ stands at the beginning of a new humanity in a similar way that Adam stood at the beginning of the old humanity.

In other words, Christ's resurrection has begun the process of reversing the spread of death caused by Adam's sin. Paul thus views Christ's resurrection as eschatological in nature—it is the

---

[43]Ladd is one of the first to trace the idea of a temporary messianic kingdom back to Ezekiel 33–39; see A Theology of the New Testament, 558.

[44]See Joseph Klausner, The Idea of the Messiah in Israel, from its Beginning to the Completion of the Mishnah, trans. W. F. Stinespring (New York: Macmillan, 1955), 48–419.

inbreaking into history of that general resurrection that was expected to occur at the end of time.[45] Jesus' resurrection is the "firstfruits" of the resurrection at the end of the age (v. 20). Since firstfruits signify both the beginning of the harvest and a pledge of more to come, his resurrection is the beginning stage of the approaching resurrection of believers, thus marking the creation of a new humanity with a new relationship to God. Therefore, one blessing already available to the citizens of the messianic kingdom is eternal life.

b. Christ's Retrieval of Adam's Lost Dominion (1 Cor. 15:23–26)

Judaism believed that Adam and Eve were created to exercise dominion over the earth, but that they forfeited that privilege when they attempted to become like God (Gen. 3; *Sirach* 49:16; *1 QS* 3:17–4:6; *Wis.Sol.* 2:23). Drawing on this background, Paul asserts that Christ has begun to retrieve that lost dominion (1 Cor. 15:25, 27a). He does so by applying two Old Testament texts (Ps. 110:1 and 8:4), often associated with Adam's lost dominion, to Christ, relating them to our Lord's present heavenly session—a reign that is in the process of defeating God's enemies (sin, Satan, and eventually death). Christ has merited this position, unlike Adam, by obediently submitting to the divine plan to die on the cross for the sins of the world (1 Cor. 15:3–4).[46] Believers, too, rule with Jesus in this messianic kingdom (v. 22; cf. Eph. 2:5–7; Col. 3:1–4; Rev. 20:6).

2. The Rule of God Has Not Yet Been Consummated (1 Cor. 15:26–28)

Even though the messianic kingdom has begun, it is temporary and will give way to the eternal kingdom of God. Whenever Paul speaks of the kingdom of God, it is often future, not having been fully manifested yet on earth (e.g., 1 Cor. 6:9–10; 15:50; Gal. 5:19–21; 2 Thess. 1:5). This means that believers are already in the kingdom of Christ but still await the *Parousia* and the coming of

---

[45]This is the major premise of Beker's work, *Paul the Apostle.*

[46]For further details on Paul's usage of these two psalms, see the author's analysis in *The Glory of Adam and the Afflictions of the Righteous,* 89–91.

God's kingdom. Two indicators in 1 Corinthians 15:26–28 confirm that the eternal rule of God has not yet been consummated on earth: (a) death is still at large (v. 26), and (b) the Son has not yet delivered the kingdom to the Father (vv. 27–28).

a. Death Is Still at Large (1 Cor. 15:26)

Verse 26 asserts, "The last enemy to be destroyed is death." Death, God's archenemy, retains its power and has not yet been completely brought under control. Although Jesus overcame death by his resurrection, God's people are nevertheless mortal and still anticipate their immortal bodies (vv. 50–57). Thus, prior to the return of Christ and the full establishment of the eternal kingdom, God's saving work is incomplete.[47]

b. The Son Has Not Yet Delivered the Kingdom to the Father (1 Cor. 15:27–28)

Verses 27b–28 lucidly show that the Son himself is subordinate to the Father in that one day he, too, will submit his authority to God: "Then the Son himself will be made subject to him who put everything under him, that God may be all in all." Is such language of subservience functional or ontological? Undoubtedly Paul intends the former, for his equation elsewhere of Christ with God eliminates the latter (Rom. 10:9; Phil. 2:11; Titus 2:13). Why, then, does Paul stress the subordinate side of the relationship between Christ and God here? The answer to this question lies in verses 21–22, where Paul has used the Adam-Christ typology. The point he wishes to make in verses 27–28 is that Christ, unlike Adam, submits himself to the plan of God. Not only did the Son obey the divine will by dying on the cross (vv. 3–4), but also even at the *Parousia* Christ will demonstrate his loyalty to God by voluntarily handing over to him the dominion of the cosmos. C. K. Barrett writes of v. 27:

> There is an element of subordinationism here . . . , which is inevitably bound up with Christ's representative fulfillment of

---

[47]As a point of interest in this regard, *4 Ezra* 7 also states that death will persist in the temporary messianic kingdom until the eternal kingdom of God is fully established.

Ps viii. According to this Psalm, man exercises his appointed lordship over the rest of creation in his being "a little lower than God." This is in harmony with the creation narrative (Gen i 28). It is when man strives to rise above his appointed place and put himself on God's level that he falls below it and loses his dominion (Gen ii 17, iii 17ff; Rom i 21; v 12–21). In the obedient service of the representative man Jesus Christ, man's dominion is being restored, but its security lies only in the unvarying submission of Jesus the Son to his Father.[48]

CONCLUSION

Taking its cue from scholars like Schweitzer and Beker, this chapter has attempted to apply the two-age structure to Pauline theology proper. Only in viewing Paul through the lens of Jewish apocalypticism will the centrality of God to the thought of the apostle be sufficiently addressed. We have seen that Paul believes that God is in the process of redeeming his world, by defeating his enemies, redeeming the new humanity, renewing creation, and establishing his kingdom. These basic spheres of reality have been forever changed for the good by the first coming of Christ. The culmination point of these activities, however, awaits the *Parousia*. With this chapter serving as the chrysalis from which Paul's thought springs, we may now proceed to examine other related categories.

---

[48]C. K. Barrett, *A Commentary on the First Epistle to the Corinthians*, 360–61.

III

PAULINE CHRISTOLOGY: MESSIAH AND THE TURN OF THE AGES

INTRODUCTION

What is the significance of the death and resurrection of Jesus Christ? Gustaf Aulén traces the three dominant approaches to this issue in his classic work, *Christus Victor: A Historical Study of the Three Main Types of the Idea of Atonement*. The first view is the "objective" view, associated with Anselm of Canterbury, whose eleventh-century work, *Cur Deus Homo?* (meaning "Why did God become man?"), argued that Jesus died in order to meet the demands of divine justice. In essence, Christ died a substitutionary death for sinners. The second approach, the "subjective view," was posed by Anselm's contemporary Abelard, who proposed the moral influence theory. Abelard maintained that God's love for sinners in sending Jesus to die so impacts them that they are motivated to repent and love others. The third type, Aulén's own view, is labeled the "classic" or "*Christus Victor*" approach because it appeals to ancient Church Fathers such as Irenaeus and encompasses more modern theologians such as Martin Luther. This model interprets the cross of Christ as the decisive moment in a cosmic drama between good and evil, in which the anti-God forces are defeated, thus liberating humanity to enjoy a new-found relationship with God. Accordingly, God is both author and object of reconciliation.[1]

---

[1]Gustaf Aulén, *Christus Victor: A Historical Study of the Three Main Types of the Idea of the Atonement*, trans. A. G. Hebert (New York: Macmillan, 1969).

As helpful as these theories are, however, none of them is sufficient to account for the wide-ranging data concerning the death and resurrection of Christ, especially as portrayed in the Pauline literature.[2] Therefore, many modern interpreters of Paul prefer to define the death and resurrection of Jesus in apocalyptic terms. That is, the death of Christ spelled the end of this age while his resurrection marked the beginning of the age to come.[3] In doing so, these scholars draw their inspiration from the role of Messiah that occurs in the pertinent Jewish apocalyptic writings.[4]

---

[2]The death of Jesus for Paul is a multi-faceted concept or, better, is multi-layered in meaning. Three strands of teaching have been identified in the Pauline literature. The first can be called the *vindicational* aspect of Christ's death. This is thought to be the contribution of the Jewish Christian church, the oldest interpretation of the death of Jesus; it maintains that the death and resurrection of Christ were inseparably related in early apostolic preaching, because the latter was the divine vindication of the former (e.g., Rom. 1:3–4; Phil. 2:5–11 [minus Paul's redaction, "death on a cross"]; cf. Acts 2:22–36; 3:15–16). The second teaching is the *sacrificial* tradition that Jesus' death was an atonement for sin (e.g., Rom. 3:25; 1 Cor. 15:3; 2 Cor. 13:4; Gal. 2:20), a doctrine originating in the Hellenistic Christian community. Third, Paul added the theology of the *cross* (e.g., Rom. 6:6; 1 Cor. 1:17–18; Gal. 3:13; Phil. 2:8). Ernst Käsemann pointed out this additional layer, arguing that the apostle used the idea of the cross polemically as a counter-message to his opponents' theology of glory and miracles (see "The Saving Significance of the Death of Jesus in Paul," in *Perspectives on Paul*, trans. Margaret Kohl [Philadelphia: Fortress, 1971], 32–59). Recently, Charles B. Cousar has called for caution in separating the teaching of Paul on the death of Jesus into such clear-cut divisions (*A Theology of the Cross: The Death of Jesus in the Pauline Letters* [Minneapolis: Fortress, 1990]).

[3]Advocates of this view include Ernst Käsemann, "The Death of Jesus in the Pauline Letters"; Beker, *Paul the Apostle: The Triumph of God in Life and Thought* (Philadelphia: Fortress, 1980); Louis Martyn, "Apocalyptic Antinomies in the Letter to the Galatians," *NTS* 31 (1985): 410–24; Cousar, *A Theology of the Cross*. A similar issue concerns the relationship in Paul between the historical Jesus, the ethics of Jesus, and his death/resurrection. It is common knowledge that Paul says next to nothing about the historical Jesus (2 Cor. 5:16 does not qualify as such a reference) and that the ethics of Jesus play only a secondary role for him (Rom. 12:14–17; 1 Cor. 9:14; cf. Acts 20:35). His emphasis is clearly on the death and resurrection of Christ. This is so because, for Paul, it is that event above all that inaugurated the age to come and, therefore, possesses eschatological import.

[4]Actually, the eschatological approach to Paul's view of the death and resurrection of Jesus nicely incorporates all three of the aforementioned views. Concerning the first, the apostle held that the death of Christ atones for sin and that a person's faith in him results in the divine verdict of "not guilty," an endtime decision now characterizing the Christian because the age to come has ar-

D. S. Russell provides a fine survey of the subject for both the Old Testament and early Judaism.[5] The word "Messiah" (the Hebrew term) or "Christ" (the Greek term) means "anointed," with reference to one who is especially set apart for God's work. As such, this word is most often applied in the Old Testament to the kings of Israel (e.g., 2 Sam. 19:21; 23:1; Lam. 4:10) and, in the postexilic period, to the priests of God (Ps. 133:2; Zech. 4:14). Emerging out of the prophetic material toward the close of the Old Testament, however, is a more general messianic hope (though the word "Messiah" is not actually used for the concept) of a future Golden Age, the future kingdom of God, in which the fortunes of Israel will be restored and the surrounding nations judged (Isa. 40–66; Ezek. 40–48; Joel 3; Zech. 14). This era of justice and peace could be associated with a coming ideal ruler (Isa. 9:6; 11:1; Jer. 23:5; Mic. 5:2; Zech. 9:9). The conclusion Russell draws from the preceding data, then, is that the role of the Messiah in the Old Testament is somewhat restricted to a nontechnical sense; that is, there is not some single individual expected as the Messiah, but rather a broad messianic expectation of the coming kingdom of God.

However, with the development of Judaism, particularly apocalyptic Judaism (200 B.C.E.–100 C.E.), the technical sense of Messiah as the long-awaited inaugurator of the kingdom of God developed, who is identified either as a Davidic-like king (*T.Jud.* 17:5–6; 22:2–3; 24:1–6; *Ps.Sol.* 17:23–51; 18:6–10), a Levitical priest (*T.Levi* 18:2–7; *T.Reub.* 6:5–12), or both (as in the Qumran writings, *1QS* 9:11; *CD* 14:19; 19:10; *1QM* 12:10; 19:3). Also to be connected with the idea of the Messiah in Jewish apocalyptic literature is the figure of the heavenly Son of Man (Dan. 7:13; *1 Enoch* 37–73; *4 Ezra* 7:28–29; 12:32; 13:32, 37; *2 Bar.* 29:3; 30:1).

Conspicuously absent in the aforementioned writings, and for that matter anywhere in early Judaism, is the notion of a

---

rived (Rom. 5:1; 8:1). Second, believers in Jesus can now live a life of love, an ethic enduring for all time and now "incarnated" in the Christian by the Spirit (Rom. 5:5; 8:8; 1 Cor. 13). Third, because the cross and resurrection was the hinge of history, God's kingdom has begun the process of overcoming the evil forces of this age (1 Cor. 2:6–8; Col. 2:15).

[5]D. S. Russell, *The Method and Message of Jewish Apocalyptic* (Philadelphia: Westminster, 1964), 304–23.

suffering and dying Messiah, an incontractable problem for the New Testament.[6] In light of this, the question can be raised: Why is there no concept of a dying Messiah in Judaism? Although there is no clear answer to this query, one can hazard two guesses. (1) From a positive point of view, apparently Jews at this period believed the real key to inaugurating the kingdom of God was their efforts to obey the Torah. If they kept the divine law, God would send his kingdom, with or without a Messiah (e.g., see *CD* 4:17; *1QH* 1:32; *2 Bar.* 17:4–18:2; 51:3–7; *4 Ezra* 7:51, 89, 96; *Pirke Abot* 2:8; 6:7; *Sif.Deut.* 34; *b.San.* 97b; *p.Tan.* 64a). This last text expresses the idea succinctly, albeit in negative fashion: "If Israel repented a single day, immediately would the Son of David come. If Israel observed a single Sabbath properly, immediately would the Son of David come."

(2) In a pejorative light, any idea of a dying Messiah would undoubtedly have scandalized Jews, because it would have signified to them both weakness and sinfulness on the part of such a revered personage—*weakness* at the hands of his enemies (something the nation of Israel had long grown weary of) and *sinfulness* because death itself was perceived as the logical conclusion of sin (something with which no Messiah should be associated). Joseph Klausner poignantly summarizes the messianic idea in Israel, particularly as it was distinguished from early Christianity:

> The Jewish Messiah is the redeemer of his people and the redeemer of mankind. But he does not redeem them by his

---

[6]The only possible exceptions to this pattern are *4 Ezra* 7:28–30 (first century C.E.) and the *Targum of Isaiah* 53 (fifth century C.E.). The first mentions the death of the Messiah as climaxing the temporal messianic kingdom. However, it is important to note that the Messiah does not suffer; rather, after having lived long and well for four hundred years, he simply dies with the rest of humanity. His death, therefore, has no apparent theological significance. Nor can the Aramaic (Targum) translation of Isaiah 53 be used as evidence for the concept of a suffering Messiah, because it transposes (probably in reaction to Christianity) the afflictions of the Suffering Servant of Isaiah 53 *from* the Messiah *to* Israel and/or the surrounding Gentile nations. Moreover, both texts are dated after the birth of Christ and cannot be used as testimony for *pre*-Christian Jewish messianic understanding.

blood; instead he lends aid to their redemption by his great abilities and deeds. To be sure, Satan will be vanquished in the messianic age, not by the Messiah, but by God. Man must redeem himself from sin *not by faith alone*, but *by repentance and good works*; then God will redeem him from death and Satan. Each man is responsible for himself, and through his good deeds he must find atonement for his sins. He cannot lean upon the Messiah or upon the Messiah's suffering and death.[7]

The foregoing considerations have revealed both continuity and discontinuity between early Christianity and Jewish apocalypticism. The former, including the apostle Paul (as we will see in this chapter), is indebted to the latter for its emphasis on Messiah as inaugurator of the age to come. But it is the concept of the death of the Messiah that separates the two. Can one be more specific concerning this difference? In particular, how does Paul relate the death of Christ to the Jewish two-age structure? We may broach the discussion here by suggesting the following thesis. For Paul, this age is under the tyranny of sin, whose rule has so twisted the Law of God that it now serves the flesh, which could only be checked by the death and resurrection of Christ.

In the last chapter, we saw how the Cross initiated the demise of the anti-God forces. Such opponents, along with death, we can label the *external* foes of humanity. Accordingly, we can identify *sin*, the *flesh*, and the *law* as the *inward* counterpart of those enemies. These are the hostile powers that enslave the people of this age. For Paul, even Jews who think they obey the divine law are to be identified as participants of this age and consequently are in bondage to the flesh. With the death and resurrection of Christ, however, the age to come dawned and, with it, the defeat of sin and the fleshly propensity toward evil, together with the liberation of the law.

This chapter, therefore, will examine the key Pauline texts on the death and resurrection of Jesus from an apocalyptic frame of reference. It is not coincidental that these texts are clustered around the three components of the inner evil alliance: sin, the flesh, and the Law (unwilling member of this "trinity" that it is).

---

[7]Joseph Klausner, *The Idea of the Messiah in Israel, From Its Beginning to the Completion of the Mishnah,* trans. W. F. Stipespring (New York: Macmillan, 1955), 530.

This threefold classification will serve as a guide to the ensuing discussion.

A. THE CHRIST-EVENT AND SIN

In this first category, we include the major Pauline references to the death and resurrection of Christ as it is related to sin: Galatians 1:4–5; 1 Corinthians 15:3–4; Romans 3:21–26; Colossians 1:13–23; Ephesians 1:7–12; Titus 2:11–13. The point to be made from our survey of these texts is that the Christ-event has broken the back of sin, the ruler of this age. Though the terminology may differ from passage to passage concerning this momentous occasion, the reality is the same—the cross and resurrection effected the shift of the two ages.

1. Galatians 1:4–5

The credit for raising the consciousness of Pauline interpreters to the presence of apocalypticism in Galatians belongs to J. Louis Martyn, whose essay "Apocalyptic Antinomies in Paul's Letter to the Galatians"[8] has proven to be a seminal study. His analysis demonstrates that this letter presents the reader with eschatological, cosmic pairs of opposites, or antinomies—including the duality of the old and new creations effected in baptism (3:27–28), the earthly and heavenly Jerusalems (4:21–31), the warfare between the Spirit and the flesh created by the advent of the Messiah (5:16–17), and, above all, the shift from the old age to the age to come via the cross. Martyn writes of this, "The motif of the triple crucifixion—that of Christ, that of the cosmos, that of Paul—reflects the fact that through the whole of Galatians the focus of Paul's apocalyptic lies not on Christ's parousia, but rather on his death."[9]

The concept of the transition of this age to the age to come is inherent in Galatians 1:4–5. The former is signaled by the phrase, "to rescue us from the present evil age" (v. 4); the latter by the words, "according to the will of our God . . . to whom be glory" (v. 5). This shift has occurred because of Christ's death ("who

---

[8]Louis Martyn, "Apocalyptic Antinomies in Paul's Letter to the Galatians," *NTS* 31 (1985): 410–24.
[9]Ibid., 420.

gave himself for our sins," v. 4) and resurrection ("God . . . who raised him from the dead," v. 1). An investigation of this passage falls naturally into two parts.

(1) Christ's death marked the defeat of this age. Two items in verse 4 are germane to this point. Paul specifies this current era as "the present . . . age" (*aiôn*) and, in doing so, obviously draws on the idea of the Jewish two-age structure. Furthermore, Paul brands this present age as "evil," an expression paralleled in Jewish apocalyptic writings. For example, the Qumran commentary on Habakkuk designates this age as the "epoch of wickedness," during which Belial, the anti-God force, is let loose (*1QpHab.* 5:7). A similar description is contained in *4 Ezra* 7:12: "The entrances of this world are narrow and painful and toilsome; they are . . . evil, full of dangers. . . ." The Western text of Mark 16:14 echoes the same sentiment: "This age of lawlessness and unbelief is subject to Satan."

(2) Paul's label in verse 4, "this present evil age," in conjunction with his comment concerning atonement for sin, follows the apocalyptic pattern found elsewhere of personifying sin as an alien intruder who reigns over this world as its despotic king (cf. Rom. 5:12; *T.Dan.* 6:2, 4; *1QS* 3:17f.; *1QM* 13:10; 18:1; Rev. 9:11). However, by virtue of Jesus' death and resurrection believers have been "rescued from this present age," a statement affirming that this age has been subdued. With the words "raised . . . from the dead" (v. 1), Paul attests to the inauguration of the age to come within history. He attributes two characteristics to this event: it redounds to the glory of God (v. 5) and it accords with the will of God (v. 4). As was mentioned in the first chapter, *glory* is an apocalyptic-laden term. In the Old Testament, it refers primarily to the radiance of God's presence, thereby inspiring awe and worship among the people of God (Ex. 24:16–17; 40:34–35; Pss. 29:2; 84:5; 96:8; Isa. 40:5; 60:1). The logical development of this idea included the notion that those who live righteously will one day stand before God, clothed with his glory in the age to come (Dan. 12:2; *1 Enoch* 62:15, 16; *2 Enoch* 22:8–10; *2 Bar.* 51:3–11; *4 Ezra* 7:88, 95–98). Such is the connotation of the term as Paul uses it in Galatians 1:5. This is confirmed by 1:12, 15–17, verses that recall Paul's encounter with the risen, *glorious* Christ on the road to Damascus.

In addition to the glory of God, Paul's phrase "according to the will of our God" is probably similar to the apocalyptic setting of Romans 12:2, in which Christians are challenged not to be conformed to this age, but to be renewed in their minds in order to experience the will of God. Regarding this connection, F. F. Bruce writes of Galatians 1:4 that it may imply not only "that believers' deliverance from the 'present evil age' is in accordance with God's will but that such deliverance enables them to live in conformity with God's will."[10] In other words, the arrival of the age to come through the Christ-event results in the performance of God's will by the people of the new age, the death-knell of sin.

2. 1 Corinthians 15:3–4

The creedal statement of 1 Corinthians 15:3–4[11] is embedded in the apocalyptic milieu of the chapter as a whole and, accordingly, encapsulates the idea that the death and resurrection of Christ precipitated the turn of the ages. That the phrase in verse 3, "Christ died for our sins according to the Scriptures," draws on the sacrificial imagery of the Old Testament and thus attributes atoning significance to the death of Jesus is clear. Yet Paul also has cosmic, apocalyptic connotations in mind with these words. Although he does not elaborate on his interpretation of Christ's death in verses 3–4,[12] he makes key remarks in the letter that suggest to the reader that the *cross of Christ* was an epoch-changing event. Three such statements come to mind. (1) Paul proclaims that the crucifixion of Christ has begun the process of overthrowing "the rulers of this age, who are coming to nothing"

---

[10]F. F. Bruce, *The Epistle to the Galatians* (NIGNTC; Grand Rapids: Eerdmans, 1982), 76.

[11]For the criteria that establish this passage as traditional material, see the discussion by Joachim Jeremias, *The Eucharistic Words of Jesus* (Philadelphia: Westminster, 1966), 101–3. Regarding other matters, such as the origin and structure of the creed, see Hans Conzelmann, *1 Corinthians* (Hermeneia; Philadelphia: Fortress, 1975), 251–54, and J. Kloppenborg, "Pre-Pauline Formula in 1 Corinthians 15:3–5," *CBQ* 40 (1978): 351–67.

[12]Beker makes a good case for integrating the two events of the death and resurrection of Christ in 1 Corinthians into a coherent whole. Thus, although Paul emphasizes the former in chapters 1–2 and the latter in chapter 15, the union of the two is presupposed by him (*Paul the Apostle*, 164, 175).

(2:6; cf. 1:18–20; see chap. 2, above). Here is clear testimony that Jesus' death spelled the end of this age and, with it, the rule of sin. (2) In 7:31b Paul continues this train of thought by announcing that "this world in its present form is passing away." "World" here is a synonym for "age" and reflects Paul's belief that the Cross has initiated the shift from this age to the age to come. (3) Finally, 15:56–57 approximates the pattern found in 15:3–4: Christ's victory (the cross and resurrection) has defeated sin's pervasive and tyrannical power.

That 1 Corinthians 15:3–4 presupposes Paul's belief that the *resurrection of Christ* effected the dawning of the age to come is easy to show. In 10:11 Paul exclaims that the early Christians are the ones "upon whom the ends of the ages [*aiônôn*] have come" (pers. tr.). In other words believers, thanks to the Christ-event, now live in the long-awaited age to come. Paul details this thought in chapter 15, where a number of Jewish apocalyptic themes typically associated with the age to come are now applied to Christians. (1) The general resurrection of the end time has been projected back into the present period in the resurrection of Christ, the firstfruits of those who have died (15:12–22; cf. Dan. 12:2–3; 2 *Bar.* 21:23; 4 *Ezra* 7:32).[13] (2) The future messianic kingdom, in which Jews expected to reign over their enemies on earth, is now being actualized through Christ's heavenly session and is shared by believers (1Cor. 15:23–28; cf. Dan. 7:22, 27; 1 *Enoch* 108:12; *As. Isa.* 9:18). (3) The hope for eschatological glory now resides in the Christian's heart, which is proleptic of heavenly existence (15:41–57; cf. 1 *Enoch* 62:15, 16; 2 *Bar.* 51:3–11; 4 *Ezra* 7:88). (4) The promise of the bestowal of the Spirit on all God's people in the age to come (Joel 2:28–32; Ezek. 36:25–28) is currently being dispensed through Christ, the "life-giving Spirit" who is the "last [*eschaton*] Adam" (15:45). In light of this, one must conclude that Paul's comments in verses 3–4 about the death of Christ for sin and his subsequent resurrection is immersed in an apocalyptic mentality.

---

[13]Important as it is, the identification of the teaching that prompted some at Corinth to deny the resurrection of the dead is not relevant to the present task. But an excellent survey of the views can be found in Martinus C. de Boer's work, *The Defeat of Death: Apocalyptic Eschatology in 1 Corinthians 15 and Romans 5* (JSNT Supp.Ser. 22; Sheffield: JSOT, 1988), 96–104.

3. Romans 3:21–26

Many interpreters think that Romans 3:21–26, a paragraph dense with theological terms related to the death of Christ, constitutes the heart of Paul's letter to the Romans.[14] It tells of two powerful forces ("sin" and "righteousness") colliding at the cross, forever changing history. A careful reading of this passage will show that Adam's fall, the perpetrator of sin in this age, has been checkmated by Christ, the inaugurator of the righteousness of the age to come.

Adam theology informs verse 23: "for all have sinned and fall short of the glory of God." Cranfield's understanding of this verse is typical of the viewpoint of many scholars: "The reference is to that share in the divine glory, which according to Jewish thought, man possessed before he fell away from his true relationship to God and which will be restored in the eschatological future (cf. 5:2; 8:18, 21, 30). As a result of sin all men lack this illumination by the divine glory."[15]

The tradition that Adam's sin resulted in the marring of the image of God as well as the loss of divine glory is well-documented in Jewish apocalypticism (e.g., *Apoc.Moses* 21:6; *1QS* 4:23; *CD* 3:20; *1QH* 17:15). The logical connection between these two concepts is lucid—sin removes the glory of God, the brilliant manifestation of his presence (recall that the first couple hid from God after their fall). Moreover, Jewish theologians reasoned from this that Adam's disobedience initiated this present age in which sin, in some way, infested all of humanity (Rom. 5:12; *Wis.Sol.* 2:23, 24; *2 Bar.* 18:1, 2; 54:19; *4 Ezra* 3:21; 4:30). In contrast to this present evil age, however, is the righteousness of God that characterizes the age to come which, according to Paul in Romans 3:21–26, has been inaugurated by means of Jesus' death and is available to all through faith. The noun *righteousness* (*dikaiosunê*)

---

[14]So James D. G. Dunn, *Romans 1–8* (WBC 38A; Waco: Word, 1988), 163; C. E. B. Cranfield, *Romans I–VII* (ICC; Edinburgh: T. & T. Clark, 1975), 199; Ernst Käsemann, *Commentary on Romans*, trans. Geoffrey Bromiley (Grand Rapids: Eerdmans, 1980), 91–92. On the issue of whether 3:24, 25–26a is pre-Pauline tradition, see the three commentators just mentioned.

[15]Cranfield, *Romans, I–VII*, 204; see also Dunn, *Romans 1–8*, 168; Käsemann, *A Commentary on Romans*, 94–95.

and the verb *justify* (*dikaioun*) share the same root word and occur seven times in these verses, thus indicating the importance of the theme[16] for that text. Two aspects of God's righteousness operate here: judicial and eschatological.

(1) Based on the sinner's faith in Christ's work on the cross, God pronounces that person righteous (v. 22). This is a judicial decision by God, the judge of the universe, and it is solely dependent on divine grace, not human achievement (vv. 19–20, 24–26). Two words highlight the gift status of justification: *propitiation* (NIV "sacrifice of atonement," v. 25), a term referring to Christ's atoning death as satisfaction for God's offended character,[17] and *redemption* (v. 24), a term emphasizing both the cost of justification (the blood of Christ) and its result (deliverance from sin).[18]

(2) Yet there is also an eschatological aspect of righteousness at work in Romans 3:21–26. In Judaism, righteousness was mainly defined in terms of conformity to God's standard of

---

[16]The literature on the subject of the righteousness of God in Paul is enormous. Cranfield provides an excellent survey of the topic as well as a useful bibliography in *Romans 1–VII*, 99–102. The attention of recent scholarship is riveted on the insightful argument of Käsemann, which claims that the righteousness of God was a technical term of late-Jewish apocalypticism for God's saving justice. As such, it reveals God's sovereign faithfulness to his covenant with Israel and to his creation by which he brings the Jews back to himself in obedience (see Deut. 33:21; 1QS 10:25; 11:12; 1QM 4:6; T.Dan. 6:10; 1 Enoch 71:14; 99:10; 101:3). Thus, the righteousness of God expresses both his gift of forgiveness and his power for obedience toward his people, the new creation. Käsemann claims that Paul inherited this conceptual background for the term and redefines it in terms of God's present reign over the world through Jesus; see "'The Righteousness of God' in Paul," *New Testament Questions of Today* (Philadelphia: Fortress, 1969), 168–82.

[17]For a good summary of the debate on whether the proper translation of the Greek word *hilastērion* in verse 25 should be "expiation" or "propitiation," see Cranfield, *Romans 1–VII*, 214–18. The two sides of the issue are represented by C. H. Dodd ("*Hilaskesthai*, Its Cognates, Derivatives and Synonyms in the Septuagint," *JTS* 32 [1931]: 352–60), who argues for "expiation," and Leon Morris (*The Apostolic Preaching of the Cross* [Grand Rapids: Eerdmans, 1955], chaps. 4–5), who convincingly demonstrates that "propitiation" is the more accurate term.

[18]The Greek word for "redemption" in verse 24 is *lytrôseôs*. Two of its more prominent uses in the Old Testament are connected with the Exodus and the manumission of slaves. Those two ideas probably join together in Romans 3:23–24: through Christ's death believers have been delivered from the enslavement of sin. Whether *lytrôseôs* involves the payment of a ransom (either to Satan or to God) is a matter of dispute.

holiness. According to the rabbis, two impulses reside in humans: the good impulse (*yetzer hatob*) and the bad impulse (*yetzer hara*). The righteous person, therefore, is one who has nurtured the former and restrained the latter by the power that comes from studying and obeying the Torah. Thus, at the Last Judgment, such people's good deeds will outweigh their bad deeds, and they will enter into the bliss of the age to come.[19] Paul, however, modifies that understanding of righteousness at two critical points. First, God justifies the *ungodly* on the basis of Christ's death (vv. 25–26). Second, God declares the sinner righteous *now*, projecting, in effect, the divine verdict of the Last Judgment into the present moment. In other words, the righteousness of the age to come has broken into this age. That being the case, justification must be apart from human works and is grounded exclusively in one's faith in Christ (cf. 4:24–25).[20]

Two further pieces of evidence confirm that Paul perceives the righteousness of God from an eschatological frame of reference in Romans 3:21–26. First, in verse 21 he asserts that the righteousness of God has been "made known" (*phanerôtai*), thereby echoing 1:17, the key statement of Romans, that the "righteousness from God is revealed [*apokaluptetai*] . . . by faith from first to last." The synonyms "made known" and "revealed" are apocalyptic in orientation and indicate that, through faith in Christ's death for their sins, sinners are justified now (cf. 5:1; 8:1). Second, in verse 26, Paul employs one of his favorite terms for the concept of salvation in history: "time" (*kairô*;[21] cf. 8:18; 11:5; 13:11). Thus Romans 3:21–26 makes it clear that through the death of Christ,

---

[19]This belief is widely attested in Jewish literature, ranging from the Dead Sea Scrolls (ca. 150 B.C.E.) to the Talmud (ca. 200–500 C.E.).

[20]The phrase "faith of Jesus Christ" in verse 26 and in other passages has traditionally been understood to mean *faith in* Jesus Christ. Richard B. Hays has recently challenged that assumption, however, arguing that the words refer to the *faithfulness of* Jesus Christ (see *The Faith of Jesus Christ. An Investigation of the Narrative Substructure of Galatians 3:1–4:11* [SBLDS 56; Chico, Calif.: Scholars Press, 1983]).

[21]See Cullmann, *Christ and Time: The Primitive Christian Conception of Time and History*, trans. Floyd V. Filson (Philadelphia: Westminster, 1950), for the classic treatment of this word.

the righteousness associated with the age to come has overpowered this age and the sin that once ruled over it.[22]

4. Colossians 1:13–23

Colossians 1:13–23 is another vital passage that contributes to our understanding of Paul's concept of Christ's death and resurrection. Verse 18 presumes the death of Christ when it says, "He is the beginning and the firstborn from among the dead." Verse 20 clarifies the nature of Christ's death as involving "his blood, shed on the cross," while verse 22 adds, "he has reconciled you by Christ's physical body through death." These remarks about the death of Jesus the Messiah occur in the context of at least three contrasts that correlate with the idea that the age to come has superseded this present age. Because of his death, Christians (1) now reign in the messianic kingdom (vv. 12–13, 16–18), (2) are forgiven of their sins (v. 14, 22), and (3) are being restored to the image and glory of God (vv. 15, 27; cf. 3:4, 10).

(1) According to verses 12–13, Christians have been transferred from the dominion of darkness into the kingdom of light. In essence, Paul applies the Old Testament language of Israel's inheritance of Canaan (Gen. 13:14–17; Num. 26:52–56; Josh. 19:9) to the church, though her possession is on a higher plane and more lasting than any earthly plot of ground. The metaphors in verses 12–13 of darkness and light identify the two realms to which humans belong and correspond to the categories of this age and the age to come vividly depicted, for example, in the Qumran literature (1QS 2:5; 1QM 1:1, 5, 11; 4:2; 13:2 ["this age is under the sway of Belial and the sons of darkness"]; 1QS 1:9; 2:16; 11:7–8; 1QH 11:11–12 ["the age to come awaits the sons of

---

[22]The same pattern delineated here is operative in Romans 5:6–10, another of Paul's passages on the death of Jesus. There, too, sin is portrayed as the ruling force of this age (thanks to Adam's sin, 5:12–21), but Christ's death inaugurated the age to come ("at the appointed time," [kairô], 5:6) and, with it, the reconciliation of sinners to a righteous God. The only significant difference between the two passages (Rom. 3:21–26 and 5:6–10) is that the latter describes the sinner's new-found relationship in terms of reconciliation. This term emphasizes the relational aspect, while righteousness/justification emphasizes the legal aspect of the believer's standing before God.

light"]). That an eschatological perspective undergirds Colossians 1:12–13 is confirmed by Paul's reference to "the kingdom of the Son he loves," undoubtedly the interim messianic kingdom hoped for by Jewish apocalyptic writers. According to the apostle, the death and resurrection of Christ inaugurated that kingdom, which encompasses the dominion of the cosmos (vv. 16–18). Christians are a part of that rule (v. 12).

(2) The theme of the death and resurrection of Christ as the turning point of the two ages continues in verse 14 and verses 21–22. The first of these texts, in effect, contrasts the redemption of the age to come with the sin of this age. This redemption from sin (v. 14) is defined in terms of deliverance from the dominion of darkness (v. 13). Such a theme of deliverance was an important tradition to Israel (see Ex. 6:6; 14:30; Pss. 33:18; 79:9) and fueled eschatological hopes for a restored land (Isa. 40–66; Ezek. 38–39). For Paul, that hope of deliverance is spiritualized (it is redemption from *sins*, v. 14) and now realized in Christ.

The second text (vv. 21–22) contrasts the enmity with God that characterizes the people of this age with those of the age to come, who have been reconciled to God because of the death of Jesus. Paul confidently speaks of this reconciliation as an accomplished fact, which, as Peter O'Brien notes, is to be understood in the light of eschatology. This assurance of a restored relationship with God rests on the teaching of the two ages; "the verb in the indicative is used to denote the decisive transfer of the believers from the old aeon to the new which has taken place in the death of Christ."[23]

(3) Because of the Christ-event believers are being restored to the image and glory of God (1:15, 27; cf. 3:4, 10). As mentioned earlier in this chapter, and as this author argued at length elsewhere, there was a strong belief in Jewish apocalypticism approximately at the time of Paul that Adam's marring of God's image and loss of divine glory would be restored in the age to come to the righteous who presently suffer.[24] That belief nicely explains

---

[23]Peter T. O'Brien, *Colossians, Philemon* (WBC; Waco, Tex.: Word, 1982), 67.

[24]I have developed this theme in greater detail in my works *Adam Christology As the Exegetical and Theological Substructure of 2 Corinthians 4:8–5:21* (Lanham, Md.:

his use of the terms *image* and *glory* in 1:15 and 27 respectively, as well as in 3:4, 10—except that, for the apostle, Christ is the righteous sufferer *par excellence*, whose death on the cross has already begun the eschatological process of recreating a new humanity.

5. Ephesians 1:7–12

The same idea found in Colossians 1:13–23 recurs in Ephesians 1:7–21: the death and resurrection of Christ was the catalyst for the transition from this age to the age to come. In Ephesians 1:20–21, this idea is clear and the terminology explicit: Upon Christ's death and resurrection, he was enthroned over the cosmos (v. 20), thus effecting the change from this age to the coming age (v. 21). This has come about "through his blood" (v. 7), that is, through the cross. Accordingly, a number of blessings now grace the Christian's life. Because their eschatological nature has already been demonstrated in connection with other Pauline texts, we need only mention them here. Believers (1) have forgiveness of sins (Eph. 1:7; cf. Col. 1:14), (2) are recipients of the revelation of God's will for the future (Eph. 1:8–10; cf. 1 Cor. 2:6–16), (3) are part of the divine inheritance (Eph. 1:14; cf. Col. 1:12–13), and (4) possess the indwelling Spirit (Eph. 1:13–14; cf. 1 Cor. 14:45).

6. Titus 2:11–14

The final passage to be considered in the category of the Christ-event and sin is Titus 2:11–14, one long sentence in Greek. The death of Christ is emphasized twice in this text: verse 11 ("for the grace of God that brings salvation has appeared to all men") and verse 14 ("who gave himself for us to redeem us"). The stated purpose of that death is to equip the people of God to overcome sin—"teach[ing] us to say 'No' to ungodliness and worldly passions" (v. 12). The setting of this passage is eschatological, evoking the notion of the overlapping of the two ages.

University Press of America, 1991), with regard to 2 Cor. 4:7–5:21, and *The Glory of Adam and the Afflictions of the Righteous: Pauline Suffering in Context* (New York: Edwin Mellen, 1993), with regard to Col. 1 and other Pauline texts on suffering.

(1) In verse 12, Paul presents the two types of lifestyles that confront people in this present "age" (*aiôni*): ungodliness or righteousness. This tradition of the "two ways" is highlighted in the Old Testament (Gen. 6:5; 8:21; Deut. 8; Ps. 1), developed in the Qumran material (*1QS* 3:13–4:26), and appropriated in Christian circles (Matt. 7:24–29; Gal. 5:16–26; Col. 3:8–14; James 3:13–18; *Ep.Barn.* 18–21; *Didache* 1–6). The assumption underlying this teaching is that the children of God will distinguish themselves as a holy people in the midst of this age, which is given over to sin.

(2) According to verses 11, 13–14, the age to come has broken into this present age through the Christ-event. The death of Jesus has initiated an eschatological shift, resulting in the overlapping of the two ages. In other words, the age to come has "already" dawned, but it is "not yet" complete. The former aspect is evident in verses 11 and 14, while the latter point is attested to in verse 13.

(a) In verse 11, Paul declares that God's grace "appeared" (*epephanê*) to all men, bringing them salvation. As Philip Towner has cogently shown, the word "epiphany" in the Pastoral Letters is an expression of salvation history, the idea that the age to come is manifesting itself within this current epoch.[25] In the case of verse 11, the term showcases the "already" aspect of Paul's eschatology, with reference to the death and resurrection of Christ. Verse 14 says virtually the same thing: Christ Jesus "gave himself for us to redeem us." The language used here echoes Jesus' saying in Mark 10:45, undoubtedly referring to the sacrificial death of Christ. Verses 11 and 14, in fact, form a parallel structure, sharing the same meaning—the age to come has already manifested itself through the death of Christ:

V. 11: grace of God appeared (death of Christ)	bringing salvation (age to come dawned)
V. 14: gave himself for us (death of Christ)	that he might redeem us (age to come dawned)

---

[25]Philip H. Towner, *The Goal of Our Instruction: The Structure of Theology and Ethics in the Pastoral Epistles* (JSNT Supp.Ser. 34; Sheffield: JSOT, 1989), 66–74.

(b) However, we learn from verse 13 that the age to come is not yet complete; it awaits the *Parousia* of Christ: "we wait for the blessed hope—the glorious appearing of . . . Jesus Christ." Once again the root word *epiphany* (*epiphaneian*, "appearing") occurs, but this time with reference to the consummation rather than the inauguration of the coming age. As such, it accentuates the eschatological tension that Christians encounter because they live in the intersection of the two ages—between the already (the first coming of Christ) and the not yet (the second coming of Christ). This tension of the two ages is the basis for the ethical struggle between the two ways delineated in verse 12. Christians are called to declare their allegiance with the righteousness of the age to come instead of with the ungodliness that imprints this age. That is, they must live like the people of the age to come while residing in the midst of this present evil age.

B. THE CHRIST-EVENT AND THE FLESH

This next section examines noteworthy Pauline texts associating the death and resurrection of Christ with the "flesh": 1 Corinthians 1:18–25; 2 Corinthians 5:14–21; Philippians 2:5–11. There are other passages in the Pauline letters that deal with the impact of the Christ-event on the flesh, but they are more concerned to address the issue of the place of the Law in this age, particularly as it is used by sin to arouse the flesh (e.g., Gal. 2:19–20; 6:14–15). Therefore, those passages will best be examined in the next section of this chapter. Here the focus is on the relationship between Christ's death/resurrection and the *flesh*, a term whose definition varies from passage to passage in Paul's letters.[26] For our purpose, we may simply note that the flesh (*sarx*) has two broad meanings: physical and ethical. The former concerns the human body which, though not *ipso facto* sinful, is nevertheless under the burden of mortality (1 Cor. 15:50; 2 Cor. 4:10–11; 12:7). The latter pertains to that penchant to sin due to Adam's nature residing in all humans and can express itself in any number of ways, including immorality (Gal. 5:19–22; Col. 2:18), arrogance

---

[26]George Ladd helpfully elaborates on the meaning of "flesh" for Paul in *A Theology of the New Testament* (Grand Rapids: Eerdmans, 1974), 466–74.

(2 Cor. 11:18; Gal. 6:12–14; Phil. 3:3), and obstinacy toward God (Rom. 8:8; 1 Cor. 3:3). It is the ethical meaning that dominates the discussion in the three passages to be surveyed here.

1. 1 Corinthians 1:18–25

Paul's theology of the cross comes to the fore in 1 Corinthians 1:18–25: "For the message of the cross is foolishness to those who are perishing, but to us who are being saved it is the power of God" (v. 18); "but we preach Christ crucified: a stumbling block to Jews and foolishness to Gentiles" (v. 23). Such a message undoubtedly did not curry the favor of Paul's opponents, who espoused a theology of "glory" by boasting in human skill and achievement (1:28–29, 31).[27] However, the apostle brands all such accomplishments as "fleshly" (v. 26; NIV "human standards") and ultimately of no account before God (vv. 27–29). The only grounds for glorying should be in the crucified Messiah (2:2).

According to 1:18–25, the cross was the turning point of the ages. For Paul, it is the symbol of that great reversal of values and fortune that Jewish apocalyptic writers expected would occur when the age to come replaced this age. Such a theme is rooted in the Old Testament, which predicts divine vindication of righteous sufferers over their enemies (Pss. 6:10; 31:17; 35:4, 26–27; Isa. 53:1–12). This expectation intensifies in Jewish apocalypticism, most likely because of the persecution Jews endured at the hands of their political foes. One can easily imagine what schematic a Jew might construct using the language of verses 18–25, in terms of the two-age structure and Israel's present affliction and future deliverance.

This Age	Age to Come
1. Perish (v. 18a–19)	1. Saved (v. 18b)
2. Foolishness (vv. 20–24)	2. Wisdom (v. 25)
3. Weakness (v. 25)	3. Power (v. 25)

---

[27]The term "boast" occurs 39 times in 1–2 Corinthians—thus indicating the importance of the word for Paul—probably in reaction to his opponents, who were apparently enamored with their spirituality and abilities.

Paul, too, assumes such a view of reality, except that he significantly modifies its perspective—through the cross of Christ the age to come has manifested itself in the midst of this present age, thus producing the overlapping of the two. Using Luther's famous phrase, we might state it this way: the age to come is ironically "hidden under its opposite," this present age. This idea clarifies the paradoxical language used throughout 1 Corinthians 1:18–25, as well as explains the confusion, and even disgust, Jewish people experienced when hearing about a crucified Messiah. For them, the Messiah and the age to come meant salvation, wisdom, and power, while a crucified Messiah could only conjure up thoughts of defeat, foolishness, and weakness. It is precisely here that we encounter the heart of Paul's message—the scandal of the cross is diametrically opposed to that which the flesh holds dear. For the apostle, deliverance comes only through the cross, the epitome of foolishness and weakness. Salvation on those terms leaves no room for boasting in human merit.

One can go further in capturing Paul's argument in 1:18–25 concerning the Christ-event and the flesh, for one's response to the cross is already shaping his or her destiny. The present tense of the verbs in verse 18 is not accidental: the message of the cross is foolishness to those who *are perishing* but the power of God to those who *are being saved*. Fee encapsulates this key idea well:

> The crucifixion and resurrection of Jesus for Paul marked the "turning of the ages," whereby God decisively judged and condemned the present age and is in process of bringing it to an end. Those who still belong to it, therefore, are in process of "perishing" with it. From this "old age" point of view the message of the cross is foolishness. On the other hand, those "who are being saved" have ... come to see their present existence as the result of God's power, which was also effected by God through the cross and resurrection of Jesus.[28]

2. 2 Corinthians 5:14–17

The next passage that connects the Christ-event with the flesh is 2 Corinthians 5:14–17. The death and resurrection of Christ forced Paul to reverse his thinking about the concept of a

---

[28]Gordon Fee, *The First Epistle to the Corinthians*, 69.

suffering Messiah. No longer does he view such an idea from a "fleshly" point of view; neither should the Corinthian church look on the apostle's suffering with contempt. The hermeneutical key here is verse 17: "if anyone is in Christ, he is a new creation; the old has gone, the new has come!" This verse contrasts this age and the age to come and, together with its surrounding verses, subsumes under the two ages the principles of the flesh and the love of Christ, respectively.

a. This Age and the Flesh

When Paul quotes from Isaiah 43:18–19 in 2 Corinthians 5:17, he does so in order to establish that this age has run its course in light of the Christ-event. For the apostle, one of the dominant forces that holds sway over this age is the flesh (see vv. 12, 15–16). Verse 16 uses the Greek word *sarx* twice: of Paul's view of humans and, formerly, of Christ. In both cases, the apostle means that he does not judge people by their outward appearance any longer. In all probability, when Paul says, "even though we have known Christ according to the flesh, yet now we know him thus no longer" (pers. tr.), he is referring to his days as a rabbi when he persecuted the church because of its belief in Jesus as the *suffering* Messiah.[29] But when he encountered the risen Jesus on the road to Damascus, all such fleshly evaluation of God and humans ceased for him. So should it for the Corinthian Christians (v. 12). In that text, Paul sarcastically criticizes the fleshly standard of judgment with which the Corinthians, fueled by Paul's opponents, were operating. They demeaned his apostolic afflictions (an attitude discussed in 2 Cor. 10–13) in a way not unlike that in which Paul once looked on Christ's afflictions. In using outward appearance as a criterion, however, the Corinthians were playing into the hands of the spirit of this age (cf. 4:4). In effect, they are living for themselves (5:15a).

---

[29]This interpretation of 2 Corinthians 5:16 is preferable to the older view, which understood Paul to be saying that he once knew Christ as the historical Jesus. Paul is most likely making the statement that he once knew Christ in a fleshly way, i.e., only from a human point of view, and that he thus looked down on his death on the cross. In other words, grammatically, the phrase "according to the flesh" modifies the verb "knew," not the noun "Christ."

b. The Age to Come and the Love of Christ

In verse 17, Paul announces that the new creation,[30] or the age to come, has arrived through Christ. The controlling ethic of this new creation is love, which was the motivating factor behind Christ's death: "Christ's love compels us ... that one died for all" (v. 14; repeated in v. 15, "And he died for all"). Love is the antidote for selfishness. That being the case, Paul as an apostle of the new age can no longer live for himself; he is driven to serve others (v. 14a). So must the Corinthians (v. 15), and the place for them to begin to act out love, the ethic of the age to come (cf. 1 Cor. 13), is by accepting Paul's afflictions (which he incurs from preaching the gospel) as proof of the genuineness of his apostleship (see 2 Cor. 5:20–6:13).

3. Philippians 2:5–11 and Its Context

This last text to be considered in the category of the Christ-event and the flesh has been entitled the *"kenosis"* passage, because of the word found in verse 7 to describe Christ's humiliation in becoming human: "he emptied [*ekenôsen*] himself ... being made in the likeness of men" (pers. tr.). Moreover, most commentators today recognize verses 6–11 to be a hymn, composed of two stanzas: verses 6–8 (Christ's humiliation in his incarnation and death on the cross) and verses 9–11 (Christ's exaltation in his resurrection and *Parousia*).[31] As we will see, Paul uses this Christological liturgical piece to challenge the Philippians to emulate the sacrificial lifestyle of their Lord. In doing so, they demonstrate that the shift of the two ages is in progress. Two points surface in this text: (1) the Christ-event and the two ages, and (2) the Christ-event and the flesh.

---

[30] The words *kainê ktisis* can be translated "new creature" or "new creation," in this case probably the latter. As such, they draw on the idea that the age to come, or the new creation, is now here, in Christ.

[31] The classic investigation of Philippians 2:5–11 is the work by Ralph Martin, *Carmen Christi: Philippians ii.5–11 in Recent Interpretation and in the Setting of Early Christian Worship* (SNTMS 4; Cambridge: University Press, 1967); for the hymnic structure of the pericope, see his chapter 2.

a. The Christ-Event and the Two Ages

Although the word "age" does not occur in 2:5–11, the idea of the turning of the two ages is clearly present in this paragraph, as well as in 2:12–15. Verses 6–11 enunciate the eschatological tension existing between this age and the age to come with reference to Christ, while verses 12–15 apply the same notion to the Christian.

(1) Christ's death and exaltation has effected the transition of the two ages. His death on the cross marked the end of this age (vv. 6–8). The key to understanding this stanza is to uncover the Adam theology that undergirds it. To many modern interpreters, Paul here highlights the contrasting choices of Adam and Christ. The one wrongly attempted to become like God, the other obediently laid aside the outward form of his deity in order to save humanity.[32] The upshot of this line of reasoning is that Christ's coming into this present age of disobedience was spawned by Adam's fall.

Jesus' resurrection signaled the beginning of the age to come (vv. 9–11). As Martin points out,[33] this second stanza reflects the idea of the overlapping of the age to come with the present age. According to verse 9, Christ's resurrection/ascension witnesses to the reality that the age to come has "already" arrived. But according to verses 10–11, the age to come will "not yet" be complete until the *Parousia*. That is, while Christ has begun the temporary messianic reign, the kingdom of God still needs to be consummated.

(2) Verses 12–15 applies this paradigmatic shift to the Christian. Using such language as "salvation" (v. 12) and "God who works in you" (v. 13), Paul describes the presence of the age to come within the believer. However, this heavenly existence must be lived out in the context of this "depraved generation" (v. 15), this evil age. Thus the Christian, like Christ, experiences the eschatological tension resulting from the turning of the ages.

---

[32]See ibid., 99–133, 161–65, for a survey of those who maintain Adam theology is central to the text, as well as for an excellent analysis of the nature of the *kenosis* itself.

[33]Ibid., 266–70.

b. The Christ-Event and the Flesh

Even though Paul does not use the term *sarx* (flesh) in Philippians 2:5–11, the thought is embedded in verses 3–5, in such terms as "selfish ambition," "vain conceit" (v. 3), and "own interests" (v. 4). By following the example of Christ who sacrificed himself for others, the Philippians will shun any such behavioral tendencies (v. 5). In effect, Paul sets up here a contrast between the flesh (the characteristic of this age) and service to others (the ethic of the age to come). If Christians affirm the latter trait in their lives now, they, like Christ, will one day be exalted.

C. THE CHRIST-EVENT AND THE LAW

The third member of the evil triumvirate subdued because of the Christ-event is the law of God, as contradictory as that may sound. However, the ambiguity surrounding Paul's concept of the function of the Old Testament law begins to dissipate with verses like Romans 7:12–13. In verse 12, Paul emphatically asserts that the Law is "holy, righteous and good," but it nevertheless is the death of a relationship with God (vv. 7–11). The reason for this perplexity is stated in verse 13: sin manipulates the Law in such a way that its commandments evoke disobedience from people. This dilemma is part and parcel of being human and living in the flesh (v. 14). In reality, then, the Law itself is in need of liberation from the grip of sin so that it can perform its original purpose of fostering friendship between humans and their God. Like Darth Vader in *Star Wars*, the Law, though created to be good, fell under the influence of the "dark side of the force" and needs to be delivered from it.

For Paul, like many of his Jewish contemporaries, the answer to this difficulty lies in the arrival of the age to come, the time when Israel will finally obey God from the heart (cf. Jer. 31:33–34; Ezek. 36:25–28)—except that the apostle believed that this expectation is now being realized in light of the Christ-event and the subsequent sending of the Spirit. The purpose of this section, therefore, is to take a brief look at four texts dealing with the relationship of the death and resurrection of Christ to the Law, based on the thesis that they are removing the evil effects of the Law by superimposing the age to come over this present age.[34]

1. Galatians 2:15–21

According to this passage, one adverse effect the Christ-event is remedying concerning the Law is the replacement of condemnation with justification. That this switch is indebted to the concept of the two-age structure is made clear in verse 20, "the Son of God, who loved me and gave himself for me." These words restate 1:4: "who gave himself for our sins to rescue us from the present evil age." These two statements are parallel, suggesting that the Law is under the influence of this evil age. Verse 16 details the ominous consequence—no flesh will be justified by observing the Law, because no one is able in this age of sin to obey God's commandments. Therefore, the Law now brings only condemnation.

However, according to verses 19–21, the one who exercises faith in Christ and is therefore in vital union with the cross is fully justified before God. The Christian now lives in the resurrection power of Christ and pleases the Lord. This can be understood as nothing less than the inbreaking of the age to come, one blessing of which is obedience to God from the heart.

2. Galatians 3:13–14 and 4:4–6

Galatians 3:13–14, along with 4:4–6, enumerates another ill consequence suffered under the Law that the Christ-event alleviated: It exchanged the curse of the Law for the blessing of the Spirit. The turning point between the two occurred at the cross, when the age to come invaded this age. As Richard Hays has ably shown, these two passages are parallel texts, which have as their substructure the narrative of the death of Christ.[35] Their similarity is nicely demonstrated in chart form:

---

[34]Chapter 5 of this work elaborates on the role of the Law in Paul's thought.

[35]Richard B. Hays, *The Faith of Jesus Christ*, 86–91, who extends the parallel with Gal. 3:13–14 to include 4:3–6. The chart that follows is my own.

Cross	
This Age	**Age to Come**
Gal. 3:13: curse of the Law	Gal. 3:14: blessing of the Spirit
Gal. 4:3, 5a: elements of the world (cf. 4:9, 10)/under the Law	Gal. 4:4, 5b–6: fullness of time/the indwelling of the Spirit

The key words indicating the eschatological framework of these two passages are "the time had fully come" (Gal. 4:4). Bruce explains the concept well:

> What is emphasized here is that the nodal point of salvation-history, marked by the coming of Christ . . . , constitutes the divinely ordained epoch for the people of God to enter into their inheritance as his mature and responsible sons and daughters. Here it is the "realized" aspect of Christian eschatology that Paul presents, the "already" rather than the "not yet."[36]

As the above chart indicates, the Law belongs to this age and is a part of the bondage of the elements of the world (cf. 3:13 with 4:3, 5a, 9–10). Rather than stimulating obedience, the Law actually stirs up sin in the soul of the person, thus bringing God's wrath on the offender (3:10–13; cf. Rom. 5:20). This is why Paul can say that all who attempt to be justified by observing the Law are under the divine curse. But at the cross, Christ himself became the object of God's wrath on behalf of the sinner. Quoting Deuteronomy 27:26 and 21:23 in Galatians 3:12 and 3:13, respectively, Paul indicates that by his crucifixion Christ, the only one who ever truly kept the Law, took on himself the curse that belonged to all people for their failure to measure up to the divine standard. Thus, the death of the Messiah is nothing less than the moment of the appearance of the age to come. Such an era of forgiveness of sin and possession of the Spirit is the fulfillment of the long-awaited blessing promised to Abraham and his seed, including Gentiles (3:14; 4:5b–6).

---

[36]Bruce, *Commentary on Galatians*, 194. Compare also Herman Ridderbos', *When the Time Had Fully Come* (Grand Rapids: Eerdmans, 1957), 48, 68.

3. Galatians 6:12–15

Another foreboding effect of the Law counteracted by the cross of Christ is the overcoming of arrogance with humility. Galatians 6:12–15 makes this clear. Here two conflicting realities are delineated by Paul—the world (v. 14) and the new creation (v. 15), which correlate with this age and the age to come. For Paul, the world is that anti-God system that runs this age (cf. 1:4; 4:3); unfortunately, the Law is its unwitting partner in crime. Furthermore, those who, like the Judaizers, oppose Paul's message of grace in Galatia and mandate others to adhere to the Law (e.g., submit to circumcision) are also under the influence of the spirit of this age. The apostle exposes their ulterior motives in verses 12–13: They compel others to obey the Law in order to boast in their own zeal for the Law (which they do not keep anyway), and they do so in order to avoid being persecuted by those who are scandalized by the cross of Christ.[37]

Paul, however, will entertain no such idea. He will boast only in the crucified Messiah, before whom he humbly bows (v. 14). Only through the cross and the new age it inspired, not the Law, can a person become a new creation, equipped for a holy life before God (v. 15; cf. 5:24).

4. Ephesians 2:11–22

In Ephesians 2:11–22 Paul associates the Law with the incapacity of human "flesh" to obey God (cf. vv. 11, 15). His emphasis here is on the negative effect that the Law has on the human race, notably the racial disharmony caused by the Law. Ironically, instead of drawing people to God and toward each other, the Law did just the reverse: it excluded the Gentiles from God (v. 11) and from Israel (v. 14).[38] It thus serves as a barrier, not a bridge, in relationships (v. 14), the result of which is enmity.

---

[37]Robert Jewett makes a plausible case for connecting this motive with the Zealot uprising in the 40s and 50s of the first century C.E., "The Agitators and the Galatian Congregation," NTS 17 (1970–71): 198–212.

[38]Paul may well be alluding to the Jewish warnings posted on the temple barricade forbidding Gentiles to proceed any further on pain of death. The notices

But through Christ's death on the cross (cf. v. 13, "the blood of Christ"; v. 16, "to reconcile both of them to God through the cross"), the age to come has dawned (v. 7, "the coming ages") in this present age (v. 2, "this age" [pers. tr.]; v. 12, "in the world"). As a result, two eschatological blessings have come, reversing the adverse effects of the Law and restoring it to its original intent. (1) Christ has created a new humanity, one that lives in peace and harmony (v. 15; cf. 10). As W. D. Davies has shown, the idea informing Paul's concept of this new humanity is that of the anticipation of the eschatological restoration of the primeval unity once inherent in Adam before the fall.[39] Christians compose, in effect, the third race.

(2) Christ is the eschatological temple, whose corporate body combines Jew and Gentile in the service and worship of God (vv. 20–22). The idea underlying this concept is the Jewish apocalyptic expectation that in the end time the heavenly temple, the New Jerusalem, will descend to earth and draw both Jew and Gentile to the house of God.[40] For Paul and early Christianity, that temple is a present reality, thanks to the death and resurrection of Christ and the subsequent indwelling of the Spirit in the hearts of the people of God (v. 22; cf. 1 Cor. 3:16; 6:19; 2 Cor. 6:16–18).[41]

CONCLUSION

The bulk of the Pauline passages describing the death and resurrection of Christ have now been surveyed, and the thesis stated at the beginning of this chapter has been confirmed—the

---

were written in Greek and Latin, two of which have been discovered—one in 1871 (now in the Archaeological Museum in Istanbul) and one in 1934 (now in the Rockefeller Museum in Jerusalem).

[39]W. D. Davies, *Paul and Rabbinic Judaism: Some Rabbinic Elements in Pauline Theology* (New York: Harper & Row, 1948), 53–58. He cites such texts as *b.Sanh.* 38a; *Gen.R.* 8; *2 Enoch* 30:13.

[40]See Isa. 56:6–7; *1 Enoch* 90:29; *2 Bar.* 4:2–6.

[41]The classic study of the spiritual temple in Judaism and in the New Testament is that by R. J. McKelvey, *The New Temple* (Oxford, N.Y.: University Press, 1969).

Christ-event has effected the change of the two ages. His cross and resurrection defeated the powers that once ruled this age—sin, flesh, and the Law (manipulated by evil). Yet does this mean that Christians, as members of the age to come, are totally free from the downward pull of this world? The next chapter seeks to answer that question.

IV

PAULINE SOTERIOLOGY: SALVATION NOW AND NOT YET

INTRODUCTION

In Romans 1:16 Paul declares that the gospel is "the power of God for the salvation of everyone who believes." Such a message of hope and deliverance would have struck a responsive chord in the hearts of most people living in his day. It would have appealed to the Greco-Roman audience, who deeply desired liberation from fear of death and a sense of helplessness before fate. Certainly ancient Judaism could resonate with Paul's hope for salvation, especially freedom from its oppressing neighbors, Rome included. It is interesting that both groups tended to define salvation in terms of the restoration of the nostalgic past. For example, the Roman poet Virgil (70–19 B.C.E.) captured the aspirations and dreams of many when, in the *Aeneid*, he addresses Octavian: "Hail to you, Augustus Caesar, son of a god, who will once more establish the golden age amid the fields where Saturn once reigned." A well-known Jewish prophet echoes a similar sentiment. Speaking of the Messiah to come, Isaiah promises that that person will establish peace and safety in all the earth (Isa. 11:4), so much so that it will be like a new creation (65:17–25).

Paul, too, believed that salvation[1] would be an age in which the end of time recapitulates the beginning of history,[2] except that

---

[1]The word for *salvation* is *sôtêria* and for *to save* is *sôzô*. In Paul, the term primarily refers to the saving activity of God. The idea extends beyond the word itself to include divine deliverance from sin, the flesh, the Law, Satan, etc. (see chap. 3 for these related concepts).

[2]The classic expression of this pattern is the German idiom, *Urzeit-Endzeit* (original time-end time). An example of this principle is in Revelation 21–22, which uses

for him the golden era was no longer future, it is now present with Christ. Christians, therefore, are the people of the end time. Statements abound in his letters that show salvation is a present reality in Christ (see Rom. 11:14; 1 Cor. 1:18, 21; 7:16; 9:22; 10:33; 15:2; 2 Cor. 2:15; 6:2; Eph. 1:13; 2:8; 1 Thess. 2:16; 2 Thess. 2:13; 1 Tim. 1:15; 2:5; 2 Tim. 3:14; Titus 3:5).

But this is not the whole story, for Paul also repeatedly refers to salvation as a future possession, something not yet fully belonging to Christians (see Rom. 5:9; 11:25; 1 Cor. 3:15; 5:5; 1 Thess. 5:8; 1 Tim. 2:15; 4:16; 2 Tim. 2:10; 4:18). Furthermore, several Pauline texts juxtapose both ideas about present and future salvation (see Rom. 6:1–14; 7:14–25; 8:17–30; 13:11–14 [cf. 1 Thess. 5:8–9]; 1 Cor. 10:11–13; Gal. 5:16–18; Eph. 2:1–10; Phil. 1:6; 3:1–14; 3:20–21). We encounter, therefore, a certain ambiguity in his understanding of salvation, an eschatological tension resulting from the overlapping of the two ages. In Christ, the age to come is already here (salvation is present), but it is not yet complete (salvation is future). The best approach to investigating Pauline soteriology is to address those texts that clearly display this eschatological ambivalence.

Before proceeding to that task, however, it is helpful to point out that this combination of the "already/not yet" paradox in Paul's concept of salvation has given rise to a number of theological constructs or models of interpretation. Four quickly come to mind, the last of which is the path followed by most scholars today and which constitutes the thesis of this chapter: justification/sanctification, the indicative/imperative "moods" of salvation, covenantal nomism, and the overlapping of the two ages. It should also be mentioned that these attempts to describe Pauline soteriology are not mutually exclusive in principle. Before probing the fourth of these paths, therefore, it is helpful to define the other three briefly.

Probably the most venerable terms used to express the Pauline concept of salvation, particularly in Protestant circles, are *justification* and *sanctification*. This model adamantly asserts that justification (the event of faith in Christ's death and resurrection) precedes sanctification (the process of holy living), not the

---

Genesis 1–3. Paul likewise presupposes this divine counterpart (see Rom. 8:18–30; 2 Cor. 5:17).

reverse.[3] Beyond that, however, there is great debate as to how these two doctrines are related. Perhaps one is not wide of the mark to say that Calvinists tend to distinguish the two while Arminians tend to merge the two.[4]

The second theological construct that attempts to grasp Paul's teaching on salvation is stated in terms of the "indicative/imperative" moods of reality. Rudolf Bultmann popularized this model a generation ago. The gist of this approach is that Christians should become (the imperative mood, not yet saved) what they are (the indicative mood, already saved).[5] Undoubtedly underlying this paradoxical expression is Bultmann's existential hermeneutic—existence precedes essence.[6]

In recent years, a third model describing the Pauline idea of salvation has been proposed by E. P. Sanders, who, in his monumental work, *Paul and Palestinian Judaism*, coined the phrase "covenantal nomism" (covenant law). Sanders attempted to prove that the Judaism of Paul's day did not, in fact, teach that salvation is by works. Rather, it adhered to the following pattern: Israel entered into its covenant with God by grace through faith but maintained that relationship by good works. Using the same terminology, Sanders claimed that Paul, like his Jewish contemporaries,

---

[3]It might be claimed that traditional Roman Catholicism tended to switch the two so that sanctification (a holy life) results in justification (acceptance by God at the Great Assize). However, many Catholic scholars today demur from this sequence, positing the necessity of justification before sanctification. In any event, the recent dialogue between Catholics and Lutherans on this point is a healthy corrective to the caricature-like argumentation that formerly characterized both sides' interpretations of the other.

[4]Calvinists call themselves such because they follow the teachings of the Reformer John Calvin (1509–1564), who emphasized the sovereignty of God. Arminians champion the doctrines of Jacobus Arminius (1560–1609) as delineated in the *Remonstrance*, a document stressing the responsibility of humans. The two approaches clashed, necessitating the convening of the Council of Dort in Holland (1618–19).

[5]See Rudolf Bultmann, *The Theology of the New Testament* (New York: Charles Scribner's, 1951), 1.332.

[6]Bultmann freely admits that Martin Heidegger's existentialist categories greatly impacted his understanding of Paul and the New Testament; see his "New Testament and Mythology," in *Kerygma and Myth*, ed. Hans Werner Bartsch (New York: Harper & Row, 1961), 1–44, esp. 24–25.

believed that "salvation is by grace . . . works are the condition of remaining in."[7]

The three views just highlighted, though conveying their own respective nuances, share a commonality of thought about Paul, that salvation is a present, though not yet complete, reality. This paradox is the hallmark of the fourth model—the overlapping of the two ages, which produces the eschatological tension formative to Pauline soteriology.[8] Chapters 2 and 3 of this book have essentially demonstrated this to be the case for Paul, especially in his teaching that deliverance from the anti-God forces, sin, the Law, and the flesh have already begun but have not yet been finalized, for the Christian. Therefore, the purpose of this present chapter is not so much to reinvestigate those specific salvific expressions as it is to accentuate the thought that the reality of the overlapping of the two ages manifests itself in the idea of *struggle* in the Christian life. For Paul, the proof that a person is genuinely Christian is the fact that he or she is engaged in an inner conflict, which is nothing less than the individualization of the eschatological shift of the ages.

A. GALATIANS 5:16–18

We have already called attention to the apocalyptic substructure of Galatians. That the doctrine of the two ages exerts its influence on Galatians 5:16–18 is transparent from the terminology employed there, especially in the language about the conflict between the flesh and the Spirit. The former (*sarx*; NIV "sinful nature") is associated with this present evil age (1:4) and the elements of the world (4:3), the demise of which began at the cross (5:24). The latter (*pneuma*; "the Spirit") is the sign that the age to

---

[7]E. P. Sanders, *Paul and Palestinian Judaism: A Comparison of Religions* (Philadelphia: Fortress, 1977), 543.

[8]Those espousing this view include Gerhardus Vos, *The Pauline Eschatology* (Grand Rapids: Eerdmans, 1952); Herman Ridderbos, *Paul: An Outline of His Theology*, trans. J. R. De Witt (Grand Rapids: Eerdmans, 1975); George Ladd, *A New Testament Theology* (Grand Rapids: Eerdmans, 1974), 359–570; Richard N. Longenecker, *The Ministry and Message of Paul* (Grand Rapids: Eerdmans, 1971). All of these take their point of departure from Albert Schweitzer, *The Mysticism of Paul the Apostle*, trans. William Montgomery (New York: Henry Holt, 1931).

come has arrived, the absence of which precludes a person from entrance into the kingdom of God (contrast 5:19–21 with vv. 22–23). The terms *flesh* and *Spirit* signal to the reader that Paul has in mind the two-age structure. Two significant ideas emerge in light of this observation: (1) The struggle that results from the collision of these forces demonstrates that the Christian lives at the juncture of the two ages; (2) the solution to this internal struggle is to walk in the Spirit. Thus the Spirit is both part of the source of the problem as well as the means for its solution.

(1) The best way to highlight the idea of the overlapping of the two ages in 5:16–18 is to compare and contrast these verses with the Dead Sea Scrolls, particularly *1QS* 3:13–4:26. Both passages are rooted in an apocalyptic milieu in that they assume the twofold periodization of history and an internal conflict within the devotee's heart. But, as we will see, Galatians 5:16–18 significantly modifies the Jewish linear structure in light of the arrival of the Spirit. The following charts and explanation depict the difference between the two writings in terms of the struggle between the two ages and its resolution.

1QS 3:13–4:26

This Age	Age to Come
Struggle (two impulses in conflict: evil versus good)	Solution: obedience to the Law defeats the evil impulse and brings the final age

---

Gal. 5:16–18

This Age - - - - - - - - - - - - ▶ ◀ - - - - - - - - - - - - Age to Come

(The meeting of the two ages)
Struggle: Spirit versus flesh
Solution: walk in the Spirit

In contrasting Galatians 5:16–18 with *1QS* 3:13–4:26, Martyn pinpoints a key difference in perspective regarding when the struggle with the flesh began. For the Qumran community, the conflict between the good and bad inclinations was designed by

God at the beginning of creation: "He has created man to govern the world, and has appointed for him two spirits in which to walk until the time of visitation" (1QS 4:16); "For God has established the spirits in equal measure until the final age" (1QS 4:25). But for Galatians 5:16–18, the arrival of the Holy Spirit and the new creation in Christ were the catalyst for the conflict with the flesh. Martyn writes: "The Spirit and the flesh [are] not . . . an archaic pair of opposites inhering in the cosmos from creation, but rather [are] an *apocalyptic antinomy* characteristic of God's New Creation."[9] In other words, Paul posits here the overlapping of the two ages as the cause for the struggle between the flesh and the Spirit within the Christian. F. F. Bruce concurs with this teaching of the Pauline passage: "The antithesis between flesh and Spirit . . . belongs to that 'eschatological tension' which, so long as believers remain in mortal body, is inseparable from their life in Christ."[10] Similarly, Bruce goes on to observe of the Galatian believers: "They had received the Spirit . . . , otherwise they would have no experience of the conflict between the Spirit and the flesh. . . . 'The result of this conflict is that you cannot do the things you wish.'"[11]

(2) The two texts also differ with regards to the solution to the struggle. For the Qumran sect, the answer to the dilemma of the dual between the good and evil inclinations is for believers to obey the Law, which in turn provides them with victory over the flesh, the evil impulse.[12] As a result of adhering to the Law, the age to come will finally appear: "The fear of the laws of God may be instilled in his [believer's] heart . . . and as for the visitation of all who walk in this Spirit, it shall be healing . . . everlasting blessing . . . eternal joy without end . . . truth shall arise in the world forever" (1QS 4:1; cf. CD 2:14–16; Sirach 21:11).

---

[9]Martyn, "Apocalyptic Antinomies in the Letter to the Galatians," NTS 31 (1985): 417.

[10]F. F. Bruce, *The Epistle to the Galatians* (NIGNTC; Grand Rapids: Eerdmans, 1982), 244.

[11]Ibid., 244.

[12]The rabbinic doctrine of the evil inclination (*yetzer harah*) and the good inclination (*yetzer hatob*) originated with Genesis 6:5 and 8:21, respectively. The former refers to the evil impulse of humans while the latter, though also mentioning the evil inclination, does so in the context of divine mercy, thus paving the way for the concept of the good impulse.

A careful reading of Galatians 5:12–26, as recent commentators have noted, reveals that Paul's opponents in Galatia presupposed the same contrast found in *1QS* 3:13–4:26—the antidote to the fleshly impulse is the Law.[13] For the apostle of grace, however, the Christian's final mastery over the flesh because of the empowerment of the Law is still forthcoming. The only way to resist the evil impulse is to depend on the Spirit (Gal. 5:18), who provides the believer with the divine edge over the flesh: "Live by the Spirit, and you will not gratify the desires of the sinful nature" (v. 16). Final salvation[14] and freedom from struggle must wait until the *Parousia*.[15] Martyn expresses the difference between Paul and his opponents at Galatia well:

> It follows that Christians who are tempted to live as though the effective opposite of the fleshly impulse was the Law are in fact persons who are tempted to abandon life in the Creation that has now been made what it is by the advent of Christ and of his Spirit. It is they who are not living in the real world. For the true war of liberation has been initiated not at Sinai, but rather in the apocalypse of the crucified one and in the coming of his Spirit.[16]

B. 1 CORINTHIANS 10:11–13

The title of this work adapts a vital phrase from 1 Corinthians 10:11, "the ends of the ages have come" (pers. tr.).[17] These words attest to Paul's belief that the age to come has dawned for Christians

---

[13]See, for example, Martyn, "Apocalyptic Antinomies in Galatians," 417–18; Judith M. Gundry Volf, *Paul and Perseverance. Staying in and Falling Away* (Louisville, Ky.: Westminster/John Knox, 1990), 141–54.

[14]Though the term *salvation* is not explicitly used in Galatians 5:16–17, it is closely related to other concepts mentioned in Galatians 5—life (eternal), Spirit, and kingdom of God.

[15]Though Paul does not mention the *Parousia* in Galatians, he presupposes the idea in some of his other writings (e.g., 1 Thess. 4:13–18; 5:3; 2 Thess. 1:9–10).

[16]Martyn, "Apocalyptic Antinomies in Galatians," 417–18.

[17]The phrase here is plural, *ta telē tōn aiōnōn*, "the ends of the ages." Fee captures Paul's message in this verse: "almost all agree that Paul's point is that he and the Corinthians belong to the period that marks the end of the ages" (Gordon Fee, *The First Epistle to the Corinthians* [TNICNT; Grand Rapids: Eerdmans, 1987]), 459, fn. 45.

and, although the word "salvation" is not used there, deliverance is an attendant circumstance of that event, particularly deliverance from trials (vv. 12–13). The point Paul makes in this passage, therefore, is that the Christian lives at the intersection of the two ages, the proof of which is affliction. He develops this thought in two parts: (1) verse 11, that the age to come is already present; (2) verses 12–13, that the age to come is not yet complete, demonstrated by the fact that believers still undergo the eschatological trials of the end time.

1. The Age to Come Is Already Present (1 Cor. 10:11)

Few disagree that verse 11 refers to the arrival of the age to come. For the apostle, Israel's experiences in the Old Testament serve as a type or foreshadowing of God's climactic work in the church, the people of God of the end time. In other words, the salvation of Christians is the goal toward which history has been moving. The long time that has elapsed since Paul's day notwithstanding, the death and resurrection of Jesus began the last days. His sending of the Spirit to his body, the church, signals the beginning of the end of human history (see 1 Cor. 12–14; 15:45).

2. The Age to Come Is Not Yet Complete (1 Cor. 10:12–13)

Nevertheless, the age to come is not yet complete; this present age continues, and the juncture of the two produces the eschatological trials of the end time. There are four indicators in these two verses suggesting that Paul believed the messianic woes, or the Great Tribulation, which were expected to occur in the last days, has been, or is about to be, unleashed on Christians: (1) The dawning of the end time brings with it the *peirasmos*, a word meaning either "trial" or "temptation," the latter nuance being the case when a person does not faithfully endure his or her hardships.[18] That Paul draws here on the Jewish apocalyptic teaching that an eschatological trial will test God's people immediately prior to the coming of the Messiah (Dan. 12:1–2) is confirmed by his juxtaposing of the notions of the age to come (v. 10) and trials (vv. 12–13).

---

[18]Ibid., 460, fn. 49.

Words in the *peirasmos* word-group are used in an eschatological way in Revelation 2:10 (at that time believers will be "tested" through the onslaughts of Satan), Revelation 3:10 (the hour of "testing" is coming upon the inhabitants of the earth), Matthew 6:13 (believers are to pray to be delivered from the coming "test/temptation"), and elsewhere.[19] First Corinthians 10:13 should be included in this list.

(2) The phrase "God is faithful," as Judith M. Gundry Volf argues, is one of a group of Pauline texts using the words, *pistos ho theos*, declaring the faithfulness of God to his people during eschatological tribulation (1 Cor. 1:9; 10:13; 1 Thess. 5:24; 2 Thess. 3:3).[20]

(3) The warning in verse 12 balances the assurance that verse 13 gives—"if you think you are standing firm, be careful that you don't fall." It is akin with those apocalyptic texts predicting the coming separation of the true from the false (Matt. 25:31–46; Mark 13:6 [Matt. 24:5/Luke 21:8]; 2 Thess. 2:9–10; Rev. 13:3–4). Even now the Corinthians must examine themselves to see if they are genuinely Christian (2 Cor. 13:5). Unfortunately, the eschatological prize can be lost (see 1 Cor. 9:24–27; 10:1–10).

(4) Nevertheless, the Corinthian Christians need not be unduly alarmed because God will not allow them to be tempted beyond their capability, but will provide a way of escape in order that they can endure it (v. 13b). This language of successfully passing the test is rooted in the apocalyptic belief that God will empower his own to endure the duress of the end time (cf. Rom. 14:4; 2 Peter 2:9; Rev. 3:10), even if it means shortening the time of

---

[19]See Heinrich Seesemann's article, "πεῖρα," *TDNT*, 6:23–36. The clause, "No temptation has seized you except what is common to man," at first glance appears to mitigate against an eschatological reading of the trials mentioned in verse 13. However, two things resolve this difficulty. First, as Fee observes, this verse intends to contrast the trials that are the common lot of humans with idolatry (see 10:1–10, 14–22), a temptation for which the individual must be held accountable (Fee, *The First Epistle to the Corinthians*, 460). In other words, Paul is dividing trials into two categories: those that humans cannot avoid and those that they, can, and should. Second, the Christ-event has transformed the Christian's ordinary trials into the messianic woes. That is to say, the death of Christ on the cross, which signified the arrival of the Great Tribulation, has now recast the affliction of believers; more on this perspective in the last chapter of this work.

[20]Volf, *Paul and Perseverance*, 69–79; especially 73–74.

the testing on their behalf (Mark 13:19–20). It may even be, as Volf suggests, that the word translated "a way out" (*ekbasis*) means "the end." [21] If so, an *inclusio* frames verses 11–13: verse 11—the end (deliverance); verses 12–13a—the trials; verse 13b—the end (deliverance).[22] On this reading, verse 13b is asserting that God's people will indeed successfully endure their trials until the very end, a translation reminiscent of the apocalyptic forecast by Jesus: "but he who stands firm to the end will be saved" (Mark 13:13).

The logic of 1 Corinthians 10:11–13, therefore, flows as follows: Although the age to come has arrived (v. 11), this present age is still in operation (vv. 12–13), the proof of which is eschatological affliction. In light of this, Christians need to avoid two extremes in responding to their trials: (1) they should not overestimate their ability in resisting temptation (v. 12), and (2) they should not underestimate God's ability in delivering them (v. 13). Thus Christians live in the dynamic tension that has ensued because of the intersection of the two ages. In essence, trials witness to the fact that they are genuinely Christian.[23]

C. ROMANS 6:1–14

Romans 6:1–14 intertwines three tenses of salvation: past (juridical), present (moral), and future (eschatological). In doing

---

[21]Ibid., 72.

[22]This suggestion of an *inclusio* (the same theme frames the intervening material in a text, resulting in an A B A' pattern) in 1 Corinthians 10:11–13, centering on the idea of the end of the ages, is my own.

[23]In Jewish expectation, the messianic woes were expected to precede the coming of the Messiah. That sequence was somewhat reversed with the death and resurrection of Jesus Christ, as Schweitzer long ago pointed out (*The Mysticism of Paul*, 144). More recently, Beker has pinpointed the rationale behind this switch. According to early Christianity, because believers share an intimate union with the cross of Christ, the suffering and death he experienced as the culmination of the messianic woes now characterizes their suffering; this is the "not yet" side of eschatology. On the other hand, because believers also share an intimate union with the resurrection of Christ, the heavenly glory he now possesses belongs to them as well; this is the "already" side of eschatology (*Paul the Apostle: The Triumph of God in Life and Thought* [Philadelphia: Fortress, 1980], 146). Thus afflictions prove the genuineness of the Christian's profession of faith.

so, it constitutes something of a microcosm of the Pauline concept of salvation. Like those verses in Paul previously noted that depict salvation as an assured fact, verses 2–4a, 5a, 6a, 8a declare that because believers have died to sin by virtue of their union with Christ's death through baptism, they now share in his resurrection life. This is the juridical sense of salvation. On the other hand, verses 5b and 8b, like other verses already highlighted in this chapter, state that salvation is not yet finalized—it awaits the return of Christ. This is the eschatological sense of salvation. Verses 4b, 6b, 11, 12–14, however, make clear that salvation is also a present reality; this is the moral sense of salvation. It is this third group of verses that require extended comment here, especially verses 12–14.

Perhaps the best term to characterize the idea latent in this third group of texts is "sanctification" (see vv. 19, 22), a word meaning "holy or set apart for God."[24] A careful consideration of verses 12–14 suggests that what Paul has in mind is nothing less than an inner *holy war*, the inevitable result of the overlapping of the two ages. This is what believers face because the kingdom of Christ has invaded the dominion of sin. Through the death and resurrection of Jesus, sin's grip on this world is no longer unopposed. One finds the clash of these two kingdoms spelled out in verses 12–14:

> Vv. 12–13a: believers are to stop permitting sin
> to rule their lives.
> Vv. 13b–14: believers are to start submitting
> their lives to the reign of God.

Three military ideas are pressed into the service of Paul's language here, thereby giving the impression that an inner spiritual holy war is being described. (1) The term "master" (*kurieusei*, v. 14), along with the word "reign" (*basileuetô*, v. 12), denote the ancient

---

[24]The Greek word for "sanctification" is *hagiasmos* (from the word *hagios*, meaning "holy"). The term originated in Exodus 19:5–6, where Israel is labeled God's "holy people." Later Judaism used the term to refer to the inheritance of the messianic kingdom by the elect people of God (Dan. 7:18–27; *Pss.Sol.* 17). Thus the nomenclature applied to the New Testament refers to the church as the new people of God who are set apart for divine holy purposes.

Near Eastern idea of the monarch who rules over his kingdom. (2) The term "instruments" (*melê*, v. 13) probably means weapons of warfare,[25] referring to the believer's body as an instrument of righteousness in the service of the kingdom of God. (3) The emphasis on obedience throughout verses 12–14 also reminds one of a militaristic setting.

Thus Romans 6:12–14 (cf. vv. 4b, 6b, 11) probably draws on a familiar theme to early Jewish and Christian apocalyptic writers— the belief that at the end of the ages the saints of God will wage war against the sons of evil (see Dan. 7; 12; *1QM* 15; Rev. 19). For Paul, however, the believer's quarrel is not with flesh and blood but against the spiritual enemies of God (Eph. 6:10–16). What Romans 6:12–14 thus presents is an internal, spiritual holy war between the dominion of sin and the kingdom of God; hence the injunction to believers to align themselves with the forces of righteousness. This battle of the soul is proof positive that the kingdom of God has entered the believer's life. In the words of Jesus, "I did not come to bring peace, but a sword" (Matt. 10:34). This struggle of the heart between good and evil is a sure sign that the Christian lives between the two ages. Paul further details this opposition in Romans 7:14–25.

D. ROMANS 7:14–25

Romans 7:14–25 is an enigmatic passage, generating at least three conflicting interpretations: (1) It speaks of Paul's, and all Christians', present engagement with sin;[26] (2) it refers to Paul's past life as a rabbi, one checkered by frustration with the Law;[27]

---

[25]See Cranfield, *Romans 1–VIII* (ICC; Edinburgh: T. & T. Clark, 1975), 319. The other possible background to the thought world of verse 13 is the practice of slavery. Yet, as Dunn remarks, the two semantic fields—weapons of warfare and slavery—are not mutually exclusive because captives from war in antiquity were often consigned to military duty (*Romans 1–8* [WBC 38a; Waco, Tex.: Word, 1988], 337).

[26]Excellent defenses of this position can be found in Cranfield, *Romans I–VIII*, 342–47; 355–70; Dunn, *Romans 1–8*, 387–99.

[27]Proponents of this view include Adolf Deissmann, *Paul: A Study in Social and Religious History*, trans. W. E. Wilson (Gloucester, Mass.: Peter Smith, 1972), 92; W. D. Davies, *Paul and Rabbinic Judaism: Some Rabbinic Elements in Pauline Theology*, (New York: Harper and Row, 1948), 498.

(3) it refers to Paul's pre-conversion days of discontent as seen now through his Christian eyes.[28] We address these views in reverse order. The third view has against it the undeniable fact that the present tense is consistently used throughout verses 14–25 (in contrast to the past tense in verses 7–13), thus pointing to Paul's present Christian life experience, not his past pre-conversion days. Moreover, this interpretation stumbles on verse 25 ("So then, I myself in my mind am a slave to God's law, but in the sinful nature a slave to the law of sin"), a poignant description of Paul's contemporary experience. The second interpretation is also contradicted by the sustained usage of the present tense in verses 14–25, not to mention Paul's positive assessment elsewhere of his pre-conversion ability to keep the Law (Gal. 1:14; Phil. 3:6b).

That leaves us with the first view. The only substantial disagreement that can be voiced against this understanding of the passage is that it seems to paint too negative a picture of the Christian life, especially when it is compared with the victorious presence of the Spirit as recorded in 8:1–16. However, this criticism is more apparent than real. Actually, 7:14–25 portrays a bad side and a good side to a Christian, and their admixture is the result of the overlapping of the two ages. This produces within Christians a deep-seated struggle between obedience and disobedience to God, the resolution of which is aided by the Spirit (8:1–16). Stated another way, the eschatological tension resident within Christians is evidence that they are genuinely saved. The following chart and explanation highlight these two opposing forces as documented in 7:14–25:[29]

	This Age	The Age to Come
V. 14	Enslaved to sin	Obedience to the Law
Vv. 15–24	Practices evil	Desires to do good
V. 25	Law of sin	Law of God

(1) The first person pronoun "I" (*egô*) occurs some eight times in verses 14–25, thus identifying the theme of the text. In reading

---

[28]This understanding was earlier popularized by W. G. Kümmel, *Römer 7 und die Bekehrung des Paulus* (Leipzig, 1929) and, lately, Beker, *Paul the Apostle*, 238–43.

[29]A similar chart occurs in Dunn (*Romans 1–8*, 398), the capstone of a magnificent exposition of the passage (387–99).

them, one quickly gets a sense therein of a divided "I," a person torn between two worlds. How are we to explain this phenomenon? Paul almost gives indication of having suffered a nervous breakdown or having become schizophrenic! But such a psychological interpretation overlooks that he disavows neither personal responsibility for his actions nor the coherence of his being. It is the same Paul who speaks of both aspects of his behavior, bad and good.

Nor does the anthropological dualistic interpretation square with a proper reading of these verses. Popularized by ancient Greek philosophy, the idea that the human being is dichotomized into two components—the higher, more nobler part (the mind, reason, or soul) and the lower, less desirable part (the body or the flesh)—finds no support in the text. On the contrary, recent studies on Paul's anthropological terms reveal that he views the human being as a totality, an "embodied soul" (to use Bultmann's description), leaving no place for an ethical disparaging of the body.[30]

The most accurate view of the "I" of Romans 7:14–25, therefore, is that the two contrasting descriptions reflect a salvation-history, or eschatological, dualism whereby the Christian is seen as belonging to both the aggregate powers of the old epoch—sin, death, and perversion of the Law—and to the forces of the new epoch—grace, life, and the Spirit. Dunn puts it this way, "The 'I' is split not as a result of creation (or the fall), but primarily as the result of redemption. . . ."[31] Elsewhere, Dunn writes of this perspective on these verses:

> In Paul we are confronted with the sharpness and frustration of the eschatological tension—that is, a tension which even if present elsewhere is rendered all the sharper and more poignant by the fact that the individual (believer) has already begun to experience the possibilities and promises of a wholly Spirit-directed life.[32]

---

[30]Excellent treatments and accompanying bibliographies of Pauline anthropological terms pertinent to this point can be found in Bultmann, *Theology of the NT*, 1.190–245, and Ladd, *A Theology of the New Testament*, 457–78.

[31]Dunn, *Romans 1–8*, 394.

[32]Ibid., 389.

(2) We may take verse 14 and verse 25 together. Verse 14 encapsulates the thesis of verses 14–25: Paul is enslaved to sin but knows that he should obey the Law of God.[33] Verse 25 restates the thesis of verse 14: Paul serves two laws—the Law of God and the law of sin. What comes between these two verses is a barrage of antithetical, almost antiphonal, statements, keying in on the battle of the two ages as individualized in the apostle and every Christian. This conflict can be categorized as Paul's practicing evil (vv. 15–16a, 17–18a, 18c, 19b–21a, 23a, 24, 25b) as opposed to his desiring to do good (vv. 16b, 18b, 19a, 21b–22, 23b, 25a).[34] What Christian in his or her most honest moments does not echo the apostle's heartfelt cry? Little wonder, then, that passages like Romans 7:14–25 prompted Martin Luther to characterize the believer as *simul justuus et peccator* ("simultaneously saint and sinner").

E. ROMANS 8:17–30

The already/not yet eschatological tension inherent to Paul's thinking comes to the fore again in Romans 8:17–30. Verse 24 succinctly summarizes the theme of this paragraph: "in this *hope* we were *saved*" (italics added). The idea of salvation as now and not yet reverberates throughout the passage, expressed in terms of suffering and glory:

Vv. 12–13a:	believers are to stop permitting sin to rule their lives.
Vv. 17–18:	Suffering/glory
Vv. 19–27:	Three groanings:
(1)Vv. 19–22:	Creation groans (hope for the revelation of the sons of God).
(2)Vv. 23–25:	The believer groans (firstfruits of the Spirit/ by hope we were saved).
(3)Vv. 26–27:	The Spirit groans (the Spirit helps us in our weaknesses).
Vv. 28–30:	Suffering/glory

---

[33]Dunn convincingly shows that *nomos* in 7:14–25 should be understood as the Mosaic Law, not a generic principle (*Romans 1–8*, 392).

[34]See 2 Cor. 4:16; Eph. 4:24; Col. 3:10, where similar language is associated with being a Christian.

Verses 17–18 and 28–30, preoccupied with the themes of suffering and glory, form an *inclusio* around this passage. These two themes combined to form a prominent notion to Jewish apocalyptic writers who believed that the suffering of the people of God in the present age would bring them glory in the age to come (cf. *1 Enoch* 1:2–8; 96:3; *2 Bar.* 48:49–50; 51:3–11; *4 Ezra* 7:15–16, 95–98). In *2 Baruch* 48:49–50, a text distinctly reminiscent of Romans 8:17–18 and 2 Corinthians 4:17, the author expresses the thought well, "For surely, as you endured much labor in the short time in which you live in this passing world, so you will receive great light in that world which has no end."

Yet for Paul, as for the early Christians, the relationship between suffering and glory was no longer consecutive (the one would lead to the other) but dialectical (the one is intermingled with the other). Because of the death and resurrection of Christ, the glory of the age to come has broken into this age of suffering. Thus the two are intertwined in the Christian's life, as Romans 8:17–18 makes clear. God's glory is already the possession of the believer, even in this age of suffering. But the divine glory is presently invisible, residing in the Christian's heart. Only at the *Parousia* will it be revealed publicly in the believer's resurrection body (cf. 2 Cor. 4:16–5:10; Phil. 3:20–21; Col. 3:1–4).

Romans 8:28–30 presents the same pattern—divine glory is the present possession of the believer, but it coexists with suffering. The former aspect is delineated in verses 29–30, which showcase a dazzling display of theological terms to describe the present aspect of the Christian's salvation ("foreknew, predestined, called, justified, glorified").[35] It is not accidental that "glory" (v. 30) is the term used to conclude the list, for it returns the reader to the

---

[35]The traditional definitions of these terms may be recalled here: "foreknew"—God chose beforehand those elect who would come to him in faith; "predestined"—God has predetermined that his own would someday be conformed to the image of Christ; "called"—God's call to faith through the preaching of the gospel is effectual; "justified"—God declares the sinner righteous because of the atoning work of Christ on the cross and his victorious resurrection; "glorified"—believers can be sure that one day they will inherit the glory of the age to come. The tack taken here is that of individual salvation. For a refreshingly different view, see William Kline, *God's Chosen People: A Corporate View of Election* (Grand Rapids: Zondervan, 1990).

thought that initiated the paragraph (v. 17). The latter aspect, suffering, is the conceptual antecedent of the words "in all things God works for the good of those who . . . have been called according to his purpose" (v. 28). In context, the "all things" are the afflictions that God uses (vv. 17–25) to conform believers to the image and glory of Christ (v. 29).

The twofold motif of suffering/glory continues in Romans 8:19–27, though it is expressed in a different metaphor—groaning. Three groanings are enumerated, each of which testifies to the overlapping of the two ages. (1) In chapter 2 we examined the meaning of the groaning of creation (vv. 19–22), so we need not explain this further. Suffice it to say that eschatological tension affects creation itself—it hopes and groans in this age for the future revelation of the glory of the children of God in the age to come, which will ensure its own deliverance from Adam's corrupting influence. Creation "knows" that the death and resurrection of Christ has inaugurated the end of time, though it also knows that the *Parousia* and complete liberation are still coming.

(2) Verses 23–25 speak of a second groaning, that of believers. Such a longing is connected with two phrases, both of which witness to the overlapping of the two ages: "the firstfruits of the Spirit" and "in this hope we were saved." The first phrase refers to the sign of the arrival of the age to come—the Spirit. But the Spirit's presence in the heart of the believer is only the beginning of the end, the firstfruits.[36] Only at the *Parousia* will the Spirit replace the Christian's earthly body with a glorious resurrection dwelling (cf. 2 Cor. 5:1–5; Eph. 1:13–14). According to the second phrase, believers have been saved (i.e., the age to come has dawned), but that salvation is rooted in hope (i.e., believers still live in this age; cf. 2 Cor. 4:17–18).

(3) The third groaning, that of the Spirit (vv. 26–27), poses a problem for interpreters, especially concerning the question of whether or not the "groans that words cannot express" refer to the phenomenon of ecstatic speech. Ernst Käsemann, for example,

---

[36]The Greek word here is *haparchôn*. In biblical Greek it is used for the firstfruits of Israel's sacrifice or offering to God. God's people dedicated their gifts to him as a part of the fuller gift to come. In Paul, the flow of giving is just the opposite— God gives the Holy Spirit as a pledge of the coming resurrection body.

believes these words must mean the utterances of tongues (*glosso-lalia*) by Christians.[37] On the other hand, Cranfield seems closer to the truth with his suggestion that the unarticulated groanings are those of the Spirit, not believers, and that such utterances are not necessarily to be equated with ecstatic speech.[38] If this is the case, then we encounter once again the eschatological tension of the overlapping of the two ages. The Spirit of the end time is intimately involved with Christians' weaknesses in this present age. The believer's inability to pray according to God's will is an extension of this tension. That they desire the divine will is proof that they are citizens of the age to come, the new humanity (see also Rom. 12:1–2). However, that they do not clearly perceive that will proceeds from the fact that they still live in this age. Dunn elaborates on this point, "This is precisely the wonder and poignancy of the eschatological tension: the Spirit does not eliminate or transform believers' total inability to maintain the proper dialogue between God and man; rather the Spirit works in and through that inability."[39] Thus, the suffering/glory motif (vv. 17–18, 28–30), in conjunction with the groanings of creation, believers, and the Spirit (vv. 19–27), evokes the idea of a struggle that results from the shifting of the two ages.[40]

F. ROMANS 13:11–14

It was the reading of Romans 13:13–14 that marked the turning point in Augustine's life, and for good reason—this passage challenges its readers to embrace the Lord Jesus Christ by faith, thereby opening themselves up to the eschatological rule of God in their hearts. When it comes to salvation, eschatology and ethics go hand in hand. This text tracks the critical turn of the ages for the Christian.

---

[37]Ernst Käsemann, *Commentary on Romans*, trans. Geoffrey Bromiley (Grand Rapids: Eerdmans, 1980), 226.

[38]Cranfield, *Romans I–VIII*, 423.

[39]Dunn, *Romans 1–8*, 477–78.

[40]Romans 5:2–5 is similar in structure to 8:17–30 concerning the intimate relationship between glory and suffering in the experience of the believer: hope (of glory), v. 2b; suffering, vv. 3–4; hope, v. 5a.

1. Salvation and Eschatology (Rom. 13:11–12a)

Verses 11–12a emphasize the indicative aspect of salvation—by virtue of the Christ-event, the age to come has drawn near and, with it, the salvation of believers. Three temporal clues here confirm this to be the case. (1) The word "time" (*kairon*, v. 11) is one of Paul's choice terms for referring to the dawning of the eschaton (cf. Rom. 3:26; 5:6; 1 Cor. 7:29). (2) The words "already the hour" (pers. tr. of *êdê hôra*, v. 11) convey a definite eschatological overtone, drawing their inspiration from Daniel's idea that God has appointed a time for fulfilling his promise of the arrival of his kingdom (Dan. 8:17, 19; cf. 1 John 2:18; Rev. 3:3, 10). (3) The clause "our salvation is nearer now than when we first believed" (v. 11) is full of eschatological terms. "Now" (*nyn*) refers to the presence of the age to come (cf. Rom. 3:21; 5:9; 2 Cor. 6:2), and "salvation" (*sôtêria*) refers to the Christian's redemptive wholeness and spiritual deliverance, a process begun by faith and soon to be culminated at the *Parousia*. This salvation has drawn "near" (*engyteron*), a term recalling Jesus' proclamation of the arrival of the kingdom of God, the age to come (Mark 1:15; 13:28, 29; cf. James 5:8; 1 Peter 4:7). These temporal terms, then, indicate that salvation and the end time have already dawned for the believer.

2. Salvation and Ethics (Rom. 13:12b–14)

However, the salvific message of verses 11–12a occurs in the context of this present age; hence Paul's emphasis in verses 12b–14 on the necessity for Christians to live holy lives. It is clear that, for the apostle, eschatology forms the basis for Christian ethics. Accordingly, two general commands are issued: Christians are to put off the deeds of darkness (vv. 12b–13) and put on the weapons of light (vv. 12c, 14).[41] This respective shunning of unrighteousness and donning of righteousness reflect the ongoing struggle that believers experience because they live in between the two epochs. The metaphor of the conflict between darkness and light reminds one of the eschatological battle between the unrighteous and the righteous envisioned in the Qumran literature (*1QM* 1:1, 8–14;

---

[41]Most Pauline scholars today agree that his language of "putting off/putting on" originated in a baptismal setting (e.g., see Dunn, *Romans 9–16*, 790).

13:5–16; cf. also *1QS* 1:9–10; 3:24–25; 4:7–13), as well as 1 Thessalonians 5:1–9.

G. PHILIPPIANS 1:6; 3:1–14, 20–21

In the previous chapter we touched on Philippians 2:12–13 and its portrayal of salvation as that which is present within the believer but which needs to be worked out—the already/not yet eschatological tension inherent to Paul's thinking on salvation. Three other passages in this letter proceed along the same line of thought: 1:6; 3:1–14; 3:20–21.

(1) Philippians 1:6 makes two basic points: God has begun a good work in believers, and this work will persevere until the day of Christ. These two ideas are rooted in the overlapping of the two ages. The "good work" that God has begun in the Christian is none other than salvation, the initiation of the age to come. More often than not, good works in Paul refers to human effort, whether toward God (Rom. 2:7, 10) or others (Rom. 13:3; 2 Cor. 8:9; Eph. 2:10; 2 Thess. 2:17; 1 Tim. 2:10; 5:10, 25; 6:18; 2 Tim. 2:21; 3:17; Titus 2:7, 14; 3:1, 8, 14). There are two exceptions to this pattern: Romans 14:20, which attributes a good work to God, and the present passage. That "good work" in Philippians 1:6 refers to divine salvation is clear from the way Paul frames the verse with the term "gospel" (vv. 5, 7).[42] It seems, then, that the good work that God initiated in the Philippians' hearts is synonymous with the notion that the deliverance of the age to come has already been inaugurated (cf. 2:12–16). Paul then makes a second point in 1:6: though the final attainment of the believer's salvation is sure, it is nevertheless future in that it awaits "the day of Christ Jesus," the *Parousia*. Verses 9–11 expand on the meaning of verse 6: Paul prays for the Philippians' progress in sanctification as they prepare for the day of Christ and the testing associated with that day. This is the not yet aspect of salvation; it must be worked out in the context of this present era.

---

[42]Volf provides excellent grounds for understanding the "good work" here as synonymous with salvation, *Paul and Perseverance*, 45–47.

(2) Philippians 3:1–14 has the same eschatological tension, though there Paul uses different terms: the righteousness of the age to come now belongs to Paul by faith, not by the keeping of the Law (vv. 1–11). Nevertheless the apostle, like all Christians, must continually strive forward toward the goal of final salvation, because he still lives in this present age (vv. 12–14). Such striving, in effect, is the product of the interplay of the two ages and serves to correct the claim by some at Philippi of being perfect spiritually. Thus verses 12–14 form part of Paul's eschatological reservation, reminding believers that they continue to live at the juncture of the two epochs. The age to come has not yet fully replaced this present age.

(3) Philippians 3:20–21 repeats the above pattern: the believer's commonwealth currently exists in heaven (v. 20a), but the consummation of that salvation is deferred until the *Parousia* (vv. 20b–21). Here one finds a merger of realized and future eschatology. The former is evident in v. 20a, especially in the claim that the believers' commonwealth is in heaven. The Hellenistic term Paul uses here, *politeuma* (NIV "citizenship"), denotes the nuance of commonwealth, as Lincoln carefully demonstrates in his analysis of the word; as such, it is not unrelated to the concept of the Jewish idea of "kingdom."[43] The term possessed special significance for the Philippians because their city was designated a Roman colony by Emperor Octavian in 42 B.C.E. Drawing on this proud heritage, Paul implies the following analogy: Just as the city of Philippi was a commonwealth of Rome (its language was Latin, its coinage was Roman, its magistrates were appointed in Rome, its legal jurisdiction was administered as if on Italian soil), so heaven is the true home right *now* of Christians, who should thereby regulate their conduct accordingly. Lincoln pinpoints the realized aspect of the age to come inherent in Paul's phrase here:

> Although not yet fully manifest for what it is, the heavenly commonwealth is a present reality. Though expressed in Hellenistic political terminology, Paul's conception corresponds to the apocalyptic motif . . . in which the benefits of salvation awaited at the end are already present in heaven (cf. *4 Ezra* 7:14, 83; 13:2; *2 Bar.* 21:12; 48:49; 52:7).[44]

---

[43]Andrew Lincoln, *Paradise Now and Not Yet* (SNTSMS 43; Cambridge: University Press, 1981), 97–101.

[44]Ibid., 101.

Nevertheless, the consummation of the believer's salvation awaits the future *Parousia* (vv. 20b–21). Only at that time will Christians exchange their earthly, humble existence for glorious resurrection bodies. In other words, believers still live in this alien world. Their *exemplar* is Christ, who first endured the sufferings of this age in order to enjoy the glory of the age to come. The word "humble" (*tapeinôseôs*) links 3:21 with 2:8 (*etapeinôsen*). In other words, the Christological pattern of humble suffering as the path to glory (2:8–11) is applied to believers (3:21). Thus the humiliation motif for Christians is a sign that they exist in between the times of this age and the age to come.

H. EPHESIANS 2:1–10

We conclude this chapter by considering Ephesians 2:1–10, a passage that uses explicit "age" terminology in rehearsing God's plan of salvation. The text falls naturally into three segments, each of which corresponds to a particular time frame: (1) verses 1–3: this age and the need for salvation; (2) verses 4–7: the age to come and the provision of salvation; (3) verses 8–10: the overlapping of the two ages and the present/future aspects of salvation. The first two segments are best understood by means of a chart that contrasts the two:

2:1–3: This Age	2:4–6: The Age to Come
(1) V. 1: dead because of sin	Vv. 4–5: saved from sin/ alive from the dead
(2) Vv. 2–3: dominated by sin	Vv. 6–7: dominion over sin

Paul explicitly contrasted the two ages in 1:21 ("the present age" and "the one to come"); he repeats the contrast in 2:2 ("the age of this world"; pers. tr.) and v. 7 ("the coming ages"). In Paul's thinking, the age to come provides the desperate need of salvation for those enslaved to this age. He delineates two counteractions in verses 1–7. (1) In response to humans being alienated from God and spiritually dead because of this age (v. 1), faith in Christ brings them salvation and new life, qualities of the coming age (vv. 4–5). (2) Whereas sinners were once dominated by the ruler of this age so that they were at his beck and call (vv. 2–3), now, by God's grace, they have been raised to the heavenlies in order to rule with

Christ (vv. 6–7). Undoubtedly, informing this concept of reigning with Christ is the Jewish apocalyptic idea that the righteous will enter God's eschatological dominion, receive life in the age to come, and sit on heavenly thrones over their enemies (Dan. 7:22, 27; *1 Enoch* 108:12; *Apoc.Elijah* 37:3–4; *As.Isa.* 9:18; *1QH* 11:10–12; cf. also Rev. 3:21; 20:6). For Paul, the historical enemies of God as specified in Judaism are spiritualized and transformed into the Devil and his host (cf. Dan. 10:20; Eph. 6:10–17).

In addition to the "this age/age to come" identified in verses 1–7, verses 8–10 allude to a third time period—the overlapping of the two ages. This segment serves to highlight the present and future aspects of salvation. The already side of salvation is emphasized in verses 8–9: Christians have been saved by the grace of God alone, apart from human merit. The perfect tense of the verb "saved" (*sezôsomenoi*, v. 8) heightens the actuality of the believer's salvation ("you have been and continue to be saved"). Nevertheless, the book is not closed on salvation; it is still in process, as verse 10 makes clear. Christians have been delivered from their sin in order to work for God and others (believers are God's "workmanship," created "to do good works"); this is the divine plan for their lives. The emphasis on ethics in this verse constitutes the not yet side of salvation. This is in keeping with Paul's futurist eschatology elsewhere in Ephesians (1:14; 4:30; 5:5, 27, 6.8, 13), of which the admonitions to grow and mature are a part (2:21; 3:9; 4:13, 15–16). Lincoln catches this aspect of Pauline eschatology in Ephesians; what he writes about the aforementioned verses can be said about the concept of Pauline salvation generally:

> In this way the tension between "already" and "not yet" is retained. The relationship between these two poles is similar to that between the Pauline indicative and imperative with its "become what you are." The force of the emphasis on realized eschatology with its spatial terminology in this letter is to highlight what believers are and have in Christ. But this stands side by side with the future references and neither pole should be played down.[45]

---

[45]Ibid., 167.

V

PAULINE ANTHROPOLOGY: FROM PLIGHT TO SOLUTION

INTRODUCTION

With respect to Paul's thought, G. Eichholz writes, "One can hardly understand his theology, if one does not grasp his theology of the Torah."[1] Yet Paul's view of the Law continues to elude the grasp of the best of scholars. N. J. McEleney writes of this: "Uncertainty remains concerning Paul's position vis-à-vis the Law, forcing interpreters to return to the question again and again in the hope that their new studies may shed some small light upon the texts by which their colleagues may see the problem in new perspective."[2]

As a rabbi, Paul clearly cherished the Torah (Phil. 3:4–6); therein lies the seed of his thought on the Law. In the Old Testament one discovers that, "thanks" to the Fall (Gen. 2–3), the human race inherited a problem. That quandary can be stated chiastically—the heart of the problem was the problem of the heart. In short, sin spelled disaster for the relationship between human beings and their God (Gen. 4–11). However, the divine solution to this human plight surfaced with the founding of Israel (Gen. 12–50), together with the gift of the Torah—the written expression of God's will—to his people, as described in the Pentateuch. In effect, therefore, the Old Testament itself provides one with the remedy for a spiritually skewed anthropology—obey the Law and live (Lev. 18:4).

---

[1]G. Eichholz, *Die Theologie des Paulus im Umriss* (Neukirchen-Vluyn: Neukirchener Verlag, 1972), 178.

[2]N. J. McEleney, "Conversion, Circumcision and the Law," *NTS* 20 (1973–74): 319.

But early on in the Old Testament, a growing awareness developed that the Law, though of divine origin, was in and of itself insufficient to produce holiness and righteousness in the hearts of the people of Israel. This concern is ominously conveyed even at the inception of the Law, for when Moses descended from Mount Sinai with the fresh revelation of God, he discovered, much to his horror, that Israel had already broken the supreme commandment of worshiping no other god but Yahweh (Ex. 32). Such concern on the part of Moses was not ill-founded, for again and again the Hebrews forsook their God and his law, their only hope of salvation. The Old Testament is replete with stories of Israel's rebellion (e.g., Num. 11:4–6; Jer. 2:22; Ezek. 20; Hos. 5:5–6), so much so that Rudolf Bultmann has characterized the Old Testament plot as a history of failure.[3] It is as if Israel found herself still to be in Adam despite having the Law.

However, alongside this checkered history of Israel's obedience stood the hope of a better day, when God's people would be restored to both their Lord and their land (e.g., Isa. 42:13; 48:21; Jer. 31:31–34; Ezek. 36:26–32; Hos. 3:4–5). Frank Thielman well captures this twofold theme of the Old Testament when he writes:

> [The Old Testament] viewed the history of God's people largely as a history of failure to do God's will. Often this failure was expressed in terms of Israel's continual violation of God's Law or covenant. Many of the same passages in which this failure was expressed, however, also extended the hope that at some future time God would intervene to destroy the vicious cycle of sin and rebellion and produce a people who would obey him from their hearts.[4]

That hope in the Old Testament and early Judaism for a brighter tomorrow became equated with the coming of the messianic age, a time when God's word would be incarnated in his people. Leaving aside for the moment the question of whether the form

---

[3]Rudolf Bultmann, "Prophecy and Fulfillment," in *Essays on Old Testament Hermeneutics*, ed. Claus Westermann (Richmond, Va.: John Knox, 1963), 72–75.

[4]Frank Thielman, *From Plight to Solution. A Jewish Framework for Understanding Paul's View of the Law in Galatians and Romans* (Supp.Nov.T 61, Leiden: E. J. Brill, 1989), 36.

of that future revelation would be the old Law internalized or a new law replacing the old one, W. D. Davies' conclusion about the role of the Torah in the messianic age still stands, "Our sources revealed the expectation that the Torah in its existing form would persist into the messianic age when its obscurities would be made plain"[5] and, one might add, when its precepts would be obeyed.

This Jewish background material is a significant component for properly interpreting the role of the Law in Paul's writings because, in documenting the ambiguity of the relationship between Israel and the Torah, it provides a mirror-image of the ambiguity in Paul's own thought concerning the place of the Law. That ambivalence has obsessed and confused Pauline scholars for hundreds of years in their attempts to sort out the issue. It is necessary, therefore, to survey the main views scholars have proposed on the role of the Law in Paul before turning to an examination of the pertinent texts.

A. SURVEY OF THE LEADING VIEWS OF PAUL'S VIEW OF THE LAW

As Brice L. Martin's recent study highlights, the most striking feature about the data concerning the role of the Law in Paul's writings is that the apostle speaks about it in both negative and positive ways.[6] From a negative perspective, the Law brings a curse (Gal. 3:13), wrath (Rom. 4:15), sin (Rom. 7:7–13), and death (Rom. 7:9–11; 2 Cor. 3:6–9); produces transgressions (Rom. 4:15; Gal. 3:19); enslaves (Rom. 6:14; 7:4–6, 23–25; Gal. 3:23; 4:5, 21–31); and is fatal (Rom. 3:20; 6:14; Gal. 3:11; 5:4). From a positive point of view, the Law is of divine origin (Rom. 7:22, 25; 8:7; 9:4); contains the will of God (Rom. 2:17–18); is holy (Rom. 7:12, 14, 16) and loving (Rom. 13:8–10; Gal. 5:14); is established by faith (Rom. 3:31; 9:30–10:4); and is obeyed in the power of the

---

[5]W. D. Davies, *Torah in the Messianic Age and/or the Age to Come* (SBLMS 7; Philadelphia: Society of Biblical Literature, 1952), 84.

[6]Brice L. Martin, *Christ and the Law in Paul* (Supp.Nov.T 62; Leiden: E. J. Brill, 1989), 19–20.

Spirit (Rom. 8:4). This sense of ambivalence about the role of the Law extends to Christians themselves, who on the one hand are no longer obligated to keep the Law (Rom. 6:14; 7:4, 6; Gal. 2:19; 3:13), but on the other hand are expected to fulfill its ideals (Rom. 2:12–16; 5:14; 6:2; 8:4; 13:8–10).

No doubt the reader will have observed that the preceding picture of the Law is drawn primarily from the two letters in which the topic is clustered—Galatians and Romans. Furthermore, it is interesting, if not vital, to note that one cannot confine the positive or negative statements to a particular letter. Martin observes that in Galatians the comments are predominantly negative, though 5:14 and 6:2 are quite positive, while in Romans there is a more balanced mixture of negative and positive remarks about the Law.[7]

The interpretation of this data has generated vast and vexing views about Paul's understanding of the Law, the tracking of which would require a Herculean effort.[8] We propose, therefore, to paint only the broad strokes of the debate by conveniently classifying the discussion under three general approaches: discontinuity, continuity, and discontinuity/continuity. Simply put, those who see Paul emphasizing a discontinuous relationship between the Christian and the Law stress the negative texts in Paul on the subject, while those who emphasize the continuous aspect of the Law in the Christian life stress those passages providing a positive perspective on the Law. Finally, those authors who perceive both negative and positive strands in Paul's teaching on the Law want to maintain a balance between the themes of discontinuity and continuity. I find myself in agreement with this third category, especially with those who attribute the tension in Paul's thought over the Law to the overlapping of the two ages.

---

[7]Ibid., 20.

[8]Excellent recent summaries of that debate can be found in Thielman, *From Plight to Solution*, chap. 1, and Stephen Westerholm, *Israel's Law and the Church's Faith: Paul and His Recent Interpreters* (Grand Rapids: Eerdmans, 1988), chap. 1.

1. Discontinuity

Three well-known representatives of the discontinuous view require discussion: Martin Luther, Albert Schweitzer, and C. G. Montefiore.

a. Martin Luther

We resume our earlier critique of Luther by calling attention to his view of the Law in Paul's thought. Three aspects concerning the Law recur in his works: the inadequacy of the works of the Law, justification by faith, and the deliverance of the Christian from the Law. Luther especially develops these ideas in his commentary on Galatians. We follow Stephen Westerholm's excellent summary of that material.[9] (1) In contrast to the Judaism of Paul's time, as well as the Roman Catholic Church of his own day, Luther claimed that the works of the Law were inadequate for obtaining salvation. From his own monastic experience and his reading of Paul, Luther made it clear that humans are depraved and therefore cannot obey the requirements laid down by the Law.[10] (2) Therefore, the only means of acquiring righteousness before a holy God is through faith. In fact, the works of the Law and justification by faith are diametrically opposed. To Luther, justification by faith is "the principal doctrine of Christianity," just as its opposite, justification by the works of the Law, is "the fundamental principle of the world, the devil, and the Pope."[11] (3) The function of the Law, therefore, is a negative one—it convicts sinners of their sin and drives them to solace in Christ, by faith alone.[12] This is true for Christians as well; since believers are simultaneously sinners and saints, the Law continues its negative role by forcefully reminding them that

---

[9]Stephen Westerholm, *Israel's Law and the Church's Faith: Paul and his Recent Interpreters* (Grand Rapids: Eerdmans, 1988), chap. 1. Westerholm gives an excellent analysis in this chapter on, among others, Luther, Schweitzer, Montefiore, Stendahl, and Räisänen, all discussed below.

[10]Martin Luther, *Luther's Works* (Galatians), vols. 26–27, ed. J. Pelikan (St. Louis: Concordia, 1963–64), 26.273–74, 387–88, 398, 404–6; 27.13.

[11]Ibid., 26.106; 27.146–47.

[12]Ibid., 26.310, 314–16, 336.

they are still in the flesh and thereby continually drives them back to faith in Christ.[13]

Luther's view of Paul and the Law is beset by two problems. First, as William Wrede pointed out, Paul's teaching on justification by faith is a polemical doctrine, one growing out of the heat of debate with the Judaizers who taught that salvation was by faith plus works. This point, together with the fact that the teaching only dominates two of Paul's letters (Galatians and Romans), should warn against elevating it to the status of being the center of the apostle's thought.[14] Second, as Stendahl has shown, Luther's approach does not take into account Paul's positive statements about the Law, especially relative to the Christian. Paul had a far more "robust" conscience about the Law's observance than Luther allowed.[15] Furthermore, as E. P. Sanders has insightfully shown, the Judaism of Paul's day in large part perceived itself as keeping the Old Testament law by faith, thus nullifying Luther's assertion that Paul's doctrine of justification by faith was unique and therefore anti-Judaistic.[16]

b. Albert Schweitzer

For Schweitzer, eschatology is the key to Paul's thought, and it is against that background that one should interpret the Pauline concept of the Law. According to the view of Jewish eschatology current in the apostle's day, evil in the world was attributed to the demons, including the Law: "the Law was given by angels who desired thereby to make men subservient to themselves"[17] (cf. Gal. 3:19; 4:1–11). However, this state of affairs will cease with the inbreaking of the age to come, the messianic kingdom. At that time sin and the Law will be done away with.

---

[13]Ibid., 26.350; 27.85–86.

[14]William Wrede, *Paul* (Lexington: American Library Association Committee on Reprinting, 1962), 64.

[15]Krister Stendahl, "The Apostle Paul and the Introspective Conscience of the West," *HTR* 56 (1963): 199–215.

[16]Sanders, *Paul and Palestinian Judaism: A Comparison of Religions* (Philadelphia: Fortress, 1977).

[17]Schweitzer, *The Mysticism of Paul the Apostle,* trans. William Montgomery (New York: Henry Holt, 1931), 69–70.

But for Schweitzer, the death and resurrection of Jesus, the Messiah, did not materialize the age to come on earth. Paul's attempt to cope with this failure consisted of his postulating the mystical doctrine of literally dying and rising with Christ, effected in baptism. That is, if the age to come did not come to Christians, then Christians can go to the age to come—those who are in Christ have already begun to experience "the cessation of the natural world through their participation in Christ's death; and, by sharing in his resurrection, they experience the dawning of the supernatural world."[18] Consequently, although the messianic kingdom did not arrive eschatologically, for Paul it nonetheless could be experienced mystically. The Law, therefore, as a part of this present age, has been removed as far as the Christian is concerned.[19]

Schweitzer's erudite theory notwithstanding, two criticisms call into question his view. First, as W. D. Davies carefully demonstrated, the Judaism surrounding Paul's time did not teach that the Law would cease with the advent of the messianic kingdom. In reality, the arrival of the age to come was expected to engender unparalleled obedience to the Torah.[20] Second, though Paul does seem to attach an inferior status to the Law by virtue of its having been mediated by the angels (Gal. 3:19), nowhere does the apostle label it as unholy. It is, after all, the Law of God. Therefore, Schweitzer neglected to perceive the positive aspect of the Law in Paul's writings, not to mention its continuing relevance for the Christian (see, for example, Rom. 8:4). As we saw in the previous chapter, although the Law has itself been subjected to sinful misuse in this evil age, it is nevertheless intrinsically good (e.g., Rom. 7:12).

c. C. G. Montefiore

With the Jewish scholar C. G. Montefiore, the debate over Paul's view of the Law took a new turn.[21] That author argued

---

[18]Ibid., 23.
[19]Ibid., 25.
[20]See note 5.
[21]C. G. Montefiore, *Judaism and St. Paul* (London: Max Goschen, 1914).

that Paul's teaching on the Law radically differed from rabbinic Judaism at three key points. First, rabbinic Jews regarded the Law as the gracious gift of a loving God to his people, whose design was their joy and good. For Paul to suggest otherwise misinterprets the true nature of things.[22] Second, rabbinic Judaism provided for repentance and forgiveness in the event that God's people disobeyed the Law, something conspicuously absent in Paul's writings.[23] Third, rabbinic theology as a whole was far more positive than Paul's pessimistic worldview that this age is under the sway of Satan and sin.[24] In other words, Paul's assumption that humans are totally depraved does not square with Judaism's teaching about the goodness of God and humankind. For Montefiore, Paul's mentality is more akin to Hellenistic, rather than rabbinic, Judaism, influenced as the former was by pagan religion.[25]

Provocative as Montefiore's work was, it suffered from a misinformed reading of rabbinic Judaism, as another Jewish scholar, H. J. Schoeps, later pointed out. Schoeps rightly criticized Montefiore on at least two grounds, First, rabbinic Judaism was not a unified whole. Even though the Talmud gives the impression that post–70 C.E. and pre–70 C.E. (the fall of Jerusalem being the dividing line) rabbinicism was the same, it was not. For example, pre–70 C.E. rabbinicism was open to Jewish apocalypticism, something that post–70 C.E. rabbinic thinking was not.[26] In other words, in pre–70 C.E. there was no "normative Judaism"; it was multifaceted, and thus Paul's thought on the Law may have been quite tolerated by his Jewish contemporaries. Second, Schoeps argued that one could not assume that in the first century C.E. there was "an irreconcilable opposition between Hellenistic and Rabbinic Judaism."[27] In this he anticipated the definitive work of Martin Hengel that documents the inter-

---

[22]Ibid., 29–30.

[23]Ibid., 42, 44, 70, 78, etc.

[24]Ibid., 69, 78.

[25]Ibid., 95, 97, 100.

[26]H. J. Schoeps, *Paul: The Theology of the Apostle in the Light of Jewish Religious History* (Philadelphia: Westminster, 1961), 26.

[27]Ibid., 26.

penetration of Judaism and Hellenism in the period under consideration.[28] In any case, notes Schoeps, Paul was immersed in Palestinian Judaism from an early age (Acts 22:3).[29]

2. Continuity

Like a pendulum, the scholarly perception of Paul's understanding of the Law swung from a discontinuous to a continuous relationship. Two pairs of scholars leading the way in this approach can be identified: Krister Stendahl and Lloyd Gaston, and C. E. B. Cranfield and James D. G. Dunn. The former of these restrict Paul's prohibition of the works of the Law to the Gentiles, while the latter interpret Paul's strictures against the Law to be aimed at Jewish legalism, not the Torah per se.

a. Krister Stendahl and Lloyd Gaston

Krister Stendahl's popular article, "The Apostle Paul and the Introspective Conscience of the West," raised the consciousness of scholars to the positive treatment that the Law receives in Paul. The apostle's robust conscience was favorable to the Law before and after his conversion, as 1 Corinthians 4:4; 2 Corinthians 1:12; 5:11; and Philippians 3:6 indicate (cf. Acts 23:1). It is a Western introspective conscience, initiated by Augustine and exploited by Luther, that has turned the Law into something dreadful for Paul.[30] But such a mindset distorts the real issue concerning the Law for Paul, which was that the *Gentiles* should not be expected to keep the Torah to be saved. Paul's entire point was that Gentiles could "become part of the people of God without having to pass through the Law."[31] On this reading of Paul, the Law serves a positive function so long as it is not misused to exclude Gentiles from salvation.

Lloyd Gaston takes this perspective to its logical conclusion, claiming that Paul did not believe that faith in Christ was

---

[28]Martin Hengel, *Judaism and Hellenism*, 2 vols. (Philadelphia: Fortress, 1974).

[29]Schoeps, *Paul*, 40.

[30]Krister Stendahl, *Paul among Jews and Gentiles* (Philadelphia: Fortress, 1976), 16–17, 83, 85.

[31]Ibid., 9.

necessary for Jews. Jews could maintain their faithfulness to the Torah as the means of salvation. Faith in Jesus Christ, according to Paul, was merely a way of including Gentiles in the people of God. Paul's contention with certain Jews was not that they rejected Christ but that they refused to see that Gentiles could be saved apart from the Law, by faith in Christ alone.[32]

Although one lauds the attempts of these two authors to establish rapprochement between modern Jews and Gentiles, their argumentation obviously smoothes over the tension inherent in the Pauline statements on the Law. For example, it is hard to read Romans 3:21–31 and not come away thinking that the "all" who have sinned and who can therefore only be saved by faith in Christ, apart from the Law, involves both *Jew* and Gentile (see also Rom. 1:16; Gal. 2:15–21; 3:10–14). For all their good intentions to accentuate the continuing relevance of the Law for the thought of Paul, Stendahl and Gaston appear to have overlooked the negative aspect, a stubborn fact to dismiss.

b. C. E. B. Cranfield and James D. G. Dunn

C. E. B. Cranfield tries to play down any tensions in Paul's thought about the Law by arguing that it is not the Torah itself that is criticized by the apostle but rather the Jewish misunderstanding and misuse of the Law, which was perverted by some Jews into a legalistic code requiring meritorious deeds.[33] This thesis is akin to the one later put forth in the magisterial work of E. P. Sanders, who maintained that much of Judaism contemporary with Paul taught that salvation was by faith and that "staying in" salvation was contingent on obeying the Law.[34] To Cranfield, phrases like "the works of the Law" are subject to mis-

---

[32]Lloyd Gaston, *Paul and the Torah* (Vancouver: University of British Columbia Press, 1987).

[33]C. E. B. Cranfield, *The Epistle to the Romans, I–VIII* (ICC; Edinburgh: T. & T. Clark, 1975), 851. See his earlier treatment of the subject, "St. Paul and the Law," *SJT* 17 (1964): 43–68.

[34]See Sanders, *Paul and Palestinian Judaism*. It should be mentioned here that Sanders' approach to Paul and the Law is the reverse of what is being set forth in this chapter. His perspective is "from solution to plight," indicating that Paul started with the solution (participation in Christ), which, in turn, automatically rendered the Law insufficient for solving the human problem of sin. In other

interpretation by the modern reader, because in Paul's day there was no word group corresponding to the ideas of legalism and legalist. Thus, when Paul speaks of the works of the Law, he is depreciating the Law as perverted into legalism by some Jews, not the Law itself.[35]

Similarly, James D. G. Dunn argues that Paul is not teaching the abrogation of the Law for the Christian, but rather rejecting some Jews' attempts to impose the "nationalistic badges" of circumcision, sabbath keeping, and food laws on Gentiles. These cultural markers amount to a legalistic misinterpretation of the Law, and it is that which condemns, not the Law per se.[36]

Although Cranfield and Dunn have provided a healthy corrective to a one-sided reading of Pauline statements about the Law, it must be admitted that negative remarks about the Law still remain in Paul. Thus, Cranfield cannot rid the difficulties posed for his view by a passage like Galatians 3:15–20, where the Law is said to be inferior to the Abrahamic promise because it is later, temporary in nature, and mediated by angels, and because it serves a negative purpose.[37] Nor can Dunn's attempt to restrict Paul's critique of the Law to only nationalistic badges be sustained. As Thielman observes, Galatians 5:2–3 seems to single out circumcision as the focal problem of the Law in general, while Romans 3:13–20, in its declaration that the works of the Law do not justify, encompasses deceit, murder, and blasphemy. Ironically the three nationalistic markers of circumcision, food laws, and Sabbath-keeping are not mentioned there, nor elsewhere (e.g., Rom. 7:7–25).[38]

---

words, in Sanders' analysis, the failure of humans to keep the Law did not concern Paul. The approach offered here is based on Thielman's work, *From Plight to Solution*, and moves from the quandary of human inability to keep the Law because of sin to the solution—obedience to the Law through the power of the Spirit and the arrival of the age to come.

[35]Cranfield, *Epistle to the Romans I–VIII*, 853.

[36]James D. G. Dunn, "The Incident at Antioch (Gal 2:11–18)," *JSNT* 18 (1983): 2–57. Dunn followed up this article with, among others, "Works of the Law and the Curse of the Law (Galatians 3:10–14)," *NTS* 31 (1985): 523–42. His two-volume commentary on Romans systematically follows this viewpoint (WBC; Waco, Tex.: Word, 1988).

[37]The critique is Heikki Räisänen's, *Paul and the Law* (Tübingen: J. C. B. Mohr [Paul Siebeck], 1983), 43.

[38]Thielman, *From Plight to Solution*, 24.

3. Continuity/Discontinuity

The third classification of scholarly interpretation of Paul's understanding of the Law accepts the presence of both negative and positive statements in the apostle's writings, though it splinters into at least three different perspectives in providing a rationale for such tension. These positions are represented by the following writers: John Drane and the developmental view, Heikki Räisänen and the contradictory view, Frank Thielman and the eschatological view.

a. John Drane and the Developmental View

In his title, *Paul: Libertine or Legalist?*, John Drane asks whether Paul should be considered a libertine (against the Law) or a legalist (for the Law). His answer is that it depends on which letter one is reading. More specifically, Drane hypothesizes that Paul's thought underwent change in the course of his writing the letters of Galatians, 1 Corinthians, and Romans. That is, Paul moved from antinomianism in Galatians to legalism in 1 Corinthians, and eventually arrived at a moderating stance in Romans, which balanced "the teaching of Galatians, that Christ had abolished the Law once and for fall, and his teaching in 1 Corinthians that the principle of Law as such was necessary for the Christian, so that while he may not be 'under the Law,' he was 'under the law of Christ' (1 Cor. 9.21)."[39]

Drane's position has two difficulties, however. First, Drane wrote at a time when scholars were enamored with the concept of "developmentalism" in Paul. But such an approach smacks more of the Hegelian dialectic (thesis = Galatians; antithesis = 1 Corinthians; synthesis = Romans) than it does of careful exegesis. Second, there is too much positive said about the Law in Galatians to support Drane's antinomian reading of that letter. Thielman notes that Galatians contains ten quotations from the Old Testament, nine of which come from the Pentateuch. Furthermore, Galatians 5:4 seems to be saying that Paul expects that his readers will fulfill the "whole Law" by obeying Leviticus 19:18, "You shall love your neighbor as yourself."[40] Moreover,

---

[39]John Drane, *Paul: Libertine or Legalist?* (London: SPCK, 1975), 133.
[40]Thielman, *From Plight to Solution*, 49.

Peter Tomson has recently identified numerous sayings from Jewish oral tradition that Paul approvingly quotes, including statements in Galatians. If Paul can draw on that material favorably, how much more so the Torah?[41] If Galatians proves not to be antinomian, Drane's development theory collapses.

b. Heikki Räisänen and the Contradictory View

If Ralph Waldo Emerson's quip is true, "a foolish consistency is the hobgoblin of little minds," then Paul, according to Heikki Räisänen, did not suffer any such malady. For this scholar, Paul's thought on the Law did not develop; rather, it was both continuous and discontinuous because it was essentially contradictory. That author traces a number of inconsistent views on the Law found in Paul. (1) Sometimes the apostle speaks as though the Jews alone are under the Law (Rom. 2; 1 Cor. 9:20–21; Gal. 2:15), while other times he says the Gentiles too are subject to the Law (Rom. 7:4–6; Gal. 3:13–14; 4:5, 6).[42] (2) Paul believed that the Law is both valid (Rom. 8:4; 13:8–10; 1 Cor. 9:9; Gal. 5:4) and invalid (1 Cor. 8; 10; 2 Cor. 3; Gal. 3).[43] (3) Obedience to the Law is both impossible (Rom. 1:18–3:20; Gal. 3:10) and possible (Rom. 2:14–15, 26–27).[44] (4) The Law is directly from God (Rom. 7:22; 8:7; 9:4; 1 Cor. 9:8–9) and mediated by angels (Gal. 3:19).[45] (5) The purpose of the Law was to give life (Rom. 3; 7:10; 8:3) and to incite sin (Gal. 3:21).[46] (6) "Works of law" and "faith in Christ" are two rival principles of salvation in Paul's thought, and they are not to be harmonized.[47]

Two comments are appropriate regarding Räisänen's radical approach. First, the author's thoroughgoing attempt to uncover inconsistencies in Paul appears to foist a modern "deconstructionist" hermeneutic onto ancient texts. Second, while ancient writers were perfectly capable of writing incoherently, "that assumption should be . . . a hypothesis of the last resort, and will

---

[41]Peter Tomson, *Paul and the Jewish Law: Halakha in the Letters of the Apostle to the Gentiles* (Minneapolis: Fortress, 1990).

[42]Räisänen, *Paul and the Law*, 16, 21, etc.

[43]Ibid., 82.

[44]Ibid., 167.

[45]Ibid., 132–33.

[46]Ibid., 141.

[47]Ibid., 176–79.

be strongest when supported as well by other features of the writing than conceptual 'inconsistencies.'"[48] Therefore, it seems only fair to assume that Paul is a coherent writer unless proven otherwise. Frank Thielman has provided an avenue of thought which, we believe, indicates that Paul is consistent in holding together a discontinuous and continuous stance toward the Law. We therefore conclude this brief survey of the issue of Paul and the Law by tracing his proposal.

c. Frank Thielman and the Eschatological View

W. D. Davies, in his study of the Torah in the messianic age, convincingly argued that the old Torah would be operative and obeyed in the age to come. Frank Thielman, in his *From Plight to Solution*, has continued that line of thinking by rooting Paul's ambiguous attitude to the Law in eschatological ideas that he inherited from the Old Testament and Judaism. Thielman arrived at this position in light of the clearer grasp of Judaism that scholars have attained since the work of Davies. We highlighted his perspective in the beginning of this section; thus here we only restate his conclusion, leaving his treatment of Galatians and Romans for our discussion of the pertinent texts. After studying the Old Testament, the Dead Sea Scrolls, and apocalyptic Judaism, Thielman concludes that the plight of the inability of humans to keep God's Law will find its solution in the arrival of the eschaton. But since Paul believed that the death and resurrection of Jesus Christ has inaugurated that era, the overlapping of the two ages accounts for the tension in his thought regarding the Law.[49]

B. AN EXAMINATION OF THE PERTINENT PAULINE TEXTS ON THE LAW

The major texts relative to the topic under discussion are clustered in Galatians and Romans. Our method will be to classify the key passages on the Law into three time frames: this age,

---

[48]Michael E. Stone's, "Coherence and Inconsistency in the Apocalypses: The Case of 'the End' in 4 Ezra," *JBL* 102 (1983): 243.

[49]See chapter 2 in *From Plight to Solution*.

the age to come, and the overlapping of the two. This procedure will demonstrate that the ambiguity in Paul's thought regarding the Law is intimately related to the two-age structure.

1. The Law in Galatians

a. This Age (Gal. 2:15–16; 3:10–14; 3:19–5:1)

These texts in Galatians are critical of the Law, or at least heighten its negative impact. A careful consideration of them convinces one that they are statements made concerning the old age. Thielman insightfully captures this setting when he argues that Paul, in these three passages, speaks negatively about the Law in order to jar the Galatians into realizing that their desire to accept circumcision is tantamount to placing themselves back under the bondage of this age. Or, to put it another way, by these remarks Paul does not suggest the Law has been abrogated; rather, that the purpose of the Law to enclose humanity in sin has now been rendered obsolete with Christ's advent.[50] We can do no better here than recap Thielman's exegesis of the three texts.

Thielman's thesis for 2:15–16 is intriguing: Paul asserts that, for those who participate in the old age, keeping the Law is impossible, something every Jew knows.[51] In arriving at this conclusion, Thielman effectively refutes the typical Lutheran exegesis of these verses. Luther's view of Paul that faith in Christ, not the works of the Law, is the only path to justification is partially true.[52] The problem, however, is that this perspective assumes that Paul's comments are directed against Judaism in general when, in reality, they are aimed at Jewish-Christians. Paul is reminding Jewish-Christians of what every Jew should know— that no one can be justified before God by keeping the Law. Thielman writes: "Paul's point is simply that to deny justification to Gentiles unless they *do* something other than put their faith in God is to deny the commonly accepted Jewish teaching that God justifies the sinner because God is gracious, not because the sinner somehow deserves justification."[53]

---

[50]Thielman, *From Plight to Solution*, 60–65.
[51]Ibid., 62.
[52]Ibid., 62.
[53]Ibid., 62–65.

The key to Thielman's interpretation, like Martyn before him,[54] is that the teaching of the two ages is the foundation of Galatians, and it is through that grid that one must understand Paul's apparently pejorative statements about the Law. Galatians 2:15–16, then, does not really denigrate the Law, but rather says that with the coming of Christ the era of disobedience to the Law is drawing to a close, for those who believe in Christ have been delivered from "the present evil age" (1:4), in which the flesh and sin control one's existence. The operative word in verse 16 is "flesh" (*sarx* at the end of the verse, omitted in NIV translation), referring to the disobedience that can only be overcome by the Spirit. This idea is consonant with the Old Testament's belief that the Law cannot be kept in this age, but that in the eschaton it will be kept by the power of the Spirit (cf. 3:1–5, 14; 4:29; 5:16–25 with Jer. 31:31–34; Ezek. 36:25–28).[55]

Thielman next examines Galatians 3:10–14. He begins by delineating the points on which scholars agree in the interpretation of that passage. Paul in some way associates the Law with a curse, claims that Christ has redeemed believers from that curse, and concludes that the Gentiles receive the blessing promised to Abraham through faith rather than the works of the Law (3:14a), and that Christ's death has initiated the eschatological age of the Spirit (3:14b).[56]

Beyond those commonly accepted elements, however, the scholarly consensus breaks down. After dismissing five major attempts to interpret the passage, especially how the curse of the Law is related (or rather contrasted) to faith in Christ, Thielman provides his own viewpoint. To him, most commentators of these verses have not taken seriously the fact that Paul is developing his argument from the context of the Old Testament passages he quotes here: Leviticus 18:15 (Gal. 3:12); Deuteronomy 21:23 (Gal. 3:13); Deuteronomy 27:26 (Gal. 3:10); and Habakkuk 2:4 (Gal. 3:11). Simply stated, these texts attest to ancient Israel's longing for the coming of the eschaton, the only solution to the plight of their inability to keep the Law. In fact, argues Thielman,

---

[54]See Martyn's "Apocalyptic Antinomies in Paul's Epistle to the Galatians."

[55]Thielman, *From Plight to Solution*, 65.

[56]Ibid., 66.

Israel knew very well that the curse pronounced on those who do not keep the Law began with God's judgment on the Israelites by sending them into exile in Babylonia.

Thus, in both the Pentateuch (Lev. 18:15; Deut. 21:23; 27:26) and in Habakkuk, it seems apparent that because Israel lived in this present evil age, it was not able to obey the divine law, the consequence of which was judgment. However, in both the Pentateuch and Habakkuk (as well as other passages in the Old Testament), the hope of a future era of obedience is offered to Israel. According to Paul, that era has dawned in Christ's death (Gal. 3:13), and the promises inherent in it are extended to Gentiles (v. 14a). This is nothing less than the fulfillment of the promise of the eagerly awaited Spirit, who alone produces obedience to the Law (v. 14; 5:13–25). To submit to circumcision, therefore, as the means of keeping the Law, rather than obeying God by faith through the Spirit, is to align oneself with the old rather than the new age.[57]

Interpreters of 3:19–5:1 have customarily stressed four parts of this section that supposedly suggest that Paul abrogates the Law and replaces it with the principle of faith. Thielman provides the following rebuttals to those criticisms, grounding them, once again, in the context of this age. That is to say, Paul does not teach that the Law is finished; rather, the curse of the Law is what has been terminated for those who believe in Jesus the Christ.[58]

(1) In response to those who understand 3:19–22 to say that the Law, having served its purpose of convicting humanity of its sin, is now finished because of the work of Christ, Thielman reasons that it is only the negative aspect of the Law that has ceased, not the Law itself. This age has rendered the Law inferior (it was ordained by angels and mediated through Moses, vv. 19–20) and inadequate to empower humans to abide by its precepts (vv. 19, 21–22). In short, the Law functioned to enclose Israel in sin (v. 22); but now that the eschatological era has arrived, the curse of the Law has been canceled. Thielman writes: "The temporal limitation in this passage is placed not upon the

---

[57]Ibid., 67–72.
[58]Ibid., 72–73.

Law as a whole but upon the law's ability to 'besiege' humanity 'under sin.' This *function* of the Law began at Horeb and ended with the coming of Christ."[59]

(2) In response to the typical reading of 3:23–4:7 that Paul equates the Law with a pedagogue whose stern responsibility ceased with the coming of Christ, Thielman replies that it is the *curse* of the Law, not the Law, that has been rendered obsolete with the arrival of the age to come. These verses, then, amplify what Paul had said in 3:19–22, using the added metaphors of the pedagogue, slavery, and sonship. For the Galatians to submit to the Law as delineated under the old age is to retrogress from maturity to childhood, from the ability to live according to God's will to the period of reprimand and punishment.[60]

(3) Against those who interpret 4:3–11 to say that the Law, as a component of the "basic principles of the world," has been jettisoned because of the coming of Christ, Thielman once again distinguishes between the Law per se, which continues into the messianic era, and the curse of the Law, which does not. On this reading, the elements of the world pertain to humanity at odds with God because of sin, thanks to the convicting work of the Law. Yet now, those who are in Christ Jesus no longer experience that aspect of the Law; rather, through the enabling power of the Spirit, they fulfill its divine intent.[61]

(4) Thielman disagrees with the assumption that Paul's allegory in 4:21–31 equates slavery to sin with slavery to the Law. Rather, what Paul subsumes under the rubric of slavery to sin is humanity convicted by its inability to keep the Law, not the Law itself. This idea (or the allegory by which it is expressed) is not unique to Paul. Elsewhere (e.g., Isa. 54; *4 Ezra* 9:38; 10:59; *Ps.Sol.* 1), earthly Jerusalem is portrayed as a mother who laments the sinfulness of the city but who nevertheless perseveres in the hope of eschatological renewal. Thus the imagery of Hagar, Mount Sinai, and present Jerusalem need not be set in opposition to the heavenly Jerusalem. It can be understood to correspond to the two ages—this age, the earthly Jerusalem, under

---

[59]Ibid., 76.
[60]Ibid., 78–79.
[61]Ibid., 80–83.

the bondage of sin that results from not keeping the Law, and the age to come, the heavenly Jerusalem set free from the curse of the Law and empowered by the Spirit to obey God's will. Thus the pattern of plight and solution evident in Isaiah 54; *4 Ezra* 9:38; 10:59; *Psalms of Solomon* 1 also obtains for Galatians 4:21–31.[62] Thielman concludes his discussion of Galatians 2:15–16; 3:10–14; and 3:19–5:1, by observing:

> [These texts] do not propose the cancellation of the Law, the *sine qua non* of Judaism. They are instead statements about the Law motivated from the conviction that the time of God's redemption of Israel, and of all humanity, from sin has arrived. These passages serve as reminders to the Galatians of the time in which they should be living as those who believe in Jesus Christ, and thus they serve as arguments to persuade the Galatians not to submit again to the yoke of bondage of sin (5:1) by undertaking circumcision, food laws, and Sabbath keeping as if they had some value for justification before God (5:3).[63]

b. The Age to Come (Gal. 5:14; 6:2)

Galatians 5:14 poses a problem for those who interpret this letter as Paul's *magna carta* of liberty from the Law. Some resort to semantic maneuvers like distinguishing the "doing" of the Law in Judaism from the "fulfilling" of the Law in 5:14 in order to overcome the difficulty,[64] while others view 5:16 to be blatantly contradictory to 2:15–16; 3:10–14; 3:19–5:1.[65] However, it is better to approach this text with Paul's eschatological perspective in mind: With the advent of the messianic age/the age to come and its accompanying gift of the Spirit, God's people are now capable of obeying the Law. Galatians 6:2 complements this interpretation; Christians are to fulfill the Law (Torah) of Christ (Messiah).

---

[62]Ibid., 83–86.

[63]Ibid., 86.

[64]Hans Dieter Betz, *Galatians. A Commentary on Paul's Letter to the Churches in Galatia* (Hermeneia; Philadelphia: Fortress, 1979), 275; cf. the similar approach by Westerholm, *Israel's Law and the Church's Faith*, 202, 204.

[65]Räisänen, *Paul and the Law*, 62–64.

Critics of the eschatological approach may respond that such a view involves Paul in a certain amount of discrepancy. After all, how can the apostle distinguish between obeying the Law on the one hand (5:14), and not advocating adherence to the ceremonial commands of the Law on the other (6:15)? Thielman decisively answers this question by proving that, long before Paul, Hellenistic Jewish theologians had already begun to discriminate between the essence of the Mosaic Law (the moral commands) and its peripheral concerns (the ceremonial regulations; see *Letter of Aristeas* 128–67; *Pseudo-Phocylides* 2.9–69; *T.Iss.* 7:2–6; *T.Zeb.* 8:1–4; Josephus' *Ant.* 20:38–48). Paul's opponents in Galatia, however, were arguing against dividing up the Law and required the observance of both moral and ceremonial aspects in order to be justified.[66] Nevertheless, the thought of the apostle to the Gentiles was still at home with one stream of Hellenistic Jewish thought—that one that said that love fulfills the Law. Thielman expresses it well:

> Thus, when Paul implies that those who belong to the eschatological age of the Spirit fulfill the Law better than those who do not belong to it (5:14; cf. 3:10–13) and at the same time says circumcision for Gentiles is of no value (5:6; 6:15), he does not make a quantum leap out of Judaism into another religious system. He argues within the conceptual world of Hellenistic Judaism that the eschatological age predicted by the Scriptures has arrived.[67]

c. The Overlapping of the Two Ages Within the Christian (Gal. 5:16–18)

Thielman does not capitalize on the role that 5:16–18 plays in Paul's eschatological perspective of the Law, especially as it relates to the overlapping of the two ages. However, in chapter 4 of this work, we attempted to make that connection by calling attention to the two ideas operative in these verses: (1) The struggle that results from the collision of the two forces ("flesh" and "Spirit") attests to the fact that the Christian uniquely lives at the

---

[66]Thielman, *From Plight to Solution*, 54–59.
[67]Ibid., 59.

juncture of the two ages, and (2) the solution to this internal struggle is to walk in the Spirit (who provides the potential for fulfilling the Law, the ultimate resolution of which awaits the *Parousia* and the full realization of the age to come).

2. The Law in Romans

There are numerous references to the Law in Romans, prohibiting an extensive treatment of each text. Thus, we will group the appropriate passages together, taking note of the influence of the two ages on Paul's perspective on the Law. The following chart will serve as the basis of our discussion:

(1) This age: works/ disobedience of the Law	The age to come: faith/ obedience of the Law
(2) 2:17–25	2:12–16/26–29
(3) 3:19–20	3:21–4:25
(4) 5:12–14	5:15–21
(5) 7:7–13	7:1–6/8:4
(6) 9:31–33/10:1–3, 5	9:30/10:4, 6–13
(7) 13:12b–13	13:8–12a/14

a. This Age and the Age to Come

(1) We propose that the alternating negative and positive statements Paul makes about the Law in Romans correspond to this age and the age to come, respectively. Those who attempt to establish their own righteousness through the works of the Law actually disobey the Law, because they are members of this age; those who receive divine righteousness by faith are the ones who obey the Law, because they are members of the age to come. The brief look at the pertinent texts in Romans confirms this hypothesis.

(2) A cursory glance at Romans 2:17–25 reveals that many Jews have not obeyed the divine law; in fact, their flagrant violation of it has profaned the name of God. According to Paul, these Jews are not truly the people of God; they are only outwardly so, having merely the external ritual of circumcision in which to boast (v. 28). In effect, they are members of this age. In stark

contrast are those Gentiles who perform the Law from the heart (2:12–16, 26–29). That these are Christian Gentiles seems apparent, especially since their obedience of the Law in the heart and by the Spirit matches the description of Jeremiah 31:33 and Ezekiel 36:26, 27.[68] The messianic era these two prophets anticipated has arrived; it is based on faith, and it includes even the Gentiles.

(3) Paul's indictment of law-breakers involves all of humanity (3:19–20), for all who attempt to be saved by the works of the Law are under the curse that the Law invokes. Such is the primary task of the Law toward those of this age, since their flesh perverts them from adhering to its just demands. However, the age to come is the divine remedy for this quandary (3:21–4:25). We earlier noted that "the present time" in 3:26 refers to the age to come that has been inaugurated by Christ. Romans 3:21–4:25, therefore, provides hope for humanity in the midst of disobedience.

This age to come, with its new-found obedience to God, was anticipated in the Old Testament itself. Romans 3:21–31 provides a statement of that hope while 4:1–25 presents Abraham as an example. The gist of the former passage is that righteousness by faith in Jesus Christ was witnessed to by the Law and the prophets (v. 21); it was that righteousness, not one's own works of righteousness, that fulfilled the Law (vv. 27–31). Thus people in Old Testament times were saved by faith because of the coming messianic era, and only thereby kept the Law (vv. 22–25). The same principle pertains in light of the Christ-event (v. 26).

The supreme example of this is Abraham (4:1–25). He received the righteousness of God by faith, because he was a sinner and could be saved no other way (vv. 1–8). Such salvation occurred before the promulgation of the Law (vv. 9–13) and anticipated the messianic age (vv. 14–25). To conclude from this, however, that the Law has been abrogated would be a hasty decision, for two reasons. (1) In 3:31 Paul asserts that faith "upholds," not "nullifies," the Law. In other words faith, both before and after Christ, is the means of fulfilling the Law, the former being anticipatory of and dependent on the latter. (2) To assume

---

[68]Cranfield provides a thorough defense of this position in *Romans I–VIII*, 155–59, 172–76.

that the Law's coming after Abraham and the promise meant that it was a temporary stage in salvation history is not accurate. The Law was, in fact, operative at the time of Abraham, as two facts indicate. (a) In order for Abraham to be classified a sinner, there must have been a divine law that he broke, because there can be no sin without law (4:15). (b) The fact that people died between Adam and Moses reveals that the Law was operative before Abraham for the same reason—death results from sin, which, in turn, is the consequence of breaking the Law (5:12–14). To be more accurate, therefore, we should understand Paul to say that, although the Law was not inscripurated and promulgated until the time of Moses, God's law was in the world in unwritten form, and therefore is not really a temporary feature in the program of salvation.

(4) In Romans 5:12–21, Paul contrasts the epochs of Adam and Christ, which correspond to the periods of disobedience and obedience of the Law, respectively. Verses 12–14 make clear that God's law was operative at the time of Adam (cf. 7:9–11) and was the catalyst for his sin (5:20a). Thus, this age, begun by Adam's transgression, has fallen heir to the first man's disobedience of the law. Verses 15–21 accentuate Christ's obedience to God, which inaugurated the messianic age, with its attendant righteousness. There is no suggestion here that the Law has ceased. What has ceased for those in Christ and the age to come is the Law's curse.

(5) This same line of reasoning continues in 7:1–13. Many commentators believe 7:7–13 relates the story of the disobedience of Adam, especially his breaking of the law not to covet (v. 7). The rabbis believed that the whole Mosaic Law was adumbrated in the divine command to the original couple not to covet the Tree of Knowledge of Good and Evil. Adam and Eve's failure to follow the divine injunction involved them in ultimately attempting to become like God.[69] Thus 7:7–13, like 5:12–14, depicts the Fall as the beginning of this age of disobedience to the law of God.

Romans 7:1–6, however, envisions that Jesus Christ has brought in the new age, and with it a new-found freedom from the curse of the Law. It is important to note here that the Christian

---

[69]See Dunn's treatment of this theme, *Romans 1–8*, 379–90.

has died, not to the Law, but to the "flesh" (*sarx* in vv. 5–6; NIV "sinful nature"). Any doubts about this are clarified by 8:4: Christians are those who fulfill the requirements of the Law because they walk in the power of the eschatological Spirit (cf. 7:6).

(6) Romans 9:30–10:13 is reminiscent of 2:12–29, in that it contrasts Israel's failure with the Gentiles' success at receiving the righteousness of God. In 9:31–33, 10:1–3, 5, Paul alerts the reader to the reason for Israel's failure—God's covenant people attempted to earn righteousness through observing the Law. While at first glance the apostle appears to be calling for the termination of the Law, 9:32 suggests that Israel's problem was that they tried to keep the Law by their own ability instead of observing it by faith, as originally intended. Any attempt, however, to rely on one's own competence to follow the Law is doomed to fail because no one is good enough to adhere to all the Law (10:5), regardless of how zealous one might be (10:1–3).

On the other hand, those Gentiles whose faith is in Jesus Christ ironically find the righteousness of God (9:30). For them, the goal of the Law has been met in Christ, who alone has kept the Law perfectly. Moreover, those who are in Christ and the age to come have experienced the end of the curse of the Law (not the Law per se) in this age.[70] According to 10:6–13, fulfilling the Law by faith was a principle already established in Deuteronomy 8:1–9:6, a passage warning Israel not to think that it kept the Law by its own power or righteousness. More specifically, I suggest that Paul applies the rabbinic hermeneutical technique of *gezerah shewah*[71] in Romans 10:6–13. Thus this text interprets Leviticus 18:5 and Deuteronomy 30:10–14, which prescribe the keeping of the Law in order to live, through the lens of

---

[70]The classic treatment of Romans 10:4, especially concerning the issue of whether *telos* means "goal" or "end," is by Robert Badenas, *Christ the End of the Law: Romans 10:4 in Pauline Perspective* (JSNT Supp.Ser. 10, Sheffield: JSOT, 1985). He concludes that *telos* means "goal" and does not, therefore, indicate that the Law is ended. Rather, only the Law as a means of works righteousness is ended; for those in Christ, the Law is fulfilled by faith. This perspective is congruent with my reading of Romans 10:4.

[71]*Gezerah shewah* was a technique the ancient rabbis followed when two or more Old Testament verses contained the same key word(s)—in this case, "keep my statutes and live." The verses were thereby considered mutually interpretive.

Deuteronomy 8:1–9:6, which teaches that the Law can only be kept by God's power, not human effort. In other words, Paul views these three famous Old Testament passages on keeping the Law as anticipating the principle that the Law can only be obeyed by faith is that principle, or law of faith (cf. again Rom. 3:27–31), by which Gentiles are currently receiving the righteousness of God.

(7) Finally, in Romans 13:8–14 we see the two ages and their corresponding relationships to the Law delineated. That Paul has in mind the two-age structure in this passage was explored in the previous chapter. The words "time," "salvation," "day," and "slumber," "night," "darkness" correlate with the age to come and this age, respectively. Interestingly, it is against this background that the apostle discusses the moral law of Moses (13:8–10). The breaking of the divine law characterizes this evil age (vv. 12b–13: carousing, drunkenness, sexual immorality, strife, jealousy), but adherence to the Old Testament commandments depicts the lifestyle of those who are citizens of the messianic age (vv. 8–11: not committing adultery, murder, theft, and coveting, but loving others). Verse 14 provides the key—to be in Christ is to break the hold of the sinful flesh, the real culprit behind disobeying the Law.

b. The Overlapping of the Two Ages

As we noted in chapter 3, the transference of the Christian out of this age into the age to come is not yet complete; Romans 7:13–25 is a powerful reminder of that fact (see chapter 4). That passage could be the testimony of any genuine Christian, in whom resides a deep-seated struggle between obedience and disobedience to the law of God resulting from the overlapping of the two ages. Only by submitting to the Spirit can such a tension be resolved (8:1–16), but even that entails constant struggle in this life. Only in the after-life will victory be ultimately secured (8:17–25).

CONCLUSION

This chapter has attempted to make a modest contribution to the thorny issue of Paul's understanding of the Law—his negative and positive statements regarding the Law are directly related to the two-age structure that forms the conceptual framework of his thought. More than that, the presence of both themes of discontinuity and continuity stems from Paul's view that the Christian lives in the intersection of the two ages. The curse of the Law characteristic of this age is terminated for believers because they are members of the age to come. Yet, the struggle to obey the law of God from the heart continues because Christians still live in this age. This eschatological underpinning sufficiently explains other Pauline texts on the Law, such as 1 Corinthians 9:20–21; 2 Corinthians 3:1–4:6; and Philippians 3:1–21, but this chapter has rightly centered on the two letters containing sustained treatment of the matter—Galatians and Romans.

VI

PAULINE PNEUMATOLOGY: THE SPIRIT AS THE PRESENCE OF THE FUTURE

INTRODUCTION

This study has already addressed the subject of the Holy Spirit in Pauline thought with regards to the struggle involved in living the Christian life that the presence of the Spirit produces (chap. 4) and the obedience to the Law in the messianic era that the Spirit generates (chap. 5). This brief chapter furthers the discussion of the relationship between the two-age structure and Paul's concept of the Holy Spirit.

That Paul, like the early church, perceived the Spirit to be an eschatological phenomenon is a commonplace in scholarship today. For example, Herman Ridderbos writes, "It is precisely the Spirit who is the great Inaugurator and the gift of the new aeon that has appeared with Christ."[1] George Ladd observes, "Life in the Spirit means eschatological existence—life in the new age. This is established by the fact that the presence of the Holy Spirit in the church is itself an eschatological event."[2] French Arrington notes that the Spirit was the sign to the early church that the end of time had arrived.[3] J. Christiaan Beker argues that Paul's major contribution to the early church's understanding of

---

[1]Herman Ridderbos, *Paul: An Outline of His Theology*, trans. John Richard Dewitt (Grand Rapids: Eerdmans, 1975), 215.

[2]George Ladd, *A Theology of the New Testament* (Grand Rapids: Eerdmans, 1974), 483–84.

[3]French Arrington, *Paul's Aeon Theology in 1 Corinthians* (Washington, D.C.: University Press of America, 1978), 132–35.

the eschatological nature of the Spirit rests in the "already/not yet" tension—the Spirit is the proleptic sign of the kingdom of God, the presence of the future. Thus the Spirit is proof that the age to come has dawned, though it is not yet completed.[4]

We will find that Beker is correct in his evaluation of this matter as we summarize five aspects of Paul's teaching on the Spirit, noting particularly the eschatological tension associated with the coming of the Spirit: the indwelling of the Spirit, the gifts of the Spirit, the fruit of the Spirit, the filling of the Spirit, and the intercession of the Spirit.

A. THE INDWELLING OF THE SPIRIT

Compared to the New Testament, the Old Testament's presentation of the Spirit is unclear. The Spirit (Heb., *ruah*) of Yahweh is not understood to be a separate entity, that is, the third member of the Trinity, but rather God's power.[5] The divine rationale behind this probably lies in the concern not to confuse Yahweh with the religious pantheons of the day. Three aspects of God's Spirit as portrayed in the Old Testament contributed to an eschatological longing for a new day. (1) The Spirit only came on select individuals, such as the builders of the tabernacle (Ex. 31:3), the judges (Judg. 3:10; 6:34; etc.), the prophets (2 Kings 2:9; Ezek. 3:12; 8:3), and people like Joshua (Num. 27:18) and Daniel (Dan. 6:3). But not all God's people possessed the Spirit—hence Joel's anticipation of the day when God's Spirit would be poured out on all (Joel 2:28–29). (2) In the Old Testament the Spirit seems to have temporarily and sporadically come upon people; not until the messianic era would he permanently indwell and empower God's own (Isa. 11:1–5; Jer. 31:31–34; Ezek. 36:26–27; 37:14; *Pss.Sol.* 17:42; 18:8). (3) From the postexilic period on, Judaism complained about the cessation of the Spirit and prophecy, eagerly awaiting their return in the age to come (Ps. 74:9; Lam. 2:9; Zech. 13:4–5; Mal. 4:5; *B.Sotah* 48a; *Cant.R.* 43).

---

[4]J. Christiaan Beker, *Paul the Apostle: The Triumph of God in Life and Thought* (Philadelphia: Fortress, 1980), 281–82.

[5]Werner Bieder, "πνεῦμα," *TDNT*, 6:359–75.

Thanks to progressive revelation, things became more clear in the New Testament. The Spirit was now recognized to be a person, not just an attribute (Matt. 28:19; Eph. 1:1–14; 1 Peter 1:2). Most importantly, the early church experienced the long-awaited arrival of the Spirit in full measure on Pentecost. The Spirit had now come to indwell permanently all God's people (Acts 2:16, 33, 38–39). It is against this backdrop that we must grasp Paul's understanding of the indwelling presence of the Holy Spirit, especially the eschatological tension that results for the believer. The Spirit has taken up residence in the Christian's body and thereby transforms it into the temple of the Lord. However, the process now begun will only be complete with the future resurrection body.

1. Present Temple

At the moment of faith, the sinner receives the gift of the Spirit (Gal. 3:2), who, in turn, places or baptizes that person into Christ (1 Cor. 12:13); hence, there is a close connection in Paul's thought between the phrases "in Christ"[6] and "in the Spirit" (see Rom. 8:9; 2 Cor. 3:17). One of the most significant metaphors the apostle uses to describe the habitation of the Spirit within the believer is the temple of the Lord. That idea is applied by Paul to both the individual Christian's body (1 Cor. 6:19) and to the corporate church, the body of Christ (1 Cor. 3:16; 2 Cor. 6:16; Eph. 2:21).

The eschatological importance of these statements should not be overlooked. Although God's dwelling with and among the people of Israel is a pervasive Old Testament theme (Lev. 26:12; Ps. 114:2; Ezek. 37:27), Israel is never identified with God's temple; such an identification was relegated to the anticipated age to come (Isa. 28:16; Ezek. 40–48; Jub. 1:18; 1 Enoch 91:13;

---

[6]Adolf Deissmann popularized the notion that the phrase "in Christ" is a formula in Paul expressing mystical fellowship (Paul, A Study in Social and Religious History, 2d ed., trans. W. E. Wilson (Gloucester, Mass.: Peter Smith, 1972). One of the finest surveys of the subject is the work by Ernst Best, One Body in Christ. A Study in the Relationship of the Church to Christ in the Epistles of the Apostle Paul (London: SPCK, 1955); see his critique of Deissmann's position, 8–12.

4 *Q.Flor.*). Therefore, for Paul to announce that the Christian and the church now constitute the temple of God was nothing short of an eschatological pronouncement—the temple of the end time has now arrived.[7] At the more personal level, the term Paul consistently employs for the Christian/church as the temple is *naos*, the actual sanctuary of the deity, as distinguished from the generic word *heiron*, the word for the temple and its precincts. Paul's unabashed claim is that the Christian's body has become the *locus* of God's dwelling, an extension of Christ himself, the new eschatological temple (cf. Mark 14:58; John 2:19–21; 2 Cor. 5:1–5).[8]

2. The Future Resurrection

Paul speaks of the Spirit as the "deposit" (*arrabôn*; see 2 Cor. 1:22; 5:5; Eph. 1:14) or the "firstfruits" (*aparchê*; see Rom. 8:23). He does not say that we *have* a deposit or firstfruits of the Spirit, as if Christians only possess a portion of the Spirit; rather the Spirit himself *is* the deposit/firstfruits. The word *arrabôn* was used in antiquity to denote an earnest deposit or down payment on property, which served as proof that there was more to come.[9] The word *aparchê* derived its meaning from the Old Testament Feast of Firstfruits, in which the priest waved the firstfruits of wheat before the Lord, both in dedication to him and in expectation of the full harvest. Thus these two words communicate two realities: They provide assurance that the believer's destiny is secure, and they serve to remind believers that they have not yet arrived at their heavenly goal—the future resurrection body (see Rom. 8:23; 2 Cor. 1:22; 5:5; Eph. 1:14). The Spirit, then, offers a double reminder—that the present bodies of believers, temples though they are, are frail and mortal, but also are a guarantee of the future, glorious resurrection. Some of Paul's congregations needed to hear this latter point especially, because, in their new-found en-

---

[7] For further discussion on the church as the eschatological temple of the Spirit, see Arrington, *Paul's Aeon Theology in 1 Corinthians*, 129–32.

[8] See Pate, *Adam Christology as the Exegetical and Theological Substructure of 2 Corinthians 4:7–5:21* (Lanham, Md.: University Press of America, 1991), chap. 4, for the overlapping of three layers of temple traditions in 2 Corinthians 5:1: (1) the eschatological temple; (2) Jesus, the new temple; (3) the Christian's resurrection body as a member of Jesus, the new temple.

[9] Johannes Behm, "ἀρραβών," *TDNT*, 1:475.

thusiasm over the Spirit, their tendency was to assume that the kingdom of God had fully arrived and that they had *already* received the resurrection body (see Rom. 8:17–25; 1 Cor. 15:12–28; 2 Tim. 2:18). Beker expresses this correction by Paul well:

> Paul's interpretation of the Spirit reaffirms early Christian experience in a new vein. The early Christians experienced the gift of the Spirit as the proleptic presence and signal of the imminent coming of the kingdom, manifest in such things as glossolalia, prophecy, and healings. Paul now articulates the experience of the Spirit in terms of a theological distinction between the Spirit and the final glory so as to prevent a premature fusion between the Spirit and the kingdom of God. This achievement is often called Paul's so-called "eschatological reservation."[10]

B. THE GIFTS OF THE SPIRIT

The previous quotation of Beker leads to a second aspect of the Spirit in Paul's thinking—the gifts of the Spirit. There are three key texts on the subject in his writings: Romans 12:3–8; 1 Corinthians 12–14; and Ephesians 4:7–16. Several general observations can be made concerning the gifts. (1) The word for "gifts" (*charismata*) refers to an endowment to believers by God's grace, which is to be used for his glory and the good of others (Rom. 12:3; Eph. 4:7–16). (2) The gifts are distributed to believers by the Spirit; they are "Spiritual" gifts (1 Cor. 12:10–11; 14:1). (3) Every believer possesses at least one gift (1 Cor. 12:7; Eph. 4:7). (4) It is through the diversity of the gifts that the body of Christ matures and is unified (Rom. 12:4; 1 Cor. 12:12–31; Eph. 4:7–18). (5) Spiritual gifts are eschatological in nature and, in particular, are stamped by the already/not yet dialectic. Justification for this last observation follows below as two points are examined: The gifts are a sign that the *eschaton* has already dawned, but they should be exercised in love, which is itself eternal and therefore belongs to the consummation of the age to come.

---

[10]Beker, *Paul the Apostle*, 282. The phrase "eschatological reservation" was coined by Ernst Käsemann, "Primitive Christian Apocalyptic," in *New Testament Questions of Today* (Philadelphia: Fortress, 1965), 132.

1. The Gifts Are a Sign of the Dawning of the Eschaton

Though it is rarely noticed by commentators, the spiritual gifts Paul mentions are a sign that the age to come has dawned. We will briefly comment on the relationship to the individual gifts to the *eschaton*.

Prophecy is of paramount importance to Paul; it heads the list in Romans 12:6–8 and receives extensive treatment in 1 Corinthians 14. Drawing on its meaning in the Old Testament, the early church considered prophecy to be inspired speech (1 Cor. 14:1–5). Moreover, with the cessation of prophecy and the Spirit at the close of the Old Testament, the belief arose that in the age to come the two would return (Ps. 74:9; Lam. 2:9; Joel 2:28–32). Undoubtedly, then, the spiritual gift of prophecy was interpreted by the early church and by Paul as a sign of the arrival of the *eschaton* (see Acts 2).

Related to prophecy was the gift of apostleship. Beginning with the disciples of Jesus and extending to Paul (e.g., Rom. 1:1; Gal. 1:1) and perhaps others (Rom. 16:7), that gift constituted the foundation ministry of the church (Eph. 2:20). The verb from which "apostle" is derived (*apostellô*) means "to send," referring to those people officially sent out to preach the gospel. That the gift of apostleship was perceived as an eschatological sign is made clear in Ephesians 3:1–13 (esp. v. 5). There Paul announces that the apostles and prophets are the recipients of the divine mystery that has been planned from eternity past (vv. 3, 9–11). Raymond Brown has carefully shown that the concept of "mystery" was a Jewish apocalyptic idea in Paul's day, referring to the revelation of divine secrets to the holy men of God. That disclosure of truth was itself a proleptic experience of the age to come (cf. Luke 8:9, where the same term is applied to the apostles of Jesus).[11] For Paul, the divine mystery consisted of the truth that Jew and Gentile would form one worshiping community in the end time (Eph. 3:6).

The gifts of wisdom and knowledge (1 Cor. 12:8) were similarly connected with the apocalyptic concept of mystery (2 *Bar.*

---

[11]Raymond Brown, *The Semitic Background of the Term "Mystery" in the New Testament* (FBBS 21; Philadelphia: Fortress, 1968).

54:13; *1 Enoch* 63:2, 32; 48:1, 49; *4 Ezra* 14:25; 38–40), ultimately deriving their inspiration from passages like Daniel 2:20–23.

Gifts such as teaching (Rom. 12:7; 1 Cor. 12:28), evangelism (Eph. 4:11) and pastor-teacher (Eph. 4:11) were eschatologically oriented by virtue of the content of their message. As C. H. Dodd so perceptively demonstrated, the *kêrygma* ("preaching") of the early church was eschatological in nature, consisting of some six elements: the messianic age has dawned (Acts 2:16; 3:18, 24); it centers in the ministry, death, and resurrection of Jesus (2:23); Jesus is now exalted at God's right hand as messianic head of the new Israel (2:33–36; 3:13); the Holy Spirit is the sign of the presence of the *eschaton* as well as the proof that Jesus currently reigns in heaven in power and glory (2:33); the messianic age will shortly reach its consummation in the return of Christ (3:21); an invitation is extended for people to receive Christ and the life of the age to come (2:38–39).[12] The three gifts mentioned above attest to this eschatological message: The "teacher" expounded the Old Testament to show its expectation of the coming Christ and the messianic era, while the "evangelist" and "pastor-teacher" proclaimed that message.

The gift of discernment of spirits distinguished truth from error (1 Cor. 12:10, 29; 1 Thess. 5:22) and was an ability suited to the last days (1 Tim. 4:1; 2 Tim. 4:1–5; cf. 1 John 4:1–3).

Tongues and interpretation of tongues (1 Cor. 12:30; 14:26–28) were associated with heavenly worship (1 Cor. 13:1); as Gordon Fee argues, they were most likely viewed by the Corinthian church as indicative of the fact that the age to come had fully arrived.[13] In a similar vein, David Aune has insightfully demonstrated that Jewish and Christian apocalyptic groups looked on their worship as a proleptic restoration of paradise, which was to occur at the end of time.[14]

The gifts of faith (1 Cor. 12:9; cf. 13:2), miracles (12:10, 28), and healings (12:9, 28) continued the ministry of Jesus in the

---

[12]C. H. Dodd, *The Apostolic Preaching and Its Developments* (New York: Harper, 1944), 38–45.

[13]Gordon Fee, *The First Epistle to the Corinthians* (TNICNT; Grand Rapids: Eerdmans, 1987), 627–28.

[14]David Aune, *The Cultic Setting of Realized Eschatology* (Supp.Nov.T 27; Leiden: E. J. Brill, 1972).

early church (Acts 1:1; 3:1–10; 12:1–17; 13:1–12). In both cases, the extraordinary power displayed signaled the invasion of the messianic kingdom, reclaiming the earth for God. They were, in reality, a witness to the presence of the new creation.[15]

The service gifts—exhortation (Rom. 12:8), ministry (12:7), administration (1 Cor. 12:28), governance (Rom. 12:8), helps (1 Cor. 12:28), mercy (Rom. 12:8), and giving (12:8)—can be treated together. They refer to service for the sake of others and, as a passage like Romans 12:9–21 makes clear, their impetus originated with Jesus, the Servant. According to Luke 4:17–21, Jesus' mission fulfilled the long-awaited coming of the Servant of the Lord in Isaiah, with its meeting of human needs. Christ's church was expected to do the same. Furthermore, the service gifts are reminiscent of the Sermon on the Mount with its call for mercy and ministry to others (cf. again Rom. 12:3–8 with vv. 9–21), ethics characteristic of the eschatological kingdom of God.

2. Love as the Completion of the Age to Come

Fee has captured the primary reason for the intervention of the "love chapter" (1 Cor. 13) between Paul's discussion of spiritual gifts in chapters 12 and 14. It provides an important corrective to the Corinthians' assumption that the spiritual gifts, especially tongues, were proof that the age to come had already fully arrived. Paul's emphasis on love in that chapter shows that the gifts of the Spirit, though eschatological in nature, have not yet completed the *eschaton*. That is a privilege reserved only for love.

According to Fee, 1 Corinthians 13 can be summarized in this manner. Verses 1–4 depict spiritual gifts not benefiting the person who, though exercising them, does not do so in love. After describing love in terms of the Corinthian situation (vv. 4–7), Paul contrasts it with selected *charismata*, emphasizing the eternal nature of love and the temporal nature of the gifts and placing that contrast in the context of the Corinthians' already/not yet eschatological existence (vv. 8–13). Fee concludes:

> This does not make *charismata* less valuable for life in the present as one awaits the consummation, but it posits against

---

[15]See Ladd's treatment of the subject, *A Theology of the New Testament*, 48–53.

their 'overrealized' spirituality that these things have a relative span (for the 'already' only), while love is both for new
and forever.[16]

We concur with Fee's evaluation of 1 Corinthians 13, adding that
Paul also incorporates the theme of love in his other two lists of
the gifts: Romans 12:9–10, 13–21 and Ephesians 4:15–16 (cf.
3:18–19; 4:2, 32; 5:2, 25). This fact suggests that love alone will
complete the age to come and is, therefore, the *sine qua non* of
Christian behavior.

C. THE FRUIT OF THE SPIRIT

According to Paul, the Spirit performs a number of significant works on behalf of the believer. For example, he creates
faith in the cross of Christ (1 Cor. 2:6–13), provides a sense of
sonship for the believer (Rom. 8:15, 16; Gal. 4:6), leads Christians
into true worship (Phil. 3:3), guides in prayer (Rom. 8:26; Eph.
6:18), empowers for service (Eph. 5:18–21; Col. 3:16–17), and
seals the believer as a mark of divine ownership (Eph. 1:13–14).

One of the well-known ministries of the Spirit is the spiritual fruit he generates in the lives of believers (Gal. 5:22–23), the
chief of which is love. Such *agape* love manifests itself toward
others in terms of patience, kindness, goodness, faithfulness,
gentleness, and self-control. Coupled with the fruit of love are
joy and peace. Together these form a triad of spiritual qualities
and should be seen in light of Paul's eschatology. They confirm
that the age to come has already dawned, but the context in
which they occur—suffering—attests that the age to come has
not yet been consummated.

1. Love, Joy, and Peace and the Dawning of the Age to Come

We have already highlighted the eschatological significance
of love for Paul in our discussion of 1 Corinthians 13. Love for
God and others is the distinguishing mark of the citizens of the

---

[16]Fee, *The First Epistle to the Corinthians*, 628.

kingdom of God (cf. Rom. 12:9–21; Eph. 4:15–16; 5:2). Joy (*chara*) is also eschatological in orientation. One of the long-awaited qualities that the Old Testament expected to accompany the kingdom of God was joy (Isa. 54:1–3; 65:17–19; Joel 2:21–27), a concept also emphasized in the New Testament (Luke 14:7–24; 15:6–7, 9–10, 23, 32; Rev. 19:7–8). Paul shared that sentiment: "For the kingdom of God is . . . joy in the Holy Spirit" (Rom. 14:17; 15:13; cf. 5:3–5; Phil. 3:1; 4:4; 1 Thess. 1:6).

The same is true of peace (*eirenê*), likewise associated in the Old Testament with the coming kingdom of God (see Isa. 11:6–8; 66:20–25). According to Paul, peace was realized in the reconciliation Jesus brings between sinners and God (Rom. 5:1; 14:17; 15:13; Eph 2:11–18). Thus, not only love, but also joy and peace must be interpreted from an eschatological frame of reference.

2. Love, Joy, and Peace and Suffering

Paradoxically, the fruit of love, joy, and peace occur in the context of suffering and affliction, the reality of which is a poignant reminder that the age to come is not yet complete. This is clearly the case for love, for God's love for believers is demonstrated in the midst of the afflictions of this age (see Rom. 5:3–5; 1 Thess. 1:3–7). Similarly, peace with God (Rom. 5:1–5) and the peace of God (Phil. 4:6, 7) come precisely in the setting of trials, as does joy (Phil. 1:12–20; 2:17, 18; Col. 1:24; 1 Thess. 1:6; 5:3–5).

In summary, the Christian triad of love, joy, and peace are subjective signs that the messianic era has been inaugurated, but they are experienced in the conflict setting produced by this present age. In other words, the Christian's experience of love, joy, and peace along with suffering results from the overlapping of the two ages.

D. THE FILLING OF THE SPIRIT

Another well-known ministry of the Holy Spirit referenced by Paul is the filling of the Holy Spirit. Although he explicitly mentions this teaching only once (Eph. 5:18), at least three other texts contain the same idea: Colossians 3:16; 1 Corinthians 14:26–40; and 1 Thessalonians 5:16–22. All four passages are informed by eschatological tension, particularly in the way the themes of spontaneity (the age to come has already dawned) and structure (the age to come is not yet complete) are juxtaposed.

1. Ephesians 5:18

Paul's talk in Ephesians 5:18 about being "filled with the Spirit" brings to mind the spontaneous empowering of select individuals in the Old Testament by God's Spirit (see "The Indwelling of the Spirit," above) and Joel 2:28–29. According to Ephesians 5:18–21, the "charismatic" results of the believer's empowerment with the Spirit are joy, thanks, and submission—qualities signifying the presence of the messianic age.

Nevertheless, believers have not yet been removed from the sphere of this age, with its hierarchical order and authoritative structure. A passage like 1 Corinthians 7:17–31 reminds Paul's Christian audience of that sobering reality. There he tells the Corinthians, and all his churches (v. 17), that even though they are citizens of the age to come, they are bound to their appointed roles in this present age (vv. 18–29). The rationale behind this assertion is that this present age has been shortened because of the inbreaking of the age to come and will soon pass away (vv. 29–31).

Such a command to obey the accepted structures of society also occurs in Ephesians 5:22–6:9, a passage coming on the heels of Paul's instruction to be filled with the Spirit (5:18–21). Thus, the spontaneous and delightful working of the Spirit in the believer points to the arrival of the age to come. However, since the believer must still submit to the hierarchical order of this age, he or she has not yet come to the full realization of the kingdom of God.

2. Colossians 3:16

The same eschatological tension imprints Colossians 3:16, the companion passage to Ephesians 5:18. Although Paul does not mention the Spirit there, "let the word of Christ dwell in you richly" echoes that notion. Moreover, the charismatic results of the filling of the Spirit (Eph. 5:18–21) and the indwelling of the word of Christ (Col. 3:16–18) are the same: joy, thankfulness, and submission. So also is the injunction to submit to the authoritative structures of this age: wives to husbands, children to parents, slaves to masters (cf. Col. 3:18–4:1 with Eph. 5:18–6:9). Thus, like Ephesians, Colossians 3:16–4:1 combines the already aspect of the age to come (the filling of the Spirit) with the not yet aspect (submit to the structure of this age). Undoubtedly, Paul includes the submission motif in both passages to check any unbridled enthusiasm on the part of his Spirit-filled listeners.

3. 1 Corinthians 14:26–40

First Corinthians 14:26–40 obviously deals with the working of the Spirit in the church at Corinth, and Paul's eschatological perspective is once again operative. The spontaneous ministries of the Spirit referred to therein—psalms, teachings, revelations, tongues, interpretations, and prophecies (vv. 26, 29–30, 39)—demonstrate that the age to come is realized in the act of worship. However, intermingled with these charismatic workings is Paul's command for structure and order (vv. 27, 28, 29, 30, 31, 32, 33, 34–38, 40), an indication that the age to come has not yet been completed (cf. 7:17–31).

4. 1 Thessalonians 5:16–22

First Thessalonians 5:16–22 continues in the same vein. It too deals with the workings of the Spirit in the context of worship and combines the themes of spontaneity and structure, evidencing the eschatological tension of the already/not yet aspects of the age to come. The former (spontaneity) is manifest in the charismatic operations of prophecy, joy, prayer, and thanksgiving—all of which are the by-products of not quenching the Spirit's activity (vv. 16–20). The latter is evident in Paul's charge to evaluate the ongoings of the worship service, to ensure things are done right (v. 21). The motivation for doing so is the continuing reality of evil (v. 22), a remark akin to Ephesians 5:16 ("making the most of every opportunity, because the days are evil") and Galatians 1:4 ("the present evil age"). Paul's emphasis, then, on the need for a structured expression of the Spirit forms part of his eschatological reservation.

E. THE INTERCESSION OF THE SPIRIT

A number of Pauline texts speak of the intercessory ministry of the Spirit on behalf of Christians (Rom. 8:26–27; Eph. 5:18) or a related idea (Eph. 1:13–23; 3:14–21; Col. 1:8–12). Once again, the eschatological tension created by the overlapping of the two ages influences Paul's comments on the subject.

1. Romans 8:26–27: The Intercession of the Spirit and Weaknesses

That Romans 8:17–30 breathes the language of apocalypticism needs no justification (see chapter 2). The suffering/glory motif is the result of the overlapping of the two ages—the glory of the age to come has broken into the suffering of this present age. Correlated to this is the Spirit's presence within, and prayer for, the believer in the face of human weakness (vv. 26–27). Whatever the meaning of the enigmatic words, "the Spirit himself intercedes for us with groans that words cannot express," they at least indicate that the Spirit's indwelling is a sign that the age to come has arrived, but that his intercessory ministry on behalf of believers is needed because they still partake of the human frailties that characterize this age. The good news is, however, that the Spirit can use those weaknesses to benefit Christians in conforming them to the image of Christ (vv. 28–30).

2. Colossians 1:8–12 and Ephesians 1:13–23; 3:14–21: The Intercession of the Spirit and Knowledge/Wisdom

Colossians 1:18–21 and Ephesians 1:13–23; 3:14–21 are parallel passages and therefore can be treated together. A twofold pattern emerges in these three Pauline prayer texts: the indwelling, intercessory work of the Spirit is proof of the presence of the age to come, but because believers still exist in this age, they need his illuminating ministry to convince them of that truth.

(1) That Paul has in mind the believer's incorporation into the messianic kingdom is clear from such phrases as "the inheritance of the saints in the kingdom of light" (Col. 1:12; cf. v. 13), "inheritance in the saints" (Eph. 1:18), "seated him . . . in the

heavenly realms . . . above all rule and authority . . . not only in the present age but also in the one to come" (Eph. 1:20–21; cf. 2:6–7), and "to grasp how wide and long and high and deep is the love of Christ" (Eph. 3:18). One of the chief evidences of this reality is the indwelling, intercessory work of the Spirit in the lives of believers (Eph. 1:13–14, 17; 3:16; Col. 1:8). It is fascinating that Paul specifically prays in all three passages that the Spirit will enlighten his audience with knowledge and wisdom concerning their exalted status (Eph. 1:17–19; 3:18–19; Col. 1:9–10).

This conjunction of the Spirit and knowledge/wisdom is rooted in the Old Testament (Ex. 31:3; 35:31, 35; Deut. 34:9; 1 Chron. 22:12; Isa. 11:2) and is accorded an eschatological nuance in significant Qumran texts (*1QS* 4:3–4; *1QSb* 5:25). That is, the Qumran community believed that it was living in the last days and that, as the true recipient of the kingdom of God, it had been given the knowledge and wisdom of the Spirit.[17] This is similar to what Paul says in the passages cited above.

(2) However, the very fact that Paul has to pray that the Spirit will enlighten his audiences with the insight that they do, in fact, participate in the heavenly kingdom is testimony to the stark reality that the age to come is not yet complete. Believers need encouragement to believe that the age to come has dawned because circumstances appear otherwise. The trials and afflictions of this present evil age cause them to have a lack of confidence in and commitment to the gospel (Eph. 3:13; Col. 1:10–11, 15–23). Thus, Paul prays that believers will have both divine insight to believe they are in the kingdom and strength to live accordingly.

3. Ephesians 6:10–20: The Intercession of the Spirit and Spiritual Warfare

We conclude with a brief comment on Ephesians 6:10–20. In verse 18, Paul refers to praying in the Spirit; coupled with other remarks in the letter, this text shows that the indwelling, intercessory work of the Spirit is a sign that the age to come has

---

17Peter T. O'Brien, *Colossians and Philemon* (WBC 44: Waco, Tex.: Word, 1982), 21.

dawned (1:7–14; 2:6–22; 3:16–17; 4:4–16; 5:17–21). By praying in the Spirit, the Christian receives the necessary strength to engage in the spiritual warfare that characterizes this present evil age (cf. 5:16 with 6:10–20). The intercessory ministry of the Spirit, then, like the other operations highlighted in this chapter, amply attest to the already/not yet eschatological tension so central to Paul's thought.

VII

PAULINE ECCLESIOLOGY: THE CHURCH AS THE DAWNING OF THE AGE TO COME

INTRODUCTION

We conveniently begin the vast subject of Pauline ecclesiology with a quote from J. C. Beker concerning the eschatological nature of the church, "Because the church has an eschatological horizon and is the proleptic manifestation of the kingdom of God in history, it is the beachhead of the new creation and the sign of the new age in the old world that is 'passing away' (1 Cor. 7:29)."[1] We concur with this fundamental perception that the church is yet another sign that the age to come has already dawned, though it is not yet complete. We will develop this thesis in the various sections of this chapter.

Before proceeding, however, we need to briefly define the word *church*. The Greek word used by Paul and the early Christians for the messianic community of believers is *ekklêsia*, a term used in both political and religious senses. Politically, *ekklêsia* was used in the Greek world of an assembly of people, especially as they were gathered to conduct the affairs of the state (see Acts 19:39). Religiously, *ekklêsia* is used in the LXX and

---

[1]J. Christiaan Beker, *Paul the Apostle: The Triumph of God in Life and Thought* (Philadelphia: Fortress, 1980), 313.

in Jewish intertestamental writings to translate the Hebrew word *qahal*, a term often applied to Israel as God's people, gathered for worship. The sixty-two occurrences of this term in Paul (not to mention the rest of the New Testament), therefore, almost certainly identify the Christian community as the continuation of Israel, the Old Testament people of God.[2]

A. CHURCH AND METAPHOR

The New Testament contains many metaphors or images of the church. Paul Minear counts as many as ninety-six.[3] Five metaphors dominate Paul's concept of the church and demand our attention: kingdom of God, temple of God, people of God, body of Christ, and bride of Christ. The already/not yet eschatological tension is the hermeneutical grid through which these images should be perceived.

1. The Kingdom of God

The kingdom of God is a major theme in the Bible.[4] Its origin comes from the Old Testament, where the emphasis falls on God's kingship. God is king of Israel (Ex. 15:18; Num. 23:21; Deut. 33:5; Isa. 43:15) and of all the earth (2 Kings 19:15; Pss. 29:10; 99:1–4; Isa. 6:5; Jer. 46:18). Juxtaposed to the concept of God's *present* reign as king are references to a day when God will *become* king over his people (Isa. 24:23; 33:22; 52:7; Zeph. 3:15; Zech. 14:9). This emphasis on God's kingship continues throughout Judaism and takes on special significance in Jewish apocalypticism, which abandoned any hope for present history. Only at the end of the age will the kingdom of God come.

Many New Testament scholars consider the kingdom of God to be the central message of Jesus, with the twofold aspect of the presence and future of the kingdom forming the substruc-

---

[2]K. L. Schmidt, "ἐκκλησία," *TDNT*, 3:501–36.

[3]Paul S. Minear, *Images of the Church in the New Testament* (Philadelphia: Westminster, 1960).

[4]The following summary is indebted to George Ladd, *A Theology of the New Testament* (Grand Rapids: Eerdmans, 1974), 60–61.

ture of his thought. That is, the kingdom of God that was expected to arrive at the end of history has already arrived in the ministry of Jesus (Matt. 12:28; Mark 1:15; Luke 4:21; 10:18; 17:20), but its consummation awaits his return in glory (Matt. 6:10; 13:36–43; Luke 13:28, 29; 19:11). The early church propagated the same message: the messianic era has come, but its completion awaits the *Parousia* of Christ (Acts 2:16, 23, 33–36; 3:13, 21, 24).

Paul inherited this belief of the already/not yet aspect of the kingdom of God. For him, the temporary messianic kingdom did indeed come with the death and resurrection of Christ, who is now reigning in heaven (Rom. 14:17; 1 Cor. 15:20–28; Col. 1:13; cf. Phil. 3:21), but the consummation of that kingdom awaits the *Parousia* (1 Cor. 6:9–10; Gal. 5:21; 1 Thess. 2:12).

This theme of the kingdom of God in Paul's thought raises the question of the relationship between it and the church. George Ladd devotes a whole chapter to that issue in the larger context of the understanding of the early church. He rightly concludes that

> while there is an inseparable relationship between the Kingdom and the church, they are not to be identified. The Kingdom takes its point of departure from God, the church from men. The Kingdom is God's reign and the realm in which the blessings of his reign are experienced; the church is the fellowship of those who have experienced God's reign and entered into the enjoyment of its blessings. The Kingdom creates the church, works through the church, and is proclaimed in the world by the church. There can be no Kingdom without a church—those who have acknowledged God's rule—and there can be no church without God's Kingdom; but they remain two distinguishable concepts: the rule of God and the fellowship of men.[5]

The eschatological tension of the already/not yet reinforces the distinction between church and kingdom. The rule of God has arrived in the hearts of those who obey him as king, but it has not yet encompassed the earth. This truth rescues Paul from a couple of misinterpretations. First, it extricates him from

---

[5]George Ladd, *A Theology of the New Testament* (Grand Rapids: Eerdmans, 1974), 119.

triumphalism, which has its roots in the Augustinian tendency to equate the church with the kingdom of God. Paul's "not yet" pole will not permit such a simplistic correspondence to stand.[6] Second, the eschatological tension delivers Paul from a dire pessimism that denies the presence of the kingdom of God in the church under the postponed kingdom theory.[7] Paul's "already" pole corrects such a viewpoint. Thus, to summarize the issue of the relationship between church and kingdom: the triumphalist perspective equates the two, the pessimist view dichotomizes the two, but the eschatological approach rightly holds the two in dialectical tension.

2. Temple of God

Because this topic was treated in the previous chapter, we only briefly comment on it here. The temple of God, or the building of God, is an important Pauline metaphor for the church (see 1 Cor. 3:16–17; 2 Cor. 6:14–7:1; Gal. 4:26; Eph. 2:19–22). Once again, the already/not yet tension sheds light on its usage by the apostle.

Both the Old Testament and Judaism anticipated the formation of a new temple in the kingdom of God (Ezek. 37:26–28; 40:1–48; Hag. 2:9; 1 Enoch 90:29; 91:13; Jub. 1:17, 29). Jesus himself hinted that he was going to build such a construction (Matt. 16:18; Mark 14:58). Pentecost witnessed to the coming of the eschatological Spirit as the fruition of that dream. Paul, building on those insights, saw the Christian community as the continuing fulfillment of that promise (1 Cor. 3:16–17; 2 Cor. 6:14–7:1; Eph. 2:19–22). Galatians 4:26 probably extends the eschatological nature of the church back to the preexistent past. There Paul identifies the church as the "Jerusalem that is above," a common designation in Judaism for the preexistent heavenly Jerusalem, the prototype of the earthly tabernacle/temple (Ex. 25:40; Wisd.Sol. 9:8; Acts 7:44; Heb. 9:23–24; Rev. 21:2, 22).[8] All of the

---

[6]See Beker on this point, *Paul the Apostle*, 303–4.

[7]A characteristic of old-line dispensationalism; see Ladd, *A Theology of the New Testament*, 106.

[8]For further discussion, see R. G. Hammerton-Kelly, *Pre-Existence, Wisdom, and the Son of Man. A Study of the Idea of Pre-Existence in the New Testament* (SNTSMS 21; Cambridge: University Press, 1973), 108–11.

preceding Pauline references signal that the church is the eschatological temple/building of God that has appeared in history through the person of Jesus Messiah and the power of the Spirit.

Despite the fact that the eschatological dwelling of God has descended among humans, it is not yet a completed edifice. In these same verses Paul also talks about the church as existing in the midst of this present age. In 1 Corinthians 3:16–17, for example, the concept of the church as the temple of God comes in the middle of Paul's exhortation not to be hoodwinked by the wisdom of this age (v. 18). Second Corinthians 6:14–7:1 poses a similar warning—the members of the church, the temple of God, must separate themselves from Belial (Satan), the ruler of this age (cf. 4:4). According to Ephesians 2:19–22, though the Spirit indwells the people of God, they need to continue to grow like a building and make Christ feel at home because of their maturing faith (Eph. 3:17). Finally, in Galatians 4:26, the church is identified as the heavenly Jerusalem, but it still exists on earth, where it is subject to harassment (v. 29; cf. 1:4).

3. The People of God

Another significant Pauline metaphor for the church is "the people of God," especially as it is referred to under the title of "saints." The term *saints* (*hagioi;* lit. "holy ones") has its origin in Exodus 19:5–6, where Israel is called "a holy nation." This title was later applied to those who were to share in the blessings of the messianic kingdom (Dan. 7:18–27; *Pss.Sol.* 17; Qumran). A similar term for this reality is the term *elect* (*ekklektoi:* Rom. 8:28, 33; Col. 3:12; 2 Tim. 2:10; Titus 1:1). In calling the church the "saints" (Rom. 1:7; 1 Cor. 1:2; 2 Cor. 1:1; Eph. 1:1; Col. 1:2) and the "elect," Paul was identifying it as the eschatological people of God, who could apply the promises of salvation given to Israel, to themselves.[9]

Nevertheless, the new people of God have not been removed from this age. Two of the more common characteristics of this age—sin and suffering—continue to plague the church. Most of the Pauline references just listed are also associated with the

---

[9]See Gordon Fee's discussion in *The First Epistle to the Corinthians* (TNICNT; Grand Rapids: Eerdmans, 1987), 32–33.

struggles the church experiences in its calling as a holy, elect people. This suggests that the eschatological people of God live in the intersection of the two ages.

4. The Body of Christ

The most distinctive Pauline metaphor for the church is "the body of Christ" (Rom. 12:4–5; 1 Cor. 12:12–28; Eph. 4:7–16; Col. 1:18). Because the subject is so complex, we can only provide here the contours of the discussion. Perhaps the best way to approach it is to survey the views regarding the origin of Paul's idea of the body of Christ. Then we will be in a better position to see his eschatological tension at work in this important image for the church. Seven theories can be delineated.

(1) Eduard Schweizer called attention to the political view, which compares the body of Christ with the Greek idea that a gathered political group of people is to be associated with a human body (Livy, *Hist.* 2:32).[10] But while this view may explain the parallel (community = body), it leaves unanswered the question of why Paul speaks of the "body *of Christ*" (e.g., 1 Cor. 12:27).[11]

(2) Similarly, W. L. Knox argued that the notion of the body of Christ originated in Stoicism, "The church as a body, of which the individuals were members, was derived from the Stoic commonplace of the state as a body in which each member had his part to play."[12] But like the political theory, this suggestion cannot explain why Paul calls it the "body *of Christ*." Ernst Best points out in this regard that the comparison is not between the body and its members, but between the members as members of the body of a person. He also notes that Stoicism never expressly called the cosmos the body of God.[13]

(3) L. Cerfaux claimed that the idea of the body of Christ originated in the church's celebration of the Lord's Supper.[14] But

---

[10]Eduard Schweizer, "σῶμα," *TDNT*, 7:1024–44; 1038–39.

[11]See James Dunn, *Romans 9–16* (WBC 28b; Dallas: Word, 1988), 723.

[12]Wilfred L. Knox, *St. Paul and the Church of the Gentiles* (Cambridge: University Press, 1939), 161.

[13]Ernst Best, *One Body in Christ: A Study in the Relationship of the Church to Christ in the Epistles of the Apostle Paul* (London: SPCK, 1955), 83.

[14]L. Cerfaux, *The Church in the Theology of St. Paul*, trans. Geoffrey Webb and Adrian Walker (New York: Herder and Herder, 1959), 263–65.

the theory that the body of Christ is equivalent to the bread of Christ is based on the assumption that Paul's teaching on the Eucharist borrowed from the mystery religions' belief that partaking of the meal of the deity was tantamount to being united with the god, a hypothesis now discarded by most scholars.[15]

(4) Rudolf Bultmann popularized the position that Gnosticism informed the Pauline concept of the body of Christ. That view promoted the primal man myth, a teaching identifying individuals as pieces of an original heavenly man who, upon his fall to earth, disintegrated into myriads of human bodies. On recollecting their original spiritual state, however, those individual pieces are ultimately regathered into the one primal man.[16] Few scholars today, however, date that myth to the first century C.E. Furthermore, the myth never was monolithic in structure, contrary to the protests of Bultmann.

(5) James D. G. Dunn roots the body of Christ concept in the charismatic worship setting of the early church. As believers gathered for worship and as God manifested himself through the *charismata*, the people sensed themselves to be a corporate body, unified in Christ.[17] There is an element of truth in this suggestion, but it is too generic, especially since two other ideas are available to explain the phrase.

(6) W. D. Davies insightfully argues that the Jewish apocalyptic/rabbinic concept of the corporate body of Adam is the best antecedent to the notion of the universal body of Christ. He writes:

> Paul accepted the traditional Rabbinic doctrine of the unity of mankind in Adam. That doctrine implied that the very constitution of the physical body of Adam and the method of its

---

[15]See Best's critique of the influence of the mystery religions on Paul, *One Body in Christ*, 87–89. See also the criticisms of Gunter Wagner, *Pauline Baptism and the Pagan Mysteries: The Problem of the Pauline Doctrine of Baptism in Romans VI.1–11, in the Light of its Religio-Historical Parallels*, trans. J. P. Smith (Edinburgh and London: Oliver & Boyd, 1967). The most recent work is by A. J. M. Wedderburn, *Baptism and Resurrection: Studies in Pauline Theology Against Its Graeco-Roman Background* (WUNT 44; Tübingen: J. C. B. Mohr [Paul Siebeck], 1987), who provides a devastating critique of the purported impact of the mystery religions on Paul.

[16]Rudolf Bultmann, *Theology of the New Testament*, trans. Kendrick Grobel (New York: Charles Scribner's, 1951), 1:178–79.

[17]Dunn, *Romans 9–16*, 723–24.

formation was symbolic of the real oneness of mankind. In that one body of Adam east and west, north and south, were brought together male and female. . . . The "body" of Adam included all mankind. Was it not natural, then, that Paul should have conceived of it [the church] as the "body" of the second Adam, where there was neither Jew nor Greek, male nor female, bond nor free.[18]

There is much to commend this point of view, especially since many interpreters see the person of Adam behind the Pauline passages on the body of Christ (cf. 1 Cor. 12 with 1 Cor. 15:44–49; Rom. 12:4–5 with vv. 1–2; 5:12–21; 7:7–13; 8:17–25; Col. 1:18 with v. 15; Eph. 4:7–16 with 1:15–23; 5:22–33). The major objection to this argument is that there is no explicit mention of the "body of Adam" in the Jewish literature contemporaneous with Paul. But this objection can be adequately met by the next theory, which fits nicely with the Adamic hypothesis.

(7) A. J. M. Wedderburn[19] proposes that the roots of the idea of the body of Christ stem from the ancient Hebrew mentality of corporate personality, the belief that one person represents many and the many are incorporated in the one (Gen. 12:1–3; cf. Gen. 14:17–20 with Heb. 7:4–10; Josh. 7:16–26). This reciprocal relationship takes one a long way toward understanding the body of Christ, and it is commensurate with the Adamic theory, the representative of the fallen human race (Rom. 5:12–21). If so, then we see that the church, the corporate body of Christ, is none other than the eschatological Adam (1 Cor. 15:45), the new humanity of the end time, which has now appeared in human history.

Yet those passages referring to the body of Christ and drawing on Paul's Adam theology make it clear that the age to come has not yet fully been realized. Romans 12:3–8 comes on the heels of verses 1–2, with its challenge to Christians not to be conformed to "this world." First Corinthians 12 is buffered by 1 Corinthians 13, the love chapter, which serves notice that we

---

[18]W. D. Davies, *Paul and Rabbinic Judaism: Some Rabbinic Elements in Pauline Theology* (New York: Harper & Row, 1948), 57; cf. 53–57.

[19]Wedderburn, *Baptism and Resurrection*, 350–56. Wedderburn also convincingly responds to criticisms of the Hebrew corporate personality theory.

continue to see "but a poor reflection as in a mirror" because "perfection" (i.e., the *Parousia*) has not yet occurred. According to the context of Colossians 1:18, Paul still needs to strive to present every Christian mature before God, an indication the end has not yet come (Col. 1:28–29). Ephesians 4:7–16 continues that theme, noting that the body of Christ is still in process and that its members need to grow toward maturity.

5. The Bride of Christ

The last dominant metaphor of the church in Paul to be considered here is the bride of Christ (2 Cor. 11:2–3; Eph. 5:22–33). The imagery takes its point of departure from the Old Testament's portrayal of Israel as the wife of Yahweh (especially Hos. 1–3; cf. Isa. 54:1–8; 61:10; 62:4–5; Jer. 3:8; Ezek. 16; 23; cf. also Ps. 45; Song of Songs in later Jewish interpretation). In the New Testament, the metaphor is redefined in terms of the bride of Messiah (Matt. 25:1–13; Mark 2:18–20; Rev. 12:1; 19:1–10; 21:1–9; 22:7). In other words, the New Testament understands the metaphor as being eschatological in orientation; the church will be united to Christ as her husband in the age to come.

Paul inherits this idea, except that he accentuates the already/not yet aspect of the church's relationship to Christ. The already perspective is clear in Ephesians 5:22–33, where Paul presents the church as the new Eve, the wife of the last Adam, the bride of Christ. But in 2 Corinthians 11:2–3, Paul accents the not yet aspect; the church is betrothed to Christ. In actuality, betrothal in ancient Judaism was the modern equivalent of being married to the person, though the marriage was not yet consummated. In this passage, the church is once again compared to the new Eve. Using this comparison, Paul warns the church against succumbing, as Eve did, to temptation. Rather, she must be faithful to Christ (cf. Eph. 5:26–27).

B. CHURCH AND SACRAMENTS

The already/not yet eschatological duality is at the core of Paul's thought on the sacraments, baptism and the Lord's Supper. For him, the former is the sign of entrance into the church, the corporate body of Christ, while the latter celebrates the ongoing relevance of the sacrificial death of Christ, whose body was given for the church.

1. Baptism

We begin this discussion with a disclaimer—it is not our desire to become embroiled in the controversy often sparked by dogmatic treatments of Christian baptism. That debate has moved from one extreme (*ex opere operato*, i.e., "by the thing performed") to another (mere memorialism). Rather, it seems more appropriate to approach the Pauline view of baptism from the two broad, competing interpretations that have dominated the discussion this century: the mystical and eschatological viewpoints. It will be readily discernible from what follows that the latter perspective is the most hospitable to Paul's teaching on the subject.

a. The Mystical Interpretation of Pauline Baptism

During the first half of this century, the mystical interpretation of the relationship between the Christian's baptism and Christ's death and resurrection prevailed, which said that Paul was deeply influenced at this point by the pagan mystery religions. It was characteristic of these cults that the worshiper, through initiation rites often involving water, was thought to be united to the death and resurrection of the respective gods.[20]

But the last half of this century has witnessed a virtual rejection of that viewpoint. The apparent similarities between Pauline baptism and the mystery religions are more than offset by significant differences. Cranfield conveniently summarizes those discrepancies:

> While the mysteries were concerned with the union of the participant with a nature-deity, baptism had to do with the relationship of the believer to the historical event of God's saving deed in Christ; while the dying and rising of a nature-deity was conceived as something recurring again and again, the historical event to which baptism pointed was a once for all, unique event; while the mysteries were inclusive

---

[20]See Wedderburn's overview of the rites of the mystery religions, *Baptism and Resurrection*, 90–163.

(one could be initiated into several without offence, since they were recognized as varying forms of the same fundamental, age-old religion), baptism was altogether exclusive; while the mystery rites were magical, setting forth symbolically the god's experiences and being thought of as effecting the union with the god which they depicted, in the case of baptism the symbolism, if it was conscious at all (and as far as Paul is concerned it is far from certain that it was), was clearly not of decisive importance, since, while Rom 6.4 and Col 2.12 might suggest the thought that the Christian's immersion in the water of baptism portrays his burial with Christ (and his emergence from it his resurrection with Christ), Paul could also write I Cor 12.13 . . . with reference to baptism, and an *ex opere operato* view of baptism is ruled out by such a passage as I Cor 10.1–12; while the mysteries reflected Hellenistic dualism (the initiate being thought of as transported out of the temporal and material world into an eternal and spiritual), baptism had to do with eschatology, with the relation of the believer to the events of the salvation-history and his membership of the Church of God; and, while in the mystery cults the initiate could be regarded as having become divine (in some of them after initiation he was actually worshipped), any idea of a divinization of the believer is completely alien to Paul's thought.[21]

b. The Eschatological Interpretation of Pauline Baptism

Most Pauline scholars today, therefore, root Paul's teaching on baptism in eschatology, defining it in terms of the Christian's participation in the events of salvation history, especially Christ's death and resurrection. An examination of the Pauline texts on baptism confirm this insight, for the eschatological tension of the already/not yet expresses itself in various ways. Those passages can be arranged under the following categories: the indicative/imperative ethic (Rom. 6:3–4; 1 Cor. 6:9–11; 10:1–13; cf. Col. 2:11; Eph. 5:14–17; Titus 3:5–7), taking off the old self/putting on the new self (Gal. 3:27; Col. 3:9–10; cf. Rom. 6:6; Eph. 4:22–24), and the sealing/deposit of the Spirit (2 Cor. 1:22; Eph. 1:13–14).

---

[21]Cranfield, *Romans I–VIII*, 302.

(1) The first set of baptismal texts (1 Cor. 6:9–11; 10:1–13; Rom. 6:3–4 [cf. Col. 2:11]; Eph. 5:14–17; Titus 3:5–7) display the indicative/imperative ethic we encountered earlier in this work.[22] This paradox is rooted in the overlapping of the two ages. First Corinthians 6:9–11 juxtaposes the two ages, using the imagery of baptism.[23] On the one hand, believers have been sanctified and justified, symbolically effected in baptism ("you were washed," v. 11). This is the indicative: they are members of the kingdom of God, the age to come. However, they have not yet arrived spiritually, for they still live in this age. Hence the imperative, that they conduct themselves in holiness in order to fully inherit the kingdom of God (vv. 9–10).

First Corinthians 10:1–13 continues that theme. Believers are members of the age to come (v. 11) by virtue of their baptism into Christ by the Spirit, symbolized by water (v. 2; cf. 1 Cor. 12:13).[24] But the presence of trials and temptations in their lives (vv. 1–10, 12–13) shows that they have not yet fully come into God's kingdom. This classic Pauline passage rules out any magical view of baptism, which claims that baptism automatically guarantees one's future in the age to come.

We have already seen that Romans 6:1–13 attests to the overlapping of the two ages in terms of the indicative/imperative ethic.[25] Verses 3–4 visualize the believer's death to this age and identification with the age to come as resulting from his or her union with Christ's death and resurrection through baptism. But that the transition is still in process is discernible in Paul's reticence to pronounce that the believer's resurrection is complete (cf. Col. 2:12).[26]

---

[22]See chapter 4.

[23]For a defense of the baptismal reference behind 1 Corinthians 6:11, see George R. Beasley-Murray, *Baptism in the New Testament* (New York: Macmillan, 1962), 162–67; contra Fee, *The First Epistle to the Corinthians*, 246–47.

[24]See Beasley-Murray's arguments for water baptism in 1 Corinthians 12:13, *Baptism in the New Testament*, 167–71. This passage clearly shows that Paul associated the baptism of the Spirit with conversion.

[25]See chapter 4.

[26]See O'Brien's discussion on this point, *Colossians and Philemon* (WBC 44; Waco, Tex.: Word, 1982), 120. On this reading Romans 6:4 and Colossians 3:11 are compatible.

Ephesians 5:14–17 also presents baptism in terms of an eschatological tension. Believers, through baptism, have seen the light of Christ and the dawning of the age to come (v. 14),[27] but they must live their lives in the midst of this present age (vv. 15–17).

Finally, Titus 3:5–7 concurs with this scheme. Christians have been regenerated by the Holy Spirit through baptism,[28] but they still must live in the hope of eternal life, a sure indication that the age to come has not fully arrived.

(2) A second cluster of baptismal texts (Gal. 3:27; Col. 3:9–10 [cf. Rom. 6:6]; Eph. 4:22–24) deals with the theme of taking off the old self/putting on the new self. These texts are most likely baptismal in orientation. First, the language of taking off and putting on, as Galatians 3:27 indicates, could easily be associated with baptism, probably with reference to the custom of taking off one's clothes before baptism and then, after baptism, clothing oneself with a white robe, symbolizing righteousness.[29] Second, the old self/new self contrast is almost certainly rooted in the Adam-Christ typology so effectively demonstrated in baptism. Baptism, therefore, is a picture of the believer's transference from this age and the old Adam to the age to come and the last Adam.[30] Thus, Colossians 3:9–10 and Ephesians 4:22–24 portray baptism as an eschatological event. However, the change is not yet complete. Christians must constantly reaffirm their break with the old and their allegiance to the new (cf. Col. 3:1–8 with vv. 9–10; Eph. 4:17–21 with vv. 22–24). Seyoon Kim well summarizes a number of the baptismal texts discussed thus far:

> In faith-baptism we already "put off" the "old man" and "put on" Christ or the "new man" (Gal 3.27; Col 3.9f.). But what happened in faith-baptism is only the first-fruits of what will happen at the *eschaton*. Only at the *eschaton* will the dying of our "old man" and our attainment of the "new man" be complete.

---

[27] Andrew Lincoln makes a convincing case for a baptismal setting for Ephesians 5:14, *Ephesians* (WBC 42; Dallas: Word, 1990), 330–33.

[28] See Beasley-Murray's arguments for a baptismal context for Titus 3:5–7, *Baptism in the New Testament*, 209–16.

[29] The reader is referred to Jonathan Z. Smith's perceptive study of the baptismal setting of these texts, "The Garments of Shame," *HR* 5 (1966): 217–38.

[30] A. van Roon elaborates on this point, *The Authenticity of Ephesians* (Supp.Nov.T 39; Leiden: E. J. Brill, 1974), 329–41.

Until then we must actualize in our lives our dying and rising with Christ in faith-baptism: we must continually "put off" our "old man" and "put on" the "new man" (Eph 4.22–24; Col 3.12ff.; Rom 12.1f.).[31]

(3) The third set of texts (2 Cor. 1:22; Eph. 1:13–14 [cf. 4:32]) portray baptism in similar eschatological imagery. The sealing of the Spirit is none other than the deposit, or the down payment, of the Spirit at baptism[32] within the believer's heart, a sign that he or she is a part of the age to come (2 Cor. 1:22a; Eph. 1:13). Nevertheless, the Spirit is only the deposit, confirming that the believer still participates in this age (2 Cor. 1:22b; Eph. 1:14).

2. The Lord's Supper

We will exercise the same restraint in discussing Paul's concept of the Lord's Supper as we did for baptism relative to the various theories of what transpires in the celebration of the Eucharist. We begin with a statement with which all Christian traditions can agree—baptism is the once-for-all sign of the incorporation of the sinner into the death and resurrection of Christ, while the Lord's Supper is the continuing proclamation of the redemptive significance of his death. We have just shown how the former of these is based on the eschatological tension of the already/not yet. We now seek to do the same for the latter by briefly examining the two passages in Paul dealing with the Eucharist: 1 Corinthians 10:1–22 and 11:17–34.

a. The Already Aspect of the Lord's Supper

Paul believed that the celebration of the Eucharist was a sign that the age to come had already appeared on earth. The Lord's Supper began as a Passover meal (Matt. 26:17–19; Mark 14:12; Luke 22:14–20). In the Old Testament, the Passover (and the Exodus) was the salvation event *par excellence*, and its observance commemorated Israel's beginning as a nation (Ex. 12). So impor-

---

[31]Kim, *The Origin of Paul's Gospel* (WUNT 2, 10; Tübingen: J. C. B. Mohr [Paul Siebeck], 1981), 325.

[32]See Lincoln's circumspect defense of the baptismal allusion behind Ephesians 1:13–14 in *Ephesians*, 39–40.

tant was this feast that it became an eschatological symbol for the regathering of Israel in the end time (Isa. 43; cf. Rev. 11:6). As such, it was a theme not unrelated to the messianic banquet that righteous Israel expected to celebrate in the age to come (Isa. 65:12–14; *1 Enoch* 60:7–8; *4 Ezra* 6:49–52; *2 Bar.* 29:4; *T.Isa.* 8:11, 20; Luke 13:28–29; Rev. 19:7). Jesus' connection, then, of Passover with his passion should be viewed from this eschatological perspective. Luke 9:31 and 22:15–16 especially make this clear. The former verse refers to Jesus' passion as an exodus, while the latter text connects Jesus' eating of the Passover with the coming kingdom of God.

First Corinthians 10:1–22 and 11:17–34 continue this perspective. The former passage explicitly refers to the Lord's Supper, noting the intimacy with Christ that obtains for believers when they participate in it. Paul refers to the same rite in 10:3–4 under the heading of "spiritual food and drink," a phrase that, together with the words "baptized into Moses" (v. 2), interprets the Exodus and desert provisions as types of the two Christian sacraments, baptism and Eucharist. It is significant that coming in between these two references to the Lord's Supper is the eschatological statement of verse 11—"these things happened to them [baptism and the Lord's Supper, among other things] as examples and were written down as warnings for us, on whom the fulfillment of the ages has come." In other words, Paul views baptism and the Lord's Supper as rites that mark the inbreaking of the age to come via the death and resurrection of Christ.

First Corinthians 11:23–34 is similar to 10:1–22 in this respect. It also portrays the Eucharist as an eschatological ritual. The Lord's Supper is the fulfillment of the "new covenant" promised in the end times (11:26; cf. Jer. 31:27–34; Ezek. 36:22–28), which is to be observed until the *Parousia*—"for whenever you eat this bread and drink this cup, you proclaim the Lord's death until he comes."

b. The Not Yet Aspect of the Lord's Supper

But the already aspect is not the whole story. While the Lord's Supper reminds us that the age to come has begun, it is not yet completed, as is verified by the warnings present in both 1 Corinthians 10:1–22 and 11:23–34. The former passage warns against presuming a magical view of the sacraments, a similar mistake tragically committed by ancient Israel. Just partaking of God's provisions in the desert did not automatically ensure all Israelites of their entrance into the Promised Land. Neither will the Lord's Supper magically guarantee believers of their entrance into the kingdom of God. The latter passage reiterates this warning—observing the Eucharist casually, laxly assuming one is fully in the age to come, can be deadly. Both exhortations, in other words, confirm the continuing presence of this age. Christians must partake of the Lord's Supper with holiness before God and love for others because they live between the ages. Ridderbos's remarks serve as an apt conclusion to this section:

> [The Lord's Supper] is the spiritual food and spiritual drink for the time between the times, as manna and water from the rock after the exodus out of Egypt and before the entrance into Canaan; in its constant repetition it spans life in the present world, until he comes. It represents both the "already" and the "not yet"; it is already celebrated as the fulfilled sacrificial meal of the New Testament with bread and wine, but is yet to be celebrated both in remembrance and in expectation.[33]

C. CHURCH AND WORSHIP

Rudolf Schnackenburg encapsulates the eschatological flavor of worship in the early church, including Paul's letters:

> The central act of worship of the early church testifies to its characteristic eschatological awareness of already having experienced the happiness of the time of salvation, and yet of still looking forward to the "restoration of all things" at the Parousia of its exalted messiah (Acts 3:20f.).[34]

This section seeks to unpack the eschatological aspect of worship as reflected in Paul's writings, discussing four intimately related subjects: the spoken word, the symbolic word, the sung word,

---

[33]Herman Ridderbos, *Paul: An Outline of His Theology*, trans. John Richard Dewitt (Grand Rapids: Eerdmans, 1975), 425.

[34]Rudolf Schnackenburg, *The Church in the New Testament* (New York: Herder and Herder, 1965), 41.

and the shared word. Since the first two items have already been addressed, we will focus our attention on the last two matters.

1. The Spoken Word

The metaphor "word" is an appropriate term with which to describe Paul's, and the early church's, concept of worship. It has to do with revelation, God's spoken word to humans, which is incarnated in Jesus Christ (John 1:1; cf. 1 Thess. 2:13). One of the significant responses Christians can make to God's revelation is to worship him and to proclaim that word to others. Such was the essence of the early church's message; it was an eschatological *kêrygma* (proclamation), composed of some six elements (see chap. 6). That spoken word highlighted that the life, death, and resurrection of Jesus Christ initiated the transition of the two ages.[35]

That Paul experienced and preached the same message is obvious from his letters. It is even clear from the two words he uses to express his continuity with the *kêrygma* of the early church: "pass on"(*paradidonai*) and "receive" (*paralambanein*; see 1 Cor. 11:2; 15:1–5; Gal. 1:9; Col. 2:6; 2 Thess. 2:15; 3:6). In other words, Paul passed on to others the gospel he received from others,[36] that Jesus' death and resurrection inaugurated the age to come. There lay the foundation of Christian worship, for as Aune has shown, early Christianity believed it recaptured Paradise in the cultic setting.[37]

2. The Symbolic Word

Here we need only make mention of the fact already developed that Paul saw the two sacraments, the symbolic (or visual) word of God to his church, as rooted in the already/not yet eschatological tension. The celebration of these events—baptism immediately following conversion (cf. Acts 2:38 with Rom. 10:9), and the Eucharist celebrated weekly on Sunday (cf. Acts 2:46

---

[35]C. H. Dodd, *The Apostolic Preaching and its Developments* (New York: Harper, 1944), 38–45.

[36]Galatians 1:12 does not contradict Paul's dependence on Christian tradition; see Ladd's discussion, *A Theology of the New Testament*, 392–93.

[37]David E. Aune, *The Cultic Setting of Realized Eschatology in Early Christianity* (Supp.Nov.T 28; Leiden: E. J. Brill, 1972), 37–41, 184–93.

with 1 Cor. 11:18–22)—served to reinforce the Pauline communities' eschatological self-understanding.

3. The Sung Word

An indispensable component in early Christian worship, according to Paul, was singing to the Lord, which involved "psalms, hymns and spiritual songs" (Eph. 5:19; Col. 3:16). Many scholars hold that the content of some of those songs can be identified from Pauline material, including two of the most famous Christological hymns: Philippians 2:5–11 and Colossians 1:15–20. These liturgical pieces are grounded in the already/not yet duality.

The hymn in Philippians 2:5–11 has been called the *kenosis* passage, because it speaks of Christ's "emptying" (*ekenôsen*) himself of his preexistent glory in order to take upon himself the form of a servant (v. 7). It naturally falls into two strophes or stanzas: verses 6–8 on Christ's humiliation, and verses 9–11 on Christ's exaltation. The second strophe conveys the already/not yet eschatological tension. Christ's death and current reign in heaven has inaugurated the age to come (v. 9), but the termination of this present age awaits the *Parousia* (vv. 10–11).[38]

Colossians 1:15–20 is a hymn to the preexistent, cosmic Christ. It also divides into two strophes: verses 15–17 on Christ as the Lord of creation, and verses 18–20 on Christ as the head of the church. Like the previous song, the second strophe assumes the already/not yet tension. Because of his death and resurrection, Christ has become head of the church (v. 18) and the fullness of God (v. 19). According to 3:1–4, the companion text of 1:15–20, Christ is presently reigning in heaven, whose glory has not yet been revealed. That is, the age to come has dawned, but it is not yet complete. The day is coming when, at his *Parousia*, Christ will have preeminence over all (1:18b, 20), and at that time his glory will be manifested for all to see (3:4). As R. G. Hammerton-Kelly notes concerning these passages, we find a

---

[38]See Ralph Martin, *Carmen Christi: Philippians ii.5–11 in Recent Interpretation and in the Setting of Early Christian Worship* (SNTMS 4; Cambridge: University Press, 1967), 266–70.

mixture of realized and futurist eschatology, which is indicative of the already/not yet dialectic.[39]

4. The Shared Word

It would be easy to overlook the role that the giving of one's financial resources plays in Paul's thought, but it is a significant ingredient of worship for him. Four passages address the subject under the heading of the Gentile contribution to the Jerusalem Christians: Romans 15:25–29; 1 Corinthians 16:1–4; 2 Corinthians 8–9; Galatians 2:10. Besides the obvious humanitarian concern to meet the needs of those who are in need, there seems to be an eschatological twist to this offering collected by the apostle from the Gentiles, as Johannes Munck provocatively argued. That author developed the hypothesis that Paul perceived his work of evangelizing the Gentiles to be a trigger to initiate the end of the age. Based on the Old Testament theme that the Gentile nations will flow into Jerusalem in the end time in order to pay respect to Israel and to worship her God (Isa. 45:14; 60:5–17; 61:6; Mic. 4:13), Munck suggested that Paul viewed his ministry to the Gentiles as the catalyst for that spiritual trek. Munck went even further, claiming that Paul saw his ministry to the Gentiles as one of stirring Israel to jealousy over its Messiah, thus bringing about the end of the age (cf. Rom. 11:13–15, 25–27 with 15:16; 2 Thess. 2:6–7).[40]

While Munck has probably overstated the case, there does seem to be an element of truth in his presentation. The urgency with which Paul collected the Gentile offering is well explained by the eschatological expectation that the Gentile gift might hasten this present age to its conclusion. If so, this sense of the word being reciprocally shared by Jews with Gentiles (in the spiritual sense) and by Gentiles with Jews (in the financial sense, Rom. 15:27) suggests the beginning of the reunion of the human race in the worship of God that was considered a characteristic of the age to come.

---

[39]Hammerton-Kelly, *Pre-Existence*, 177–78.

[40]Johannes Munck, *Paul and the Salvation of Mankind*, trans. F. C. Clarke (Richmond, Va.: John Knox, 1959), 299–308.

D. CHURCH AND MINISTRY

Since we have already surveyed Paul's teaching on the ministry of the gifts of the Spirit, our concern here is to consider briefly the relationship between *charismata* (gifts) and church office.

1. The Issue of the Relationship Between Gifts and Office

It has been fashionable for some time now for biblical scholars to dichotomize the emphasis on ministry as the usage of spiritual gifts one finds in the indisputable Pauline letters from the stress on church office as the conduit of service thought to characterize the Pastoral Letters.[41] Employing the Hegelian philosophical dialectic, some hypothesized that the Pauline "charismatic" ministry reacted to the "official" ministry of the Jerusalem church; out of this conflict eventually came the episcopal structure of the second-century church, which ambiance the Pastoral Letters share.[42] Others used Max Weber's sociological principle of the routinization of the charismatic, which argued that religious organizations begin with a charismatic focus but, if they are to survive into the second generation, must make a transition into a structured organization.[43] Thus, for example, Paul's indisputable letters breathe the air of the spontaneous, egalitarian use of the gifts of the Spirit, but they give way to the ecclesiastical hierarchy of the Pastoral Letters that impede egalitarian ministry.

2. The Intimate Connection Between Gifts and Church Office in Paul's Letters

Aside from the questionable practice of a wholesale reading of modern-day philosophical and sociological theories back into

---

[41]See the bibliography in the excellent study by E. Earle Ellis, *Pauline Theology. Ministry and Society* (Grand Rapids: Eerdmans, 1989), 88, fn. 1.

[42]This was H. von Campenhausen's theory, *Ecclesiastical Authority and Spiritual Power* (Stanford, Calif.: Stanford University Press, 1969), 81–86.

[43]One of the most pervasive attempts to apply this sociological model to Pauline ecclesiology is Bengt Holmberg's *Paul and Power: The Structure of*

ancient texts, the preceding hypotheses have labored under the twofold assumption: (1) Organization did not exist in the early Pauline churches, and (2) the *charismata* were not operative in the later Pauline communities as represented in the Pastoral Letters. These assumptions are being abandoned today for two good reasons.[44]

(1) There was, in fact, organization in the early Pauline churches. We employ Ellis's list of a number of such ordered ministries.[45] (a) Paul's collection of gifts from the Gentile Christians for the saints in Jerusalem was a structured ministry, much like those collected by the Jewish synagogues. Both were gathered in the local assembly of worshipers (cf. 1 Cor. 16:1–4); both were collected by appointed envoys (cf. 2 Cor. 8:18–22); both were sent to Jerusalem (the one to help the poor saints in Jerusalem [cf. Rom. 15:26–27]; the other to pay the temple tax). (b) Paul's matter-of-fact reference to two types of officers, "over seers and deacons," in Philippians 1:1 strongly suggests the presence of structured offices in the churches he founded (cf. Acts 14:23). (c) References to those who had the right to receive financial remuneration for preaching indicates that there were paid ministers in Paul's day (1 Cor. 9:14; cf. Acts 20:17; 1 Cor. 12:28; 1 Thess. 5:12). (d) Added to this is Paul's introduction of structure and order in his churches to correct abuses that resulted from unbridled spontaneity in the services (1 Cor. 11; 14; 1 Thess. 5).

Moreover, the alleged mature and distinct expressions of church organization in the Pastorals do not hold up under scrutiny. (a) Rather than Timothy and Titus being single bishops over churches under their auspices, akin to the monarchical epis copate structure of the second century, careful exegesis of Acts 20:17, 28; 1 Timothy 4:1, 2, 8; 5:17; and Titus 1:5–7 reveals that the leadership of both earlier and later Pauline churches was plural,

---

Authority in the Primitive Church as Reflected in the Pauline Epistles (Philadelphia: Fortress, 1980), though not without qualification.

[44]These two assumptions have been criticized by, among others, J. N. D. Kelly, *A Commentary on the Pastoral Epistles* (New York: Harper & Row, 1963), 13–16 and Ellis, *Pauline Theology*, 92–116.

[45]Ellis, *Pauline Theology*, 92–100.

not singular.[46] (b) Related to this, the apparent distinction between the bishop/overseer and elders in the Pastorals does not stand. In reality, the two titles appear to be interchangeable and their qualities overlap (Titus 1:5–7; cf. Acts 20:17, 28). Thus it is likely that the offices are identical. (c) The supposed advanced order of widows in the Pastorals (1 Tim. 5:3–16) is not far removed from the practice as is earlier found in Acts 6:1–7. (d) The practice of the laying on of hands (1 Tim. 5:22) is substantively no different than what took place in the commissioning of ministers and missionaries in the early church (Acts 6:6; 13:3).

(2) There was *charisma* in the later Pauline churches as represented in the Pastoral Letters. (a) Ministry continued to depend on the gifts of the Spirit (1 Tim. 4:1, 14; 2 Tim. 1:6, 14). (b) The fact that officers had to be tested shows that conferring the office was not mechanical and automatic (1 Tim. 3:10). (c) Such offices could not be static if they needed to be protected from neglect and were in continual need of being actualized (1 Tim. 4:11–16; 2 Tim. 1:6). (d) That Paul had to lay down guidelines for women's teaching suggests that ministry was not restricted to the ecclesiastical hierarchy. (e) The corresponding word to the early Pauline term *charismata* ("gifts") in the Pastorals is "good works," which are effected by the power of the Spirit.[47]

3. The Eschatological Nature of Gifts and Office

In the last chapter, we argued that the inherent tension in Paul between the spontaneous exercise of spiritual gifts and the implementation of structure and order was rooted in the already/not yet eschatological principle. The gifts are a sign of the inbreaking of the age to come while the need for structure and order attest to the continuing influence of this age. The same idea informs the Pastoral Letters, especially the relationship therein between gifts and office.

---

[46]See Gordon D. Fee, *1 and 2 Timothy, Titus* (Peabody, Mass.: Hendrickson, 1988), 20–23; cf. Kelly, *A Commentary on the Pastoral Epistles*, 13–16.

[47]This paragraph is indebted to the analysis of Reggie M. Kidd, *Wealth and Beneficence in the Pastoral Epistles* (SBLDS 122; Atlanta, Ga.: Scholars, 1990), 186–87.

(1) The eschatology of the Pastorals, as Fee so ably demonstrates, consists of the already/not yet tension.[48] As in other letters (2 Thess. 2:3, 7), the present apostasy in the Pastorals is seen in terms of the messianic woes of the end time (1 Tim. 4:1; 2 Tim. 3:1). Like the indisputable Pauline letters, persevering through suffering and patience in light of the *Parousia* stand side by side (cf. 2 Cor. 1:4–11; Col. 1:24; 1 Thess. 1:6–7 with 1 Tim. 6:12–14; 2 Tim. 1:12). Salvation, like Paul's earlier letters, is both present and future (1 Tim. 1:16; 4:8; 6:12, 14; 2 Tim. 1:9–10, 12; 2:3–11; Titus 2:12–14). The apostle expresses in the Pastorals an ambivalence about an awareness of dying and an eagerness to be alive at the *Parousia* (2 Tim. 4:6–8; cf. Phil. 1:18–26; 3:12–14, 20–21).

(2) As Philip Towner has judiciously documented, the problem addressed in the Pastorals is much like that found in the church at Corinth—unbridled enthusiasm over the dawning of the age to come, to the point of assuming this present age is over. In both cases, therefore, Paul introduces structure and order to check the misuse of spontaneity.[49] If this is so, then the relationships between structure and spontaneity in the Corinthian correspondences and gifts and office in the Pastoral Letters are best explained by the already/not yet tension: the age to come has dawned (hence the joy of spiritual gifts), but this age continues to run its course (hence the need for structure and order to check the forces of sin at work even in the church). Until the *Parousia*, both aspects, gifts and office, are vital to the church's ministry.

E. CHURCH AND STATE

The modern issue of the separation of church and state is not a new debate; it goes back to the Reformation, to Luther's doctrine of the two kingdoms, and beyond that, even to the first Christians. Paul, as a citizen of two kingdoms—Christ's and Caesar's—was necessarily embroiled in the controversy over the

---

[48]See Fee, *1 and 2 Timothy, Titus*, 19–20.

[49]Philip H. Towner, *The Goal of Our Instruction: The Structure of Theology and Ethics in the Pastoral Epistles* (JSNT Supp.Ser. 34; Sheffield: JSOT Press, 1989), 29–42.

relationship between the two. In at least three passages he focuses his attention on the subject: 1 Timothy 2:1–2; Titus 3:1–2; and especially Romans 13:1–7. Once again, the already/not yet eschatological tension shapes his view of the stance of the church toward state. The best way to approach this topic is to offer three models of interpretation of that relationship: the church versus the state; the church equals the state; the church and the state. As will be argued below, the last one best expresses Paul's view. Perhaps a chart will help clarify the discussion:

	Church vs. State	Church = State	Church and State
Eschatological tendency:	Overlooks "already" aspect	Overlooks "not yet" aspect	Both "already/ not yet"
Historical example:	Jewish apocalypticism	Old Testament theocracy/zealots	Paul
Modern counterpart:	Millenarian groups	Protestant liberalism/ Liberation Theology	Two kingdoms of Luther/Separation of Church and State

1. Church Versus State

This model opposes continuity between God and government, church and state. Jewish apocalypticists at the time of Paul claimed that God had abandoned history and that only the establishment of the kingdom of God in the age to come would bring resolution to the problems of sin and strife in this age. In this belief they differed from the Old Testament prophets, who, while renouncing the societal evils of their day, nevertheless believed that God would intervene in the affairs of the world. This contrast between Jewish apocalypticists and the Old Testament prophets pinpoints the underlying problem of the former view with regard to the New Testament era—it overlooked the fact that God already established his kingdom on earth through Jesus Christ, embryonic though it is. The same sort of failure in perception characterizes modern millenarian movements that predict the *Parousia* and, when their prophecies fail, unknowingly display cognitive dissonance in their intensified efforts to get the next date of Christ's return right. This worldview fails to appreciate the significance of the fact that Christ already began his kingly, heavenly reign at his resurrection and ascension.

2. Church = State

This model equates the two spheres of church and state, a union not unlike ancient Israel's theocratic assumption that her nation was coterminous with God's kingdom (the Old Testament prophets knew otherwise!). This theocratic conviction reached its climax with the Zealot revolts against Rome in the first and second centuries C.E. It was fueled by the idea that God's hand could be manipulated to deliver his people, the Jews, if they engaged the enemy in conflict. Such a mentality finds a modern analogy in the nineteenth century liberal Protestant belief that the church will one day bring utopia to earth. It is also akin to some twentieth-century Catholic liberation theologies that tend to identify God's main concern with the world, not the church. In fact, if the church is to do any good, according to this perspective, it must identify with the efforts of the needy in the world to overthrow oppressive regimes.[50] Strange bedfellows that Protestant liberalism and Catholic liberation theology may be (the former is based on capitalism while the latter is grounded in socialism), they both suffer from not perceiving the not yet aspect of the kingdom of God. The age to come has not fully arrived, nor will it ever do so by human effort alone.

3. Church and State

The Pauline model holds church and state in dynamic tension, the result of the overlapping of the two ages. As such it approximates Luther's two-kingdom theory[51] and is not far removed from the current American theory of separation of church and state. Both interact with each other, but neither is to

---

[50]Ellis provides a powerful critique of this approach in *Pauline Theology*, 18–21.

[51]Heinrich Borkamm defines this doctrine as referring to "the two ways in which God effects his will in the secular and spiritual realms of the world. Both duality and unity thus seemed to be preserved" (*Luther's Doctrine of the Two Kingdoms*, trans. Karl H. Hertz [FBBS; Philadelphia: Fortress, 1966], 2). The basis for Luther's two-kingdom theory is his work *Temporal Authority* (*Martin Luther's Works*, Weimar, 1523).

rule the other. The eschatological mooring of Paul's teaching can be succinctly expressed. The church is the proleptic appearance of the kingdom of God on earth (though it is not to be equated with that kingdom); this is the already aspect. But this age continues to exist and, with it, sin. Therefore government is a political reality of this age, serving as a check to anarchy. In other words, the state serves an inevitably negative function. This is the not yet aspect.

Romans 13:1–7, 11–14, Paul's major exposition on the subject, confirms this reading of the apostle. Verses 11–14 highlight the already side of the ledger—"the hour has come"; "salvation is nearer now than when we first believed." Verses 1–7 depict the not yet pole—the state is to perform its divinely appointed function of punishing crime (vv. 3–4), and believers are to support it by taxes (vv. 6–7) and with prayer and respect (1 Tim. 2:1–2; Titus 3:1). Christians should probably not expect much more from government in this age than the protection of life and rights and a peaceful environment in which to preach the gospel (1 Tim. 2:1–4). In the event of the rise of immoral government, civil disobedience may well be a viable response (Acts 5:29; cf. Rom. 10:9); Jesus, not Caesar, is Lord. But even then, such demonstrations ought to be nonviolent, following the example of Jesus (1 Peter 2:13–23).

CONCLUSION

We conclude this chapter on a meditative note. The church means different things to different people. To some, like Paul himself at one time, it elicits threats and persecution (cf. Acts 9:1). To others, like Celsus, the famous fourth-century critic of Christianity, it is an object of scorn. To far too many, the church is an obsolete institution to be treated with benign neglect. But to all who love Jesus Christ, the church, imperfect though it is and ever in need of reform, is still God's instrument for ministry to this world and the anchor of truth in a day when there seem to be no absolutes. Paul put it well; it is "God's household, . . . the pillar and foundation of the truth" (1 Tim. 3:15). May we as Christians help her to live up to that name.

VIII

PAULINE SOCIETY: GALATIANS 3:28 AND THE NEW WORLD ORDER

INTRODUCTION

Any attempt to interpret Paul's view of society must take into account Galatians 3:28, "There is neither Jew nor Gentile; there is neither slave nor free; there is neither male and female; for you are one in Christ Jesus" (pers. tr.). In his astute analysis of this verse, Klyne Snodgrass introduces the text in this manner:

> The study of Galatians 3:28 is both exciting and frustrating. On the one hand, the verse is the most socially explosive statement in the New Testament. On the other hand, the context gives little help in interpreting these words, and a bewildering array of possibilities for interpretation appear both in technical and nontechnical studies. The problems are caused by two main facts. First, the words about slave and free and about male and female appear abruptly and without apparent relation to the situation in the Galatian church. Second, some of Paul's other statements—such as 1 Corinthians 11:2–16; 14:33–36; Ephesians 5:22–33; and 1 Timothy 2:8–15—seem to contradict Galatians 3:28. What is the relation between this passage and the other texts?[1]

This quotation sets the agenda for the chapter at hand, which seeks to understand the Pauline view of society through

---

[1] Klyne R. Snodgrass, "Galatians 3:28—Conundrum or Solution?" in *Women, Authority and the Bible*, ed. Alvera Mickelsen (Downers Grove, Ill.: InterVarsity, 1986), 161.

the hermeneutical grid of Galatians 3:28 and its companion passages. The text itself provides an outline of the social contours of Paul's world: Jew and Gentile (cf. Rom. 1:16, 18–4:25; 11:11–27; Gal. 3:1–14; Eph. 2:11–16); slave and free (cf. 1 Cor. 7:20–24; Philem. 10–17); male and female (cf. 1 Cor. 11:2–16; 14:34–35; Eph. 5:22–33; Col. 3:19–20; 1 Tim. 2:9–15). Our thesis builds especially on the recent work of E. Earle Ellis, who convincingly argues that the ambiguity reflected in the relationship between Galatians 3:28 and other passages that fall within the purview of its social parameters is to be explained by the reality that Christians live between the two ages.[2]

Before addressing the three areas of concern in this text, we first need to make three observations. (1) Galatians 3:28 must be interpreted against the cultural background of Paul's day, which, on any reading, would have required radical reassessment of societal distinctions then current. For example, consider how different the message of this verse was from an ancient Greek statement apparently condoned by the likes of Socrates and Plato, in which the speaker gives thanks that he "was born a human being and not an animal, that I was born a man and not a woman, and that I was born a Greek and not a barbarian."[3] The Jewish version of this thanksgiving, prayed three times daily by the male, read, "Blessed art thou, Lord, who hast not made me a heathen, who hast not made me a woman, and who hast not made me a brutish man."[4] Sometimes a fourth element was included in the Jewish blessing, "that I was not made a slave."[5] When Rabbi Aha b. Jacob was asked if being a woman was not the same as being a slave, he responded that a slave is more contemptible![6] Obviously Paul's statement of equality in Galatians 3:28 cut against the grain of ancient society.

(2) As an answer to one of the problems surrounding Galatians 3:28 pointed out by Snodgrass—its lack of contextual

---

[2]E. Earle Ellis, *Pauline Theology: Ministry and Society* (Grand Rapids: Eerdmans, 1989), 53–86.

[3]*Diogenes Laertius* 1:33; cf. Plutarch's *Lives, Caius Marius* 46:1.

[4]*b Menahoth* 43b.

[5]See again *b Menahoth* 43b.

[6]*b Menahoth* 43b; cf. *Tosephta Berakoth* 7:18; *p Berakoth* 9:1.

flow—the verse is likely a liturgical pre-Pauline pronouncement associated with Christian baptism. Convincing evidence for such has been supplied by Wayne Meeks, who put forth the theory that Galatians 3:28, along with 1 Corinthians 12:13 and Colossians 3:10–11, are based on a baptismal formula. (a) All three texts contain the same elements—baptism into Christ (Gal. 3:27) or into one body (1 Cor. 12:13), or putting on the new man (Col. 3:10); a simple listing of two or more pairs of opposites; and the statement that "all" are "one," or that "Christ is all." (b) The declaration is associated in every instance with baptism, though baptism is not under discussion in the letters. (c) With specific reference to Galatians 3:28, the formula stands out clearly from its context. The allusion to Genesis 1:27 ("male and female") has no obvious connection with the surrounding verses, in contrast to the phrase "Jew nor Greek."[7] Thus, entrance into the Christian life is defined by Paul in terms of spiritual equality, which, in turn, is grounded in the unity of the body of Christ.

(3) Galatians 3:28 finds its ultimate frame of reference in eschatology—it marks the dawning of the age to come, the new creation. Those who are in Christ are part of the new world order, the new humanity (cf. Gal. 3:28 with 6:15). For Paul to say in 3:28 that the annulment of the distinction between Jew and Gentile comes to those who are "in Christ" is tantamount to saying that neither circumcision or uncircumcision matters but what is important is a new creation (see 6:15). This is the already aspect of Paul's eschatology. However, 3:28 is not Paul's only word on the subject. Other passages need to be taken into consideration as well. As will be seen, the eschatological tension that has resulted from the intersection of the two ages provides a suitable explanation for the apostle's view of society.

A. JEW NOR GENTILE

That Paul's statement "there is neither Jew nor Gentile . . . in Christ" was socially provocative can be verified by the reaction

---

[7]Wayne A. Meeks, "The Image of the Adrogyne. Some Uses of a Symbol in Earliest Christianity," *HR* 13 (1974): 165–208.

such a comment elicited from early critics of Christianity. For example, Tertullian, a patristic theologian of the second century, includes in one of his writings a famous pejorative appellative heaped on Christians, implying them to be an inferior people, "But, you say, it is on the score of religion and not of nationality that we are considered to be third; it is the Romans first, then the Jews, and after that the Christians."[8] Like the derogatory name "Christian" (Acts 11:26), the term "third race" as descriptive of a spiritual new world order inaugurated in Christ stuck. In this section we investigate Paul's view of the relationship between Jew and Gentile in Christ, noting first the spiritual equality of the two (see Rom. 1:18–25; Gal. 3:1–14; Eph. 2:11–16). Yet other passages (e.g., Rom. 1:16; 11:11–27) show deference to the ethnic priority of Israel. The ambiguity between the two sets of texts is rooted in the overlapping of the two ages: Jew and Gentile are already equal in Christ; but the unity is not yet complete, because God has more work to do on behalf of Israel.

1. Spiritual Equality of Jews and Gentiles in Christ

Paul's assertion in Galatians 3:28 that in Christ Jew and Gentile are equal is paralleled in several other passages (Rom. 1:18–4:25; Gal. 3:1–14; Eph. 2:11–16). (1) The argumentation of Romans 1:18–4:25 is well known. The apostle's major concern is first to show that both Jew and Gentile are sinners and therefore in dire need of the righteousness of God (1:18–3:20). Paul then demonstrates that all have access to God's gracious provision of justification in Christ by faith alone (3:21–31). In reality, Paul argues, faith has always been the means for salvation, beginning with Abraham, the father of the Jewish nation (4:1–25). Therefore, neither Jew nor Gentile has any grounds for boasting before God. By faith, both are equal in Christ; racial status is irrelevant (cf. 1 Cor. 7:17–19).

(2) Galatians 3:1–14 forms the basis of Paul's thought in verse 28. Verses 1–5 roundly criticize the Galatians' reneging on the principle of justification by faith, having replaced it with the

[8]*Ad Nationes* I.viii. For an excellent treatment of this and related quotes, see Adolf Harnack, *The Mission and Expansion of Christianity in the First Three Centuries*, trans. James Moffatt (Gloucester, Mass.: Peter Smith, 1972), 266–78.

works of the Law. Their reason for doing so probably stemmed from pressure put on them by the Judaizers to walk in the Spirit by keeping the Law. Verses 6–14 refute that line of thinking by contrasting, or at least disassociating, the Law of Moses from the promise of Abraham. Paul's rationale is that the promise of salvation through Abraham (cf. v. 8 with Gen. 12:3) is made void concerning the Gentiles if justification comes from obeying the Mosaic Law. The latter brings a curse, not a blessing, because no one is able to observe the Law. Jesus Christ alone obeyed the Law and, on the cross, took the curse of all upon himself in order that the Abrahamic promise might rest on Jew and Gentile alike (cf. Gal. 3:16, 29). Thus the cross becomes the great leveler of society, and it can only be embraced by faith, which alone is the means for receiving the Spirit.

(3) Earlier we located Paul's discussion of Ephesians 2:11–16 within the framework of the two-age structure (see 1:21; 2:7). There Paul paints a "before and after" picture of the status of Gentiles in terms reminiscent of this age and the age to come. Before the dawning of the age to come, Gentiles were not a part of the people of God, having no hope in this age (vv. 11, 13). But now, in Christ, with the arrival of the age to come as well as the subsequent removal of the curse of the Law, Gentiles are being incorporated into the people of God, being reconciled to both God and Jews (vv. 14–16). The net result is that both Jew and Gentile have been formed into "one man," the new humanity, the third race.

2. Ethnic Deference to Jews

Although Christian Jews and Gentiles are equal spiritually, Paul still defers to the ethnic priority of Israel—"first for the Jew, then for the Gentile" (Rom. 1:16–17; cf. Acts 13:46; 18:6; 28:28). God is not yet finished with Israel. Though an older generation of scholars assumed that the church permanently replaced Israel in the plan of God, there is now a growing consensus that rejects the concept that the church, the new Israel, has replaced the old Israel as the elect people of God.[9] Cranfield typifies this new

---

[9]Karl Barth, *Church Dogmatics*, II, eds. G. W. Bromiley and T. F. Torrance (Edinburgh: T. & T. Clark, 1936), 195–305; Hans Kung, *The Church* (New York: Sheed & Ward, 1968), 132–50; Hendrik Berkhof, "Israel as a Theological Problem

understanding when he says, "I confess with shame to having also myself used in print on more than one occasion this language of the replacement of Israel by the church."[10] Two factors seem to have converged to produce this shift of thinking about the future of Israel—the historical events of the Jewish holocaust under Nazism along with the establishment of the political state of Israel, and careful exegesis of Romans 11:25–27. We will concentrate on the second of these two.

Romans 11 makes three points. (1) Israel's rejection of Jesus Messiah is partial, not total (vv. 1–10). Some Jews indeed have responded in faith to Christ ("the remnant"), Paul included. (2) Israel's rejection of Jesus Messiah actually served a merciful purpose—it paved the way for Gentiles to come to Christ (vv. 11–24). But that is not the end of the story for Israel because God will use the Gentiles' conversion to stir the Jews to jealousy to receive Jesus as their Messiah. (3) Israel's rejection of Jesus Messiah is temporary, not permanent (vv. 25–27). A day is coming when "all Israel will be saved" (v. 26).

This last idea calls for extended comment. Three hermeneutical problems are raised by verse 26. (a) What does "Israel" mean? If it means *spiritual* Israel, then the referent would include Gentiles as well as Jews, and Paul is not then necessarily saying that *national* Israel will be restored to God. But the "spiritual" Israel view is unlikely, seeing that the other ten times "Israel" is used in Romans 9–11 (9:6 [twice], 27 [twice], 31; 10:19, 21; 11:2, 7, 25) refer to ethnic Israel. For verse 26 to posit a different meaning is unlikely.[11]

(b) What do the words *"and thus* [pers. tr. of *kai houtôs*] all Israel will be saved" mean? Some take the phrase as temporal, "and then," meaning that after the spiritual hardening of Israel and the fullness of the Gentiles, *then* all Israel will be saved.[12] But

---

in the Christian Church," *JES* 1 (1969): 329–47; Herman Ridderbos, *Paul: An Outline of His Theology,* trans. John Richard Dewitt (Grand Rapids: Eerdmans, 1975), 354–56.

[10]C. E. B. Cranfield, *Romans IX–XVI* (ICC; Edinburgh: T. & T. Clark, 1977), 448, fn. 2.

[11]See ibid., 576–77; Dunn, *Romans 9–16* (WBC 38b; Dallas: Word Books, 1988), 681. Most modern commentators agree with this interpretation.

[12]F. F. Bruce, *The Epistle of Paul to the Romans: An Introduction and Commentary* (TNTC; Grand Rapids: Eerdmans, 1963), 222; C. K. Barrett, *A Commentary on the Epistle to the Romans* (HNTC; New York: Harper, 1957), 223.

a temporal rendering of *kai houtôs* is rare in Paul. Most, therefore, take the phrase comparatively— 'and so" or "and in this manner"—referring to the immediate context of verse 25. Some of these go on to suggest that verse 26 refers to the remnant (including both Jew and Gentile; i.e., the church), thereby ruling out any future conversion of national Israel.[13] It is preferable, however, to take the antecedent of verse 26 as the Gentiles coming into the community of faith, which, when completed, turns Israel to Jesus the Messiah. The future tense in "will . . . be grafted" (v. 24) and "will be saved" (v. 26) supports this conclusion.[14] On this reading, verse 26 refers to an event that will witness a national turning of Israel to Christ.

(c) What does "all Israel" mean? Three main possibilities surface. (i) Covenantal/Reformed theologians take the phrase to mean *spiritual* Israel, the elect of God including both Jew and Gentile Christians (i.e., the church). But Cranfield sufficiently refutes this perspective by exposing its problem—to say that the church will be saved is redundant (ii) Dispensationalists take the words to refer to *national* Israel, Israel as a whole, though not necessarily every individual Israelite. The phrase "all Israel" is used elsewhere to refer to the nation but without necessarily including every Jew (cf. 1 Sam 7:2–5; 25:1; 1 Kings 12:1; 2 Chron 12:1–5; Dan. 9:11; cf. *bSan* 10:1). (iii) The most recent theory is the *unified* Israel interpretation proposed by Bruce Longenecker, which builds on the second possibility. He writes:

> Instead, in 11.26 Paul is thinking exclusively of an ethnic entity, and moreover, of that entity as a whole. Throughout 9–11, Paul draws out the disparate courses of two groups— believing and unbelieving—within ethnic Israel. By the inclusive "all" in 11.26, he joins both groups together. Thus Paul looks forward to the time when not only the remnant of Israel who have believed but also those of Israel who have strayed from the course of their unbelief will be saved. When Paul

---

[13]G. C. Berkouwer's exegesis is typical of this interpretation, *The Return of Christ*, trans. James van Oosterom and ed. Marlin J. Van Elderen (Grand Rapids: Eerdmans, 1972), 335–49.

[14]See, for example, W. Sanday and A. C. Headlam, *The Epistle to the Romans* (ICC; Edinburgh: T. & T. Clark, 1895), 235.

speaks of "all Israel" in 11.26, what he has in mind is an ethnic group whose members at present are schismatically divided. In this sense, his point is not so much that all *Israel* will be saved, but that *all* Israel will be saved.[15]

In other words, "all Israel will be saved" refers to the future event of the nation of Israel's conversion to Jesus as Messiah, which will unite it with those Jewish Christians (spiritual Israel) throughout the period of the church. Truly, all Israel, united Israel, will for the first time be saved.[16]

We should also point out that Paul's collection of the Gentile offering in order to help the poor saints in Jerusalem (Rom. 15:25–29; 1 Cor. 16:1–4; 2 Cor. 8–9) probably also conveys the apostle's deference to Jews. The Old Testament underpinning of this action undoubtedly proceeded from the Jewish expectation of an eschatological conversion and pilgrimage of the Gentiles to Zion (cf. also Rom. 9:25–27 and 15:16–33 with Isa. 45:15; 60:15–17; Mic. 4:13; *Tobit* 3:11; *1QM* 12:13–15). Only at that time would the union between Jew and Gentile be complete. Until then, Jewish and Gentile Christians live in the overlapping of the two ages, between spiritual equality (already) and ethnic priority (not yet).

B. SLAVE NOR FREE

Slavery was tragically a basic element in Greco-Roman society, reaching its highest proportion in the first centuries B.C.E. and C.E. Estimates vary that from one-fifth to one-third of the population was enslaved. The slave revolts in Italy and Sicily in the late republic confirm widespread social discontent at the time.[17] Cato's account of slave labor in agriculture reveals a taskmaster mentality reminiscent of pre-Civil War American

---

[15]Bruce W. Longenecker, "Different Answers to Different Issues: Israel, the Gentiles and Salvation History in Romans 9–11," *JSNT* 36 (1989): 97.

[16]Perhaps the modern analogy of the reunification of Germany after the fall of the Berlin Wall would help to grasp the sense of Paul's concept of a unified Israel.

[17]See the article by Gager, "Religion and Social Class in the Early Roman Empire," in *The Catacombs and the Colesseum: The Roman Empire as the Setting of Pauline Christianity*, eds. Stephen Benko and John J. O'Rourke (Valley Forge, Pa.: Judson Press, 1971), 108.

slavery.[18] Seneca relates that a proposal in the Roman senate that slaves be required to follow a distinctive dress code was defeated lest the slaves discover how numerous they were.[19]

Slavery was a despicable institution, devaluing the dignity of the human being. The legal status of a slave was that of a "thing." Aristotle defined a slave as "living property" (*Politics* I.ii.4–5, 1253b) and as a "living tool and the tool a lifeless slave" (*Nicomanean Ethics* VIII.ii). In short, the slave was subject to the absolute power of his or her master.

Although early Christianity did not officially challenge slavery,[20] the gospel thankfully did sow the seeds that later produced its overthrow (or apparent overthrow). Paul's writings in particular, especially Galatians 3:28,[21] have contributed much to the cause of freedom. However, the fact that Paul was a child of his day unavoidably influenced his presentation of the issue. We find, therefore, a nuanced call in his letters for social equality that was shaped by the idea of the overlapping of the two ages. Three passages necessitate comment regarding this matter.

1. 1 Corinthians 7:22–23

This passage applies the already/not yet eschatological tension to the ancient institution of slavery. It is uncomfortably straightforward concerning the latter emphasis: "each one should remain in the situation which he was in when God called him" (v. 20; cf. vv. 17, 24). That is, Paul suggests that slaves should not aspire to obtaining freedom. He does not call the church to challenge or overthrow slavery; to have done so would have provoked the wrath of Rome on the newly established Christian

---

[18]Ibid., 110.

[19]See Everett Ferguson, *Backgrounds of Early Christianity* (Grand Rapids: Eerdmans, 1987), 46.

[20]Probably the main reason for this was the recognition that the wrath of Rome would fall on it for even suggesting the demise of an institution so vital to the structure of Roman society.

[21]Susie C. Stanley provides a fine survey of the history of the interpretation of Galatians 3:28 from the nineteenth century to the present, noting its potential liberating influence, "Response to Snodgrass' Galatians 3:28—Conundrum or Solution?" *Women, Authority and the Bible*, 181–92.

religion. Paul realized that societal institutions, slavery included, would continue to remain intact in his day, and thus Christians would have to cope with the political realities of this age.

But, as Scott Bartchy has carefully detailed, Paul's main point in 1 Corinthians 7:17–24 was not to absolutize social standings. In Paul's day, slaves could be freed by the process of manumission, and he in no way opposed that procedure. Bartchy shows that a slave could not reject the offer of manumission.[22] Thus, Paul did not intend to suggest that slaves should weigh the choice between freedom and slavery; rather, when they were able to become free, they should make the most of the opportunity. In effect, what Paul does here is to *relativize* social standings— slaves needed to realize that they were freedmen in Christ and the free needed to see that they were slaves to Christ (vv. 21–22). In other words, his point is not that change is disallowed but that it is immaterial spiritually. Seeing that one's earthly situation presents no disadvantage in fellowship with God, each person is challenged to live the Christian life at the level with which he or she is identified.[23] This is the already aspect of Paul's eschatology —in Christ there is no slave or free.

2. Philemon

Philemon, like Galatians 3:28 and 1 Corinthians 7:21–22, has received bad press in its history of interpretation, particularly regarding the institution of slavery. It was used by the anti-abolitionists in America prior to the Civil War. But this is surely a wrong reading of the letter. In fact, the correct understanding of Philemon is to view it through Paul's lens of the overlapping of the two ages. The not yet aspect is admittedly there, for Paul does indeed send Onesimus back, changed man that he was (vv. 12–16). While Paul sincerely hopes that the slave's owner, Philemon, will not require it, and while Paul expects that the new relationship between the converted slave and master will

---

[22]S. Scott Bartchy, *First-Century Slavery and 1 Corinthians 7:21* (SBLDS 2; Missoula, Mont.: Scholars Press 1971), 62–120.

[23]Ibid., 155–83.

take priority over social status, Onesimus may have to resume his servitude to Philemon in Colosse.

But Paul is not content to leave the matter there; he relativizes class status. He reverses the roles, calling himself a slave or prisoner of Christ (vv. 9–10, 13) and Onesimus a brother (v. 16). Furthermore, as a master communicator, Paul subtly tries to influence Philemon toward releasing Onesimus in a number of ways. (1) He hopes that Philemon will permit Onesimus to remain with him in the ministry (v. 13), which implies Onesimus' freedom. (2) Paul reminds Philemon that he owes him (Paul) a favor—since Philemon can thank Paul for his salvation (implied), he should set Onesimus free (v. 19). (3) Paul expresses his confidence in Philemon's judgment: "You will do even more than I ask" (v. 21; cf. v. 8). That is, Philemon will do more than just take Onesimus back with open arms; he will let him go free. (4) Probably Paul sagely relied on social pressure to help motivate Philemon to free Onesimus, inasmuch as the apostle expected that his letters would be read publicly in the house church settings and to be received as the word of God (cf. v. 2 with 1 Thess. 2:13; 5:27). Philemon would have felt social pressure to let Onesimus go. All these factors bear witness to the already aspect of Paul's eschatology; the age to come in which there is no class distinction has arrived in Christ.

3. The *Haustafel*

Martin Luther first coined the word *Haustafel*, a word meaning "house-table" or "household codes." Today the term is used for those New Testament passages that delineate the structure of ancient society, bringing to bear on it Christian conduct: Ephesians 5:22–6:9; Colossians 3:18–4:1; Titus 2:1–10; 1 Peter 2:18–3:7. One of the most insightful works done on this subject is David L. Balch's *Let Wives Be Submissive to Their Husbands*.[24] Although Balch works primarily with the husband-wife role as delineated in 1 Peter 3:1–7, his research is equally applicable to the topic of slavery as put forth in Ephesians 6:5–9; Colossians

---

[24]David L. Balch, *Let Wives Be Submissive to Their Husbands* (SBLMS 26; Chico, Calif.: Scholars Press, 1981).

3:22–4:1; Titus 2:9–10. Though he does not call it such, it is the eschatological tension of the intersection of the two ages that informs these *Haustafel*.

Balch convincingly proves that the origin of the threefold division inherent to the *Haustafel* (husbands and wives; parents and children; masters and slaves) is Greek, not Jewish or Christian. This categorization with its attendant class status and accompanying prejudicial attitudes can be traced back to Plato (*Laws* 627A; *Timaeus* 90c) and his student Aristotle (*Politics* I 1253a; *Nicomanean Ethics* VIII 1160b–1161a10). The emphasis in those philosophers' statements on the subject is less than positive.[25] The upshot of their comments is to stress the role of the subservient side of the ledger: wives are to submit to their husbands; children are to obey their parents; slaves are to serve their masters. This mentality was bequeathed to later Roman society, especially in the absolute power conveyed to the father of the household (*Paterfamilias*). Even Philo and Josephus, famous Jewish writers contemporaneous with Paul, were not able to extricate themselves from such a patriarchal attitude.[26]

This, argues Balch, is the setting in which early Christianity found itself. How was it to respond to the prevailing social norms of the day? Balch's answer is insightful—the New Testament writers utilize the *Haustafel* in an apologetic manner. Recognizing Rome's suspicion of Christianity's message of egalitarianism (e.g., the widespread formula of Gal. 3:28; cf. also 2 Cor. 5:17) and recalling the imperial government's recent strictures on some mystery religions' espousal of equal status for all its members,[27] the New Testament authors continued to employ the *Haustafel* in their writings in order to alleviate any suspicion

---

[25]For example, Plato writes of children that it is "the claim of parents to rule over offspring" (*Laws* 627a); of slaves, "slaves ought to be ruled, and masters ought to rule" (*Laws* 627a); and of women, "On the subject of animals, then, the following remarks are offered. Of the men who come into the world, those who were cowards or led unrighteous lives may with reason be supposed to have changed into the nature of women in the second generation" (*Timaeus* 90c.).

[26]For Philo, see *Special Laws* II.225–27; III.169–71; *The Decalogue* 165–67. For Josephus, see *Against Apion* II.199. For further discussion, see Balch, *Let Wives Be Submissive to their Husbands*, 52–56.

[27]Ibid., 63–116.

on Rome's part that Christianity desired to disrupt the fabric of society. We believe that Paul's attitude of slaves submitting to authority is sufficiently explained by Balch's thesis. It expresses the not yet aspect of Paul's eschatology; submission and authority are facts of this age.

However, early Christianity was not content to leave the issue there. Balch goes on to demonstrate that the New Testament writers significantly qualify the *Haustafel* by introducing into it for the first time the principle of reciprocity. The "superior" side of the ledger has its obligations, too, as Christians: husbands should love their wives; fathers are not to provoke their children; masters must treat their servants fairly. Interestingly enough, Ephesians 6:9 and Colossians 4:1 relativize the last category by reminding masters that they themselves will give an account to their heavenly Lord concerning how they treated their servants.

This principle of reciprocity surely stems from Paul's eschatological perspective: because the kingdom of God has dawned, there are no second-class citizens in its realm. All are equal in position before God. Nevertheless, the tension in Paul's thought remains: equality and authority attest to the reality that the age to come exists in the midst of this present age. Such a tension continues into modern times, knowingly or unknowingly.

C. MALE NOR FEMALE

We begin an overview of this issue by recalling one of the difficulties attached to the interpretation of Galatians 3:28 as pinpointed by Snodgrass—the matter of how that verse is to be related to other Pauline passages relevant to the topic of male and female relationships in Christ (1 Cor. 11:2–16; 14:33–36; Eph. 5:22–33; 1 Tim. 2:9–15).[28] First Corinthians 7:17–24 should also be factored into the equation. Snodgrass himself identifies four different proposals to account for that relationship.[29] (1) Paul did not really mean these words. He is quoting a pre-Pauline formula

---

[28]Snodgrass, "Galatians 3:28," 161.
[29]Ibid., 162–66.

without intending to take its words in woodenly literal fashion. Most likely Paul is correcting a more liberal tradition than his own.

(2) Paul only meant Galatians 3:28 partially. Those who take this approach claim that this verse is a soteriological statement and has nothing to do with social issues such as nations, slavery, or gender assigned in creation.

(3) Paul's true theology differed from his original insight in Galatians 3:28. For example, Betz says that Paul retracted in 1 Corinthians what he said earlier in Galatians 3:28, because the latter stirred a radical feminist movement in the church that attempted to define humanity in terms of unisex, calling for the obliteration of natural distinctions between the two sexes.[30]

(4) Paul meant what he said. However, scholars espousing this view differ in their attempts to explain how Galatians 3:28 relates to similar Pauline texts. Thus, some take 1 Corinthians 14:33–36 (and possibly 11:2–16) as later non-Pauline interpolations, while Ephesians, Colossians, and the Pastorals are considered to be the work of students of Paul, not the apostle himself.[31] Others view Galatians 3:28 as Paul's normative, transcultural perspective and other passages (e.g., 1 Cor. 14:34–35; 1 Tim. 2:9–15) as only descriptive texts and therefore culturally bound.[32] Most recently, Ellis has argued that Galatians 3:28 and the other key passages related to the subject in Paul's letters are in basic agreement and that what tension there is among them is to be explained by the overlapping of the two ages.[33] Our own view basically follows Ellis' approach. We will develop that viewpoint by considering the following trajectory of texts: Galatians 3:28;

---

[30]Hans Dieter Betz, *Galatians: A Commentary on Paul's Letter to the Churches in Galatia* (Hermeneia; Philadelphia: Fortress, 1979), 200.

[31]Typical of this view are the works by Robin Scroggs, "Paul and the Eschatological Women," *JAAR* 40 (1972): 283–303; and Elisabeth Schüssler Fiorenza, *In Memory of Her* (New York: Crossroad, 1983), 245–46.

[32]Included in this category are the works by Walter L. Liefeld, "Women, Submission and Ministry in 1 Corinthians," *Women, Authority and the Bible*, 134–54; David M. Scholer, "1 Timothy 2:9–15 and the Place of Women in the Church's Ministry," *Women, Authority and the Bible*, 193–224; and Snodgrass himself, "Galatians 3:28."

[33]Ellis, *Pauline Theology*, 53–86.

1 Corinthians 11:3–16; 14:34–35; the *Haustafel* of Colossians 3:18–19 and Ephesians 5:22–33; and 1 Timothy 2:9–15.

1. Galatians 3:28

In the introduction to this chapter, we summarized the rationale appealed to by Wayne Meeks in his proposal that Galatians 3:28 is a pre-Pauline baptismal formula. Meeks develops the proposition that behind Galatians 3:28; 1 Corinthians 12:13; and Colossians 3:10–11 resides a baptismal reunification formula that envisions the restoration of Adam's lost primeval unity as occurring in Christ via baptism. He locates the ultimate origin of this tradition in Plato's *Symposium*, 189–93. There, Aristophanes speaks about three kinds of original beings who were joined back-to-back. Each one had the faculties of two human bodies and could be masculine, feminine, or bisexual. In response to their rebellion, Zeus carved each of the three beings, splitting them into either two men, or two women, or one man and one woman. Seeing their remorse for such rebellion, Zeus rejoined the severed halves by making possible their copulation. Meeks finds traces of this Greek story in diverse texts like Philo (*Quaest.Gen.* I.25; *De Opif* 151), the Talmud (*Meg.* 9a; *Mek.Pisha* 14; *b.Erubin* 18a; *b.Ber.* 61a), the Midrashim (*Gen.R.* 8:1; *Lev.R.* 14), Gnosticism (*Gos.Phil.* 68:22–23; 70:12–18; *Gos.Thom.* 22, 106, 114), and the New Testament (Gal. 3:28; 1 Cor. 12:13; Col. 3:10–11). Pertinent to this discussion is Meeks' claim that in these citations, Genesis 1:26–28 (especially v. 27) and 2:21–24 play a major role concerning the interpretation that Adam was originally androgynous. He argues that 1:26–28 is viewed by the prior texts as referring to the original unity of the sexes in Adam, and 2:21–23 is understood as describing the separation and demise of that unity. The goal of humanity, therefore, is to be reunited into one flesh (2:24).

Three of those passages may be cited here to illustrate the point. *Genesis Rabbah* 8:1 states that God created Adam as both male and female; only the two together restore the unity of God's creation. Compare this to *Gos.Phil.* 68:22–23, which reads, "When Eve was in Adam, there was no death; but when she was separated from him death came into being. Again if [she] go in,

and he takes [her] to himself, death will no longer exist."
Gos.Phil. 70:12–18 provides a lengthier rendition of this account,
"Because of this Christ came, in order that he might remove the
separation which was from the beginning and again to unite the
two; and that he might give life to those who died in the separation, and unite them."[34]

Meeks applies this archetypal story to the pre-Pauline tradition behind 1 Corinthians 12:13; Galatians 3:28; and Colossians
3:10–11:

> The allusion to Genesis 1:26–27 is unmistakable; simi-
> larly, as we noted earlier, Galatians 3:28 contains a reference to
> the "male and female" of Genesis 1:27 and suggests that
> somehow the act of Christian initiation reverses the fateful di-
> vision of Genesis 2:21–22. Where the image of God is restored,
> there, it seems man is no longer divided—not even by the
> most fundamental division of all, male and female. The bap-
> tismal reunification formula thus belongs to the familiar
> *Urzeit-Endzeit* pattern, and it presupposes an interpretation of
> the creation story in which the divine image after which
> Adam was modeled was masculofeminine.[35]

However, Meeks suggests that Paul significantly qualified this
tradition because of its implicit rejection of the created order of
male and female. Paul agreed with the basic vision of the crafters
of the tradition concerning the spiritual equality of the sexes and
the return to the divine image, but he protested that this reunification was unattainable prior to the eschaton. Using words approaching the idea of the overlapping of the two ages, Meeks
writes:

> Therefore Paul accepts and even insists upon the equality of
> role of man and woman in this community which is formed
> already by the Spirit that belongs to the end of days. The new
> order, the order of man in the image of God, was already tak-
> ing form in the patterns of leadership of the new community.
> Yet the old order was to be allowed still its symbolic claims,
> for the Christian lived yet in the world, in the "land of unlike-

---

[34]Meeks, "The Image of the Adrogyne."
[35]Ibid., 185.

ness," until the time should come for the son himself to submit to the Father, that God might be all in all.[36]

A similar tack is taken by Dennis R. MacDonald, whose thesis is that Genesis 3:21 forms part of the exegetical substructure for a dominical saying in the *Gospel of the Egyptians*, which was used by Paul, *mutatis mutandis*, in Galatians 3:26–28. The impact of the Genesis verse on the other two authors becomes clear when they are placed side by side:

Gen 3:21 (LXX)	Gos.Eg.	Gal. 3:26–28
And the Lord made garments of skin and clothed them	When you tread upon the garment of shame	For as many of you have been baptized into Christ have put on Christ[37]

MacDonald calls attention to the impact of Genesis 3:21 on the dominical statement in the *Gospel of the Egyptians*. He notes that the Jesus saying, especially as it is used by Julius Cassianus, is influenced by Gnostic interpretations of verse 21, which viewed the fall of the soul into the world as the result of Adam's and Eve's sexual union, a behavior they learned from the serpent. For this transgression, the primeval couple was incarcerated in mortal bodies (i.e., they were clothed in coats of skin). The goal, therefore, of the faithful is to "tread" on that "garment of shame," a reference to the deliverance of the soul from the body, which is illustrated in the practice of disrobing one's garment and trampling on it before entering the baptismal waters. This midrashic interpretation of Genesis 3:21 presumes the notion mentioned above that Adam was thought to originally have been created in the image of God and endowed with divine glory (Gen. 1:26–27) but, when he sinned, was clothed with skin, a human body.

MacDonald argues that the same type of exegesis is used in Galatians 3:27, except that a more positive formulation occurs in

---

[36]Ibid., 208.

[37]The purpose here is not to enter into the debate over which came first—the *Gospel to the Egyptians* logion or Galatians 3:27–28—but to note simply the contribution of Genesis 3:21 to both texts in their baptismal settings.

that the tradition refers to being "clothed with Christ" in baptism, rather than "treading upon the garments of shame." In other words, Paul (or the pre-Pauline tradition) debunks the latter phrase with its Gnostic view of the human body. Yet the reality attested to in both phrases (clothed with Christ and tread upon the garments of shame) is the same, in that both evince hope for the restored image and glory of Adam. For the *Gospel of the Egyptians*, that entails putting off the body; for Galatians it involves putting on Christ.[38]

We suggest that further Pauline redaction of the tradition informing Galatians 3:27–28 follows: Whereas the *Gospel of the Egyptians* says, "neither male *nor* female" (which suggests a return to an androgynous primeval state), Paul in Galatians 3:28 says, "neither male *and* female." The difference is almost imperceptible, but nonetheless significant—in saying there is neither male *and* female, Paul looks to be rejecting the idea of an androgynous state.[39] In effect, then, he qualifies the tradition behind Galatians 3:28 by rejecting the obliteration of sexual distinction between male and female (cf. Gen. 1:27, on which Gal. 3:28 is based). He does, however, promote the demise of inequality between the two spiritually and socially. In other words, Paul's shaping of the teaching informing Galatians 3:28 reflects, as Meeks has noted, the already/not yet eschatological tension. Already the spiritual and social barriers between men and women in Christ are falling; but their complete disintegration is not yet accomplished, nor will it be until this age fully gives way to the age to come.

A number of commentators also see a similar emancipatory activism informing the pre-Pauline tradition behind Galatians

---

[38]Dennis Ronald MacDonald, *There Is No Male and Female* (HDS 20; Philadelphia: Fortress, 1987). The chart as it is set up here is a conflation of the two charts provided by MacDonald (32, 116). Snodgrass ("Galatians 3:28," 163, fn. 7) too cavalierly dismisses MacDonald's thesis by asserting that the logion as found in the *Gospel of the Egyptians* did not exist prior to Galatians 3:28. But this overlooks (1) the widespread popularity of the saying and (2) the antiquity of the idea informing the saying.

[39]This is a piece of information I inadvertently overlooked in my earlier treatment of the subject; see Pate, *The Glory of Adam and the Afflictions of the Righteous: Pauline Suffering in Context* (New York: Edwin Mellen, 1993), 240–46.

3:28 at work in the church at Corinth.[40] They argue that the root problem of the Corinthian church consisted of the belief that the age to come had fully arrived in the death and resurrection of Christ. The upshot of that erroneous assumption was the belief that Christians had become like the angels and were therefore genderless. Moreover, adherence to "over-realized eschatology" prompted the Corinthians to say that slavery was a passé institution and that there was no more distinction between Jew and Gentile. Scholars viewing the situation in Corinth in this light go on to argue that 1 Corinthians 7 represents Paul's "eschatological reservation" on the subject. In other words, the apostle reminds his audience that this age still exists and that the age to come at best only intersects with, not replaces, it. Thus, although the age to come has dawned and thereby relativized racial distinctions ("circumcision is nothing and uncircumcision is nothing," vv. 18–20), class status ("he who was a slave when he was called by the Lord is the Lord's freedman; . . . he who was a free man when he was called is Christ's slave," vv. 21–24), and sexual gender ("the wife's body does not belong to her alone but also to her husband. In the same way, the husband's body does not belong to him alone but also to his wife," v. 4), the Corinthians needed to bring the equality tradition into balance—they were still members of this present age ("each one should retain the place in life that the Lord assigned to him," vv. 17, 20, 24). That is, equality (a hallmark of the age to come) and authority (an undeniable reality of this present age) coexist for the Christian.

2. 1 Corinthians 11:3–16 and 14:33–35

Mention of the circumstances of the Corinthian church necessitates some discussion of the two critical texts written to that community relative to male and female relationships in light of the Christ-event. It is often asserted that 1 Corinthians 14:33–35, with its subordinationist theme, contradicts the more irenic principles enunciated in 11:3–16, so much so that some attribute the

---

[40]See A. C. Thiselton, "Realized Eschatology at Corinth," *NTS* 24 (1978): 510–26; Philip H. Towner, *The Goal of Our Instruction: The Structure of Theology and Ethics in the Pastoral Epistles* (JSNT Supp.Ser. 34: Sheffield: JSOT Press, 1989), 33–45; MacDonald, *There Is No Male and Female,* 119–26.

former to a later non-Pauline interpolator.[41] But, as we shall shortly see, Paul's eschatological perspective, especially the already/not yet tension, is operative in both passages. There is, therefore, no inherent contradiction between the two.

Concerning 11:3–16, we need not probe the linguistic labyrinth that surrounds the words "head" and "cover." The reader is referred to the fine semantic studies that exist regarding their meaning and the present context.[42] In any event, the interpretation put forth here does not turn on this or that nuance associated with those words. We offer a more generic, straightforward explanation of the passage. The Christian woman's role is shaped by the arrival of the age to come (vv. 4–5, 11–12), but such an exalted position still exists within the framework of this present age (vv. 3, 6–9, 13–16).

Regarding the first set of verses, two ideas suggest the arrival of the age to come. (1) In verses 4–5, Paul undoubtedly presents the "man" and "woman" prophesying as a fulfillment of Joel 2:28 and the dawning of the promised era of the Spirit. Any attempt to minimize the force of the word "prophesy" as applied to the woman (e.g., to restrict it to teaching) does not take the text seriously enough, for the same word is used of the man. (2) Verses 11–12 make clear that in Christ, men and women have a new reciprocal relationship, one that surpasses the old domineering one in which both parties vied for power, subtly or not so subtly (cf. Gen. 3:16b).

Paul offers a disclaimer in the second set of verses (vv. 3, 6–9, 13–16), however, affirming the continuing authority structure of the relationship between man and woman, especially in the marital bond. The wife is still subordinate to her husband, symbolized by her wearing of a veil. But that this is a functional,

---

[41]Even so stalwart of an evangelical as Gordon Fee succumbs to this temptation in *The First Epistle to the Corinthians* (TNICNT; Grand Rapids: Eerdmans, 1987), 699–708.

[42]For the meaning of "head" see the two classic treatments, S. Bedale, "The Meaning of *kephalê* in the Pauline Epistles," *JTS* 5 (1954): 211–15; and Wayne Grudem, "Does *kephalê* Mean 'Source' or 'Authority Over' in Greek Literature? A Survey of 2,336 Examples," *TJ* 6 (1985): 38–59. For the meaning of "cover" and related matters, see Fee's excellent survey of the views, *The First Epistle to the Corinthians*, 508–30.

not essential, submission is made clear in the analogy of verse 3, where Christ is said to be subordinate to God. This speaks of the ongoing reality of this present age. The intersection of the two ages, therefore, results in equality and authority.

Concerning 1 Corinthians 14:34–35, we can identify the same eschatological tension. While we do not wish to downplay the complexity of the passage (Fee identifies at least four approaches to this text),[43] once again a clear-cut interpretation seems possible. The sign of the arrival of the age to come is the presence of the Spirit within the community and the accompanying ministry of prophecy, a gift applicable to both men and women (cf. 11:4–5 with 14:4–5, 29–33). It is pointless to attempt to restrict that activity to men, for that stance flies in the face of verses 29–33. The same language of the necessity for the prophets to keep "silent" (v. 30) and "subject their spirits" (v. 32) is used of women "keeping silent" (v. 34) and "subjecting themselves" (v. 34), leaving no doubt about the nature of the activity of the women—they were engaged in prophesying.

But Paul does not stop there; he offers a stricture in verses 34–35: Women must not utter prophecies ("speak," v. 34) in the setting of public worship, undoubtedly because that would entail exercising authority over men, a violation of the created order (cf. 1 Cor. 11:3; 1 Tim. 2:12–14). Here is genuine tension, but no real contradiction. Because the age to come has dawned, women possess the Spirit which, for some, involves the gift of prophecy. Nevertheless, the hierarchy initiated with Adam and Eve is still operative in this age (cf. Gen. 2–3), therefore retaining male headship over the woman, particularly in marriage. That does not mean, however, that things will stay that way at the full disclosure of the kingdom of God (cf. 1 Cor. 13:8–13).

3. Colossians 3:18–19 and Ephesians 5:22–33

These two sections, as noted earlier in this chapter, are a part of the *Haustafel*. There we noted the eschatological tension that characterizes the slave/master relationship; thus, we only need mention here that the not yet side of the ledger—"wives, submit

---

[43]Fee, *The First Epistle to the Corinthians*, 699–708.

to your husbands" (Eph. 5:22; Col. 3:18)—is balanced by the already side—"husbands, love your wives" (Eph. 5:25; Col. 3:19). The addition of the reciprocal aspect that accompanies the latter theme is indicative of the fact that the age to come has broken into the present age, generating a dialectic between authority and equality. As such, it is fully consistent with the other Pauline passages examined thus far regarding the male and female relationship in Christ.

4. 1 Timothy 2:9–15

In this passage, Paul stresses three areas in which he believes Christian women should display an attitude of submission.[44] (1) They are to show their compliant spirit by wearing modest adornment (1 Tim. 2:9–10), a standard apparently upheld by Gentiles (see Juvenal's Satire 6; Seneca, To Helvia 16:3–4), Jews (see Prov. 7:10–17; T.Reu. 5:1–5; 1 Enoch 8:1–2), and Christians (1 Peter 3:1–6) alike. This deference in dress may well reflect Paul's abhorrence of the immodest attire that characterized the prostitute priestesses of the Artemis cult in Ephesus.[45]

(2) Christian women are to refrain from teaching or exercising authority over men (vv. 11–12). Recent exegetes of this text tend to mitigate the stringency of these words by restricting their application to the subordination of wives to their husbands[46] or

---

[44]The following three points come from Pate, The Glory of Adam, 323–25.

[45]See the recent discussion of the cultural climate of such women by Sharon Hodgin Gritz, Paul, Women Teachers, and the Mother Goddess at Ephesus. A Study of 1 Timothy 2:9–15 in Light of the Religious and Cultural Milieu of the First Century (Lanham, Md.: University Press of America, 1991), 125–28.

[46]This approach rests on the assumption that the singular form of the word pair gunaiki/andros most naturally refers to a husband and wife. But Jouette M. Bassler notes that this view is not aided by any possessive pronouns ("Adam, Eve, and the Pastor: The Use of Genesis 2, 3 in the Pastoral Epistles," in Genesis 1–3 in the History of Exegesis: Intrigue in the Garden, ed. Gregory Allen Robbins [Lewiston, N.Y.: Edwin Mellen, 1988], 62); cf. also Douglas Moo, "1 Timothy 2:11–15: Meaning and Significance," TJ 1 (1980): 63–64. Moreover, as G. Engel pointed out long ago, the logical consequence of such a prohibition would still be that at least married women would be prevented from teaching in public when their husbands were present ("Let the Woman Learn in Silence," Exp.Tim. 16 [1904–5]: 189–90).

to the forbidding of interruptions of the worship services.[47] These attempts are certainly understandable but, as Jouette M. Bassler points out, they involve "reading twentieth-century sensibilities into the text, for a comprehensive prohibition of any leadership office seems clearly indicated by the words."[48] In other words, verses 11–12, like 1 Corinthians 14:33–35, seem to restrict women from uttering prophecies or authoritative teachings in the worship service in the presence of men, in keeping with the created order (Gen. 2–3).

(3) Christian women will be saved by embracing the role of motherhood, especially the pain of childbirth (vv. 13–15). These words pose a hermeneutical thicket and have generated three basic interpretations. (a) "She will be *safely kept* through childbearing," with the term *sôthêsetai* connoting physical preservation.[49] But aside from the fact that the statement is simply not true (many Christian women have not survived childbirth), this rendering stumbles because *sôzein* conveys a theological sense in the Pastorals (1 Tim. 1:15; 2:4; 4:16; 2 Tim. 1:9; 4:18; Titus 3:5), and because *dia* (*through*) is not taken in its normal instrumental sense. (b) "She will be saved through the childbearing," i.e., through the birth of Christ through Mary, the new Eve. While a messianic reading of Genesis 3:16 is possible in the context of 1 Timothy 2, nevertheless the word *teknogonias* should be translated generically ("childbearing"), not specifically ("the childbearing"). (c) "She will be saved through childbearing." Kelly accurately expresses the resulting meaning of this approach, "Her path to salvation . . . consists in accepting the role which was plainly laid down for her in Gen. iii.16 ('in pain you shall bring forth children')."[50]

---

[47]Dibelius/Conzelmann restrict the meaning of *authentein* to "domineering" rather than the broader idea of "have authority" (*The Pastoral Epistles*, trans. P. Buttolph and A. Yarbro [Hermeneia; Philadelphia: Fortress, 1972], 47). However, Moo provides substantial support showing that the term is best understood in the latter sense ("1 Timothy 2:11–15," 66–67).

[48]Bassler, "Adam, Eve and the Pastor," 48–49.

[49]See Bassler's bibliography on this view, "Adam, Eve, and the Pastor," 63–64, note 23.

[50]J. N. D. Kelly, *A Commentary on the Pastoral Epistles* (HNTC; New York: Harper & Row, 1963), 69.

Unpalatable as this may be to contemporary thought, this third view seems to be the most natural reading of the text, both grammatically and contextually. Grammatically, this translation ascribes the customary theological sense to the word *sôzein* and the normal instrumental rendering of *dia* ("through"). Moreover, it rightly translates *teknogonias* in the generic sense—"childbearing." Contextually, this interpretation best takes into account the polemics of Paul, who undoubtedly aims his comments in 1 Timothy 2:15 and 4:3–4 at the false teachers who propagated disparaging views about marriage and sex. These people were not unlike the later Gnostics, who, as Irenaeus (*Heresies*, 1.24.2) described them, declared that "marriage and the begetting of children are of Satan."[51] According to 1 Timothy 2:13–15, Christian women express their faith, love, and holiness (v. 15b) through good works (v. 10), the most significant of which is submitting to the divine plan of bearing children, painful though it is (v. 15a). Such obedience transforms the curse of Genesis 3:16 into a blessing—it brings salvation (1 Tim. 2:15).

This subordinationist emphasis in 1 Timothy 2:9–15 bespeaks of the continuing presence of this age. But this does not mean that Paul overlooks the fact that the age to come has arrived. It is eminently possible, as recent authors have suggested, that the church at Ephesus, to whom Paul wrote 1 and 2 Timothy, believed that the age to come had fully arrived and therefore championed the casting off of all sexual distinctions. Paul thus used the submission principle to correct this emancipationist misconception. Probably two major strands of thought intersected to produce this rival message. (a) This group may well have appealed to the apostle's egalitarian attitude as identified in the tradition behind 1 Corinthians 12:13; Galatians 3:28; and Colossians 3:11. (b) The espousal of realized eschatology by these people, as William Lane, Gordon Fee, and Phillip H. Towner have shown, prompted them to proclaim the full arrival of the age to come and, with it, the new creation; hence the dissolution of all social distinctions and barriers.[52]

---

[51]Ibid., 70.

[52]William L. Lane, "1 Tim. iv.1–3. An Early Instance of Over-Realized Eschatology?" *NTS* 11 (1965): 164–67; Fee, *1 and 2 Timothy*; Towner, *The Goal of Our Instruction*.

Therefore, it can be proposed that Paul, in order to counteract this situation, responds in a twofold way here. (a) He introduces the principle of submission into the eschatological scheme of things to demonstrate that the age to come has already arrived but is not yet complete. Christians continue to live in this age. (b) More than that, he roots hierarchy and subordination in creation itself, before the Fall (1 Tim. 2:13), so that even though he believes the new creation has dawned in Christ, he operates on the assumption that it, too, must follow the divinely prescribed chain of authority.

On this reading, eschatological tension continues to characterize Paul's thoughts in 1 Timothy 2:9–15. There is no need, therefore, to posit contradiction in his thinking, nor even less to attribute to someone else the authorship of the Pastoral Letters. Furthermore, to those who accept Pauline authorship of the Pastorals and who laudably and logically argue that 1 Timothy 2:9–15, as well as 1 Corinthians 11:3–16, 14:34–35, are culture-bound, it must be said that such an approach is a moot point.

For Paul, culture will always be a concomitant of this age and will only be truly improved upon when the age to come completely arrives. Until then, the relationship between male and female, like that between Jew and Gentile and slave and free, will be one of ambiguity, checkered success, and imperfect harmony. To hope for more in this world, try as one should, is to set oneself up for disappointment.

IX

PAULINE ESCHATOLOGY: SIGNS OF THE TIMES AND THE BEGINNING OF THE END

INTRODUCTION

It is only fitting that we bring this overview of Paul's thought to a close by examining the "doctrine"[1] of Pauline eschatology, in the context of the Jewish apocalyptic expectation that certain "signs of the end times" would rapidly occur before the coming of the Messiah, signaling the end of this present age and the beginning of the age to come. For Paul, because Christ's death and resurrection initiated the age to come, those cosmic and catastrophic events have already begun; but they will not be finished until the *Parousia*. The Christian, therefore, must cope with living between the two ages, regardless of how short or long that interval may be. This approach to Paul's thought rescues him from modern date-setters of the Second Coming and from prophetic crystal ball readers, who, however sincerely motivated, only bring disrepute on the Christian message and their own testimonies by anachronistically reading twentieth-century happenings back into Paul's writings. It is difficult to understand how today's "prophetic" bards can be so certain of the date of Christ's return when he himself is not (Matt. 24:36; Mark 13:32; Acts 1:7)!

---

[1]Technically speaking, we should probably refrain from using the word "doctrine" relative to Paul's teachings because the apostle does not set out in any of his letters to delineate a full-orbed statement on his beliefs. Rather, Paul's letters are occasional in nature and therefore reflect only a part of his thinking on a particular subject. However, this does not preclude using the term "doctrine" with reference to the apostle's cardinal concerns.

The aforementioned disclaimer does not imply, however, that the events accompanying the end of time were unimportant to Paul. In fact, they were important. But those eschatological occurrences were not his chief concern. What occupied his attention more than anything else was the first coming of Christ, to which Christ's return would serve as an apt epilogue. The thesis, then, of this chapter is that the signs of the times have already begun with the death and resurrection of Jesus the Messiah, but their culmination awaits the *Parousia*.

A. THEORIES OF PAULINE ESCHATOLOGY

Once it was established that eschatology was the taproot of Paul's fertile mind, scholars proceeded in two directions. Some held to the view that Pauline eschatology remained consistent in his writings, arguing that in one way or another, the overlapping of the two ages was the key to the apostle's thought.[2] This study aligns itself with that perspective,[3] and we will spell out the details relative to the signs of the time in the second half of this chapter. Others, however, claimed that Paul's eschatology developed, or even contradicted itself, as time passed. But even the scholars espousing this approach could not agree as to the specifics of that development. At least five differing interpretations surface in the literature, of which we will offer a brief critique. Our presentation follows no particular chronology of their appearance.

1. Philosophical Influence

The venerable Jewish apocalyptic scholar, R. H. Charles, popularized the theory that Paul's eschatology changed from a

---

[2]See, for example, H. A. A. Kennedy, *St. Paul's Conceptions of the Last Things* (London: Hodder and Stoughton, 1904); Gerhardus Vos, *The Pauline Eschatology* (Grand Rapids: Eerdmans, 1952); Andrew Lincoln, *Paradise Now and Not Yet* (SNTSMS 43; Cambridge: University Press, 1981); George Ladd, *A New Testament Theology* (Grand Rapids: Eerdmans, 1974), 550–70.

[3]See also my works, *Adam Christology as the Exegetical and Theological Substructure of 2 Corinthians 4:7–5:21* (Lanham, Md.: University Press of America, 1991) and *The Glory of Adam and the Afflictions of the Righteous: Pauline Suffering in Context* (New York: Edwin Mellen, 1993), for a more extended treatment of the subject.

Jewish to a Hellenistic understanding of the end times and the life to come. According to him, Paul's earlier Jewish belief in the future resurrection of the body (1 Thess. 4:13–18) changed first to a Jewish-Hellenistic perspective (which combined resurrection body with immortal soul to equal somatic immortality; 1 Cor. 15:42–58; 2 Cor. 5:1–10), and then to the pure Greek hope of the immortality of the soul at death, excluding any future resurrection body (Phil. 1:21).[4]

Charles' once popular theory has fallen on hard times, for at least three reasons. (1) Scholars have recognized the theory for what it was—the imposing of nineteenth-century evolutionary thought on the Pauline material.[5] (2) Hengel's magnificent work on the relationship between Judaism and Hellenism in the first centuries B.C.E. and C.E. has shown an interpenetration between the two, thus ruling out a supposed linear development from Judaism to Hellenism in the self-understanding of the early church.[6] (3) Both the resurrection of the body and the immortality of the soul have been recognized as persisting from the beginning to the end of the apostle's letters.[7]

2. Circumstantial Change

Other scholars attributed development in Paul's eschatology to a change in circumstances, usually connected with the delay of the *Parousia* or the death of Christians before the *Parousia*. In short, these two events (or non-event in the first instance) caused Paul to abandon his belief in the imminent return of Christ. Regarding the delay of the *Parousia*, the typical argument claims

---

[4]R. H. Charles, *A Critical History of the Doctrine of a Future Life in Israel, in Judaism and in Christianity* (London: Black, 1899).

[5]See Pate, *Adam Christology*, chap. 1, for a more thorough refutation of the developmental approach concerning Pauline eschatology in general and 2 Corinthians 5:1–10 in particular. Compare also Lincoln, *Paradise Now and Not Yet*, 181–84.

[6]Martin Hengel, *Hellenism and Judaism*, 2 vols. (Philadelphia: Fortress, 1974). Lincoln has used Hengel's insights with regard to Pauline eschatology in his *Paradise Now and Not Yet*.

[7]See the insightful article by Ben Meyer, "Did Paul's View of the Resurrection of the Dead Undergo Development?" *JTS* 47 (1986): 363–87.

that in his early letters, Paul had a burning desire for the *Parousia*; but in Colossians, Ephesians, and the Pastorals that expectation waned, so that the thought of the Lord's return was only of incidental value to him.[8] In other words, the already/not yet tension has given way therein to an over-realized eschatology.

But the recent works of Peter O'Brien and Andrew Lincoln have rendered this hypothesis inadequate for Colossians. These two authors have carefully demonstrated that Paul's eschatological tension remains intact in that letter. Both the "not yet" (futurist) aspect (Col. 1:22, 29; 3:1–11) and the "already" (realized) aspect (1:9–13; 2:8–15) are present.[9] Clinton Arnold has done the same for Ephesians (cf. Eph. 1:15–21 [the already aspect] with 6:10–20 [the not yet aspect]).[10] And the same can now be said of the Pastorals, as Gordon Fee and Phillip H. Towner have shown (see especially 2 Tim. 1:10; Titus 2:11–14; 3:4–6, where both elements are operative).[11] That is to say, the burning desire for the *Parousia* never recedes in Paul's letters. Furthermore, scholars no longer labor under the assumption that the delay of the *Parousia* wrought havoc with the confidence of Paul and the early church. Writing on this subject as it pertains to Romans 13:10–14, C. E. B. Cranfield's insights deserve quoting in full:

> What is the meaning of this *Naherwartung* (i.e., "near-expectation")? It is well known that very many scholars regard it as an assured result that the primitive Church was convinced that the End would certainly occur within, at the most, a few decades, and that its conviction has been refuted by the indisputable fact of nineteen hundred years of subsequent history. The true explanation, we believe, is rather that the

---

[8]The classic expression of this approach is C. H. Dodd's, "The Mind of Paul: II," in *New Testament Studies* (Manchester: University Press, 1953), 112–13.

[9]Peter O'Brien, *Colossians, Philemon* (WBC 44; Waco, Tex.: Word, 1982), xlvi–xlvii, and the commentary that follows on 1:22, 28; 3:1–11; Lincoln, *Paradise Now and Not Yet*, 122–34.

[10]Clinton E. Arnold, *Ephesians: Power and Magic: The Concept of Power in Ephesians in Light of its Historical Setting* (SNTSMS 63, Cambridge: University Press, 1989), 103–22, 143.

[11]Gordon Fee, *1 and 2 Timothy, Titus* (Peabody, Mass.: Hendrickson, 1988), 19–20; Philip H. Towner, *The Goal of Our Instruction: The Structure of Theology and Ethics in the Pastoral Epistles* (JSNT Supp.Ser. 34; Sheffield: JSOT Press, 1989), 10–11, 69.

primitive Church was convinced that the ministry of Jesus had ushered in the last days, the End-time. History's supreme events had taken place in the ministry, death, resurrection and ascension of the Messiah. There was now no question of another chapter's being added which could in any way effectively go back upon what had been written in that final chapter. All that subsequent history could add, whether it should last for few years or for many, must be of the nature of an epilogue. The completeness, the decisiveness, the finality, of what had already been wrought had stamped it indelibly with this status of something added after the conclusion of the final chapter. As the interval provided by God's patience in order to give men time to hear the gospel and to make the decision of faith, its continuance depending entirely upon God's patience, it could hardly be properly characterized otherwise than as "short time." However long it should continue, it could never be more than this; and this present age, which Paul refers to as "the night," could never again have a higher status than that of something "far spent." Henceforward "the day" would always be imminent, until it should finally break.[12]

The other circumstance supposedly causing Paul to abandon the hope of the *Parousia* was the death of Christians before that event. C. L. Mearns, for instance, argues that Paul's eschatological teaching underwent a radical shift prior to the writing of the Thessalonian letters.[13] He insists that before writing 1 Thessalonians, Paul's teaching was thoroughly immersed in realized eschatology. But when some of the Christian believers died, a futuristic eschatology entered his thought. L. Joseph Kreitzer rightly criticizes this theory on three grounds. (1) Mearns assumes without further ado that Paul's original teaching at Thessalonica did not include a resurrection for dead believers. (2) He also assumes that the realized and futuristic elements were not present in Paul's original teaching, but developed later. (3) Mearns' theory naively presumes that Paul had little or no contact with the reality of Christians dying prior to

---

[12]Cranfield, *Romans IX–XVI* (ICC; Edinburgh: T. & T. Clark, 1977), 683.

[13]C. L. Mearns, "Early Eschatological Development in Paul: The Evidence of I and II Thessalonians," *NTS* 27 (1980–81): 137–58.

writing 1 Thessalonians. It stretches the imagination to say that Paul, who had already ministered for at least fifteen years within various Christian communities before penning that letter, did not encounter the death of any Christian.[14]

3. Authorial Difference

Many Pauline interpreters accepting a fundamental change in perspective between the apostle's earlier and later writings like that just delineated, attribute that divergence to differences in authorship: Paul wrote the former; students or distant admirers of his theology wrote the latter.[15] Once again the counter-arguments highlighted in the last point forcefully show the constancy of the two-age structure throughout the Pauline literature, reinforcing the apostle's authorship of those letters.

Some scholars see a special problem relative to this issue regarding 1 and 2 Thessalonians. They allege that an essential difference can be detected between the two: 1 Thessalonians portrays the *Parousia* as imminent but 2 Thessalonians prescribes certain events or signs of the time that must occur before the *Parousia* can happen. From this they conclude that Paul did not write 2 Thessalonians. However, it is more likely that, in Paul's mind, because the signs of the times had already begun (*à la* 2 Thessalonians), the *Parousia* of Christ was truly imminent (*à la* 1 Thessalonians).[16]

4. Mystical Reinterpretation

In our first chapter, we looked at Schweitzer's reinterpretation of the *Parousia* in terms of the believer's mystical union with

---

[14]L. Joseph Kreitzer, *Jesus and God in Paul's Eschatology* (JSNT Supp.Ser 19; Sheffield: JSOT Press, 1987), 177–79.

[15]The classic defense of this position would include Eduard Lohse, *Colossians and Philemon* (Hermeneia; Philadelphia: Fortress, 1971), 84–91; Andrew Lincoln, *Ephesians* (WBC 42; Waco, Tex.: Word, 1990), lix-lxxiii; Martin Dibelius/Hans Conzelman, *The Pastoral Epistles*, trans. P. Buttolph and A. Yarbro (Hermeneia; Philadelphia: Fortress, 1972), 8–10.

[16]Charles A. Wanamaker provides a useful bibliography of those advocating different authorship for 1 and 2 Thessalonians, along with a thorough refutation of the view based on the presence of both imminence and the signs of the times in both epistles (*The Epistles to the Thessalonians* [NIGTC; Grand Rapids: Eerdmans, 1990], 17–18).

Christ. According to him, because of the delay of the *Parousia*, Paul abandoned hope of a future return of Christ and subsequent resurrection of believers, replacing it with the belief that the elect have been "risen-along-with-Christ, even though they still have the external seeming of natural man."[17] In other words, the resurrection of the end time has already happened to Christians through their union with Christ. There is therefore no real need in Paul's thinking for a future *Parousia*.

Despite the brilliance and coherence of Schweitzer's thesis, there are at least two difficulties with his view. (1) As Richard Hays notes, Schweitzer's literalistic conceptualization of Christ-mysticism is naive. Schweitzer's epistemology, like many in his time, dichotomized metaphor and reality. Because he interpreted metaphor as merely an ineffective symbol, with no participation in the reality it represented, Schweitzer wrongly concluded that dying and rising with Christ was therefore non-metaphorical (i.e., literal).[18]

(2) Schweitzer's focus on consistent (futurist) eschatology, which interprets Paul to have abandoned the *Parousia* because of its delay, is too exclusivistic. It neglects the presence of inaugurated eschatology in Paul's writings. J. C. Beker catches the significance of the weakness of this position:

> If future eschatology were such a decisive matter, the delay of the *Parousia* would have destroyed the Christian faith.... In fact, Paul can adjust himself remarkably well to the delay of the Parousia . . . whereas he expects to be alive at the Parousia in 1 Thess. 4:15 and 1 Cor. 15:50–52, he seems to contemplate his death before its occurrence in Phil. 1:20 and possibly in 2 Cor. 5:1–11 (cf. 2 Cor. 1:9). Even so, he can write in what was one of his last letters, "Salvation is nearer to us now than when we first believed" (Rom. 13:11; cf. Phil. 4:4). In other words, he persists in imminent expectation, notwithstanding his awareness of the delay of the Parousia.[19]

---

[17] Albert Schweitzer, *The Mysticism of Paul the Apostle*, trans. William Montgomery (New York: Henry Holt, 1931), 112.

[18] Richard B. Hays, *The Faith of Jesus Christ: An Investigation of the Narrative Substructure of Galatians 3:1–4:11* (SBLDS 56; Chico, Calif.: Scholars Press, 1983), 48.

[19] J. C. Beker, *Paul the Apostle: The Triumph of God in Life and Thought* (Philadelphia: Fortress, 1980), 177–78.

5. Demythological Hermeneutics

The term *demythologize* is synonymous with the existential approach of Rudolf Bultmann, whose ambitious goal was to cut through the "myths" of the New Testament in order to get at the core of truth residing therein. Achieving that, moderns can then discover what the Bible says about being authentic human beings. With regards to the Pauline *corpus*, the interpreter must recognize that Paul's Jewish apocalypticism is a mythical construction, which we should not take at face value. Bultmann writes:

> This mythological method of representation is foreign to modern man, whose thinking is determined by science to whatever extent, if any, he himself actively participates in scientific research and understands its methods. We have learned the meaninglessness of speaking about "above" and "below" in the universe. We can no longer accept the thought of Christ coming on the clouds of heaven.[20]

In Bultmann's opinion, Paul himself demonstrates gradual development in his thought on the subject and takes steps toward demythologizing the *Parousia* hope. He abandons it for the Hellenistic idea of the immortality of the soul.

Though at one time scholarship was enthusiastic about Bultmann's program, few today accept it wholesale. (1) It wrongly foisted onto the New Testament and Paul Heideggarian existentialism. (2) It suffers from the false assumption that the scientific method is the only criterion for measuring reality, an evaluation with which many modern scientists themselves would feel uncomfortable. (3) As Beker observes, Bultmann's removal of apocalypticism from Paul's interpretation of the Christ-event actually distorted the gospel Bultmann claimed to love.[21]

The foregoing discussion has demonstrated the inadequacy of trying to identify substantial development in Paul's eschatology. A more promising approach can be found in identifying the eschatological tension in his literature, a task to which this book

---

[20]Rudolf Bultmann, "The Christian Hope and the Problem of Demythologizing," *ExpT* 65 (1953–54): 229.

[21]Beker, *Paul the Apostle*, 18.

has been devoted. It remains now to trace the influence of the overlapping of the two ages on Paul's understanding of the signs of the end times.

B. TOPICS OF PAULINE ESCHATOLOGY: THE SIGNS OF THE TIMES

The Old Testament and early Judaism associated the appearance of the age to come or the kingdom of God to earth with a number of events: the rise of the Antichrist, the messianic woes, apostasy of many of God's people, the kingdom of Messiah and God, the resurrection of the body by God's Spirit, the judgment of the righteous and wicked, cosmic disturbances and a new creation, a new temple, Israel's regathering to God and her land, and eternal life. All of this was subsumed under the category of the arrival of the Day of the Lord. We do not wish to give the impression that all of these attendant circumstances were treated with equal interest in the pertinent Jewish writings; in actuality some were of more concern to this or that author than others. But, in general, these events were equated with the signs of the times—hence their reoccurrence in a number of Jewish works. For Paul, these happenings fall under the rubric of the already/not yet eschatological tension. What we will say here necessarily reduplicates some of the points made earlier in this study.

1. The Rise of the Antichrist

Closely associated with the signs of the end is the figure of Antichrist, who was expected to arrive on the world scene in the last days to do battle with God and his people. Though the name *Antichrist* is the product of Christian thought, the idea of an end-time anti-God personage has its roots in the Old Testament, especially Ezekiel 38–39. There Gog of the land of Magog is identified as the leader of the forces of evil in opposition to God. Hermann Gunkel traces the concept even further back to the primeval past, to the supposed conflict between God and the monster chaos, a creature given various names: e.g., dragon (Job 7:12; Ps. 74:13; Isa. 51:9; Ezek. 2:3; 32:2); Leviathan (Job 40:15–24; Pss. 74:14; 104:26; Isa. 27:1); Rahab (Job 9:13; 26:12; Ps. 89:10; Isa. 30:7; 51:9); serpent (Job 26:13; Isa. 27:1; Amos 9:3); Tehom/Tiamat (Gen. 1:2,

6; Ps. 74:13).[22] Both of these notions, an end-time anti-God personage and a primeval chaotic beast, combined to produce the multivalent figure of the Antichrist. H. H. Rowley describes him in this manner: "Whether regarded as a mere man or as the incarnation of this demonic spirit, we have the figure of a powerful king or ruler, subduing many beneath his evil sway, filled with the sense of his own importance, setting himself up to be equal with God, claiming divine honours, and trampling on the saints."[23] References to this malevolent force abound.[24]

The key Pauline text on the Antichrist is 2 Thessalonians 2:3–12, where he is called "the man of lawlessness," a personage taken from Daniel 7 and 11. This derivation becomes transparent through three points of comparison: (1) like the beast in Daniel 7:8; 11:35–36, the man of lawlessness arrogates to himself divine status, even to the point of occupying the temple of God (cf. 2 Thess. 2:4 with the desecration of the temple described in Dan. 11:31); (2) both are characterized as being lawless (*anomias*, 2 Thess. 2:3; *anomountes*, Dan. 11:32); (3) both are revealed at a propitious time (*apokaluphthênai kairô*, 2 Thess. 2:6; *apokaluphthênai kairou*, Dan. 11:35). In 2 Thessalonians 2, however, the man of lawlessness takes on the added feature of being a parody of Christ: he will have a wondrous *Parousia* like Christ (cf. v. 9 with v. 8). He is, in the truest sense, the anti-Christ.

According to Paul, the Antichrist or man of lawlessness has not yet fully appeared on the human scene (2 Thess. 2:3–6, 8–12). But this is not the whole story, for the mystery and the spirit of antichrist has already been unleashed on the world, "For the secret power of lawlessness is already at work" (v. 7). The only force preventing the Antichrist from making his "grand" entry is "the one who now holds it back" (v. 7), whatever or whoever that

---

[22]Hermann Gunkel, *Schöpfung und Chaos in Urzeit und Endzeit* (Göttingen: Vandenhoeck and Ruprecht, 1988), 41–69.

[23]H. H. Rowley, *The Relevance of Apocalyptic, A Study of Jewish and Christian Apocalypses from Daniel to the Revelation* (London and Redhill: Lutterworth Press, 1947), 146 (for a discussion of the origin of the idea of Antichrist, see p. 30).

[24]See Dan. 7:8, 25; 11:36, 40–41, 45; *As.Moses* 8:1; *Pss.Sol.* 2:29; *4 Ezra* 5:6; *T.Isaac* 6:1; *T.Jud.* 25:3; *T.Dan.* 5:4; *Sib.Oracles* II:63, 75; 2 Thess. 2:3–12; 1 John 4:3 (cf. Mark 13:22 [Matt. 24:24]); Rev. 11:7, 13; 13:2, 5, 7.

may be.[25] This sense of realized eschatology blended with futurist eschatology is also at work in a passage like 1 John 4:3: "every spirit that does not acknowledge Jesus is not from God. This is the spirit of the antichrist, which you have heard is coming and even now is already in the world." A similar idea can be detected in Jesus' warning in the Olivet Discourse regarding the appearances of "false Christs," whose purposes will be to deceive people, even the elect of God (Matt. 24:23–24/Mark 13:21–22). Paul probably believed that the unleashing of the Antichrist was in some way connected with the cross of Christ (cf. 1 Cor. 2:6–8; 15:55–57; Eph. 6:10–16 with Luke 10:17–19; Col. 2:14; Rev. 12:7–13; see also *Jub.* 5:10f.; *1 Enoch* 16:1; *1QM* 1; *1QS* 3–4).

2. The Messianic Woes

The messianic woes refer to the time of great sorrow and tribulation that will come on God's people immediately prior to the coming of the Messiah. The concept is adumbrated in the Old Testament, in association with the Day of Yahweh (e.g., Amos 5:16–20; Isa. 24:17–23; Dan. 12:1; Joel 2:1–11, 28–32; Zeph. 1:14–2:3), and developed in Jewish apocalypticism (*4 Ezra* 7:37; *Jub.* 23:11; 24:3; *2 Bar.* 55:6; *1 Enoch* 80:4–5). However, the term *messianic woes* itself does not occur until the writing of the Talmud (e.g., *b.Shab.* 118a; *b.Pes.* 118a).

We have elsewhere analyzed the relationship of the messianic woes to Paul's thinking, where we examined the key Pauline texts dealing with the topic of suffering (Rom. 5:1–11; 1 Cor. 15; 2 Cor. 4:7–5:21; 12:1–10; Gal. 3:26–29; 4:26; 6:17; Eph. 1:15–23; 3:13; 2 Thess. 2:1–12; 1 Tim. 2:1–15; 2 Tim. 2:10–12). In doing so, three facts emerged for each passage. (1) Each one juxtaposes the themes of suffering and glory. (2) Such a twofold combination stems from Paul's belief that the two ages overlap for the Christian. Thus, on the one hand, because believers share an intimate union with the cross of Christ, the suffering and death he experienced as the culmination of the messianic woes now characterize their suffering. This is the not yet side of Paul's eschatology. On the other hand, because believers also share an

---

[25]We have attempted to make the case for identifying the restrainer as Michael, the archangel, (see Pate, *The Glory of Adam*, 308–9).

intimate union with the resurrection of Christ, the heavenly glory he now possesses belongs to them as well. This is the already side of Paul's eschatology. Yet that glory is invisible, being perceptible only to the eye of faith (see Rom. 8:24–25; 1 Cor. 2:8–16; 2 Cor. 4:17–18). Only at the *Parousia* will that glory be publicly manifested (cf. Phil. 3:20–21; Col. 3:1–4).[26] Furthermore, this twofold theme of suffering and glory is understood by Paul and his Jewish contemporaries to be Adamic in nature. That is, Adam's lost glory will be restored in the age to come to those who suffer for righteousness' sake in this age. That goal is already in the process of being realized. (3) Each of the Pauline passages on suffering gives evidence that the apostle expects that all Christians will suffer, however that may be defined.[27]

3. Apostasy

Jewish apocalypticism maintained that the end of time would witness a large scale falling away from the faith by the people of God (*Jub.* 23:14–23; *4 Ezra* 5:1–13; *1 Enoch* 91:3–10; 93:8–10; *1QpHab* 2:1; Matt. 24:12/Mark 13:5, 22a/Luke 21:6). Paul, too, believed as much. At least three of his letters attest to that belief, each of which is imprinted by his understanding that the two ages are in transition: 2 Thessalonians 2:3–12 (cf. 1 Thess. 2:14b–17); 1 Timothy 4:1–5; 2 Timothy 3:1–5 (cf. 1 Tim. 1:6–7, 19–20; 2 Tim. 2:18; 3:6); and Galatians 1:6–10.

As mentioned in connection with the Antichrist, 2 Thessalonians 2:3–12 is stamped by the already/not yet eschatological tension. This applies equally to the "apostasy"(v. 3, pers. tr.). The day is coming, says the apostle, when people will believe the lie of the man of lawlessness and refuse to be saved. God himself will permit that delusion to dupe many. That lawlessness has already begun (v. 7). It is probable that Paul had

---

[26]Pate, *The Glory of Adam*. It is debatable whether Paul thought that the church would go through the Great Tribulation. We only suggest here that the apostle believed that Christian suffering has been infused with eschatological meaning in light of the cross.

[27]Suffering apparently meant different things to Paul: e.g., persecution (Rom. 8:36–39), the trials of life (Rom. 5:2–5; 2 Cor. 4:17–18), spiritual struggle resulting from the tension between the two ages within the believer (Rom. 7:14–25), and ecological imbalance (Rom. 8:19–22).

something specific in mind with reference to the present work of lawlessness; 1 Thessalonians 2:14b–17 may be the key—"the Jews . . . killed the Lord Jesus and . . . drove us out . . . in their effort to keep us from speaking to the Gentiles so that they may be saved. In this way they always heap up their sins to the limit. The wrath of God has come upon them at last." What Paul refers to here is not ethnic resentment toward his countrymen but eschatological judgment. The Jews, the supposed people of God of old, have, in rejecting their Messiah and his messengers like Paul, become participants in the apostasy of the last days, which is already at work.

First Timothy 4:1–5 and 2 Timothy 3:1–5 bear this out. Both passages speak of the coming religious apostasy in the last days (cf. 1 Tim. 4:1, "some will abandon the faith"; 2 Tim. 3:5, "having a form of godliness but denying its power"). That this event is already in progress is evident in the way Paul perceives his opponents as having succumbed to spiritual lawlessness (see 1 Tim. 1:6–7, 19–20; 2 Tim. 2:18; 3:6).

Galatians 1:6–10 continues in the same vein of thought. Paul signals this background with his reference to "the present evil age" (v. 4). The Galatians' temptation to embrace the rival "gospel" of Paul's opponents in Galatia, the Judaizers, sounds like the deception that was expected to take hold of the professing people of God during the messianic woes (cf. Mark 13:22; 2 Thess. 2:9). In fact, the word Paul uses in Galatians 1:6, "deserting" (*metathithesthe*), is used in the LXX to refer to religious apostasy (*Ecclus.* 6:9; 2 *Macc.* 7:24; cf. Josephus, *Ant.* 20:38; *Life* 195). Also, the word "quickly" (*tacheôs*) in Galatians 1:6 approaches the status of a *technicus terminus* for the quickness with which the messianic woes will give way to the *Parousia* (see 2 Thess. 2:2; Rev. 1:1; 2:16; 3:11; 22:7, 12, 20). Moreover, the anathema Paul pronounces on his opponents who were trying to deceive the Galatians (1:8–9) has an eschatological ring to it, much like the divine wrath that was expected to fall on the false prophets and false Christs at the *Parousia* (see Mark 13:24; 1 Thess. 5:9; 2 Thess. 2:8).[28]

---

[28]As Judith M. Gundry Volf's work shows, one need not conclude from this that genuine Christians will apostasize or lose their salvation (see her *Paul and Perseverance: Staying in and Falling Away* (Louisville, Ky.: Westminster/John Knox, 1990).

4. Kingdom of Messiah and God

In light of all that has been said in this work, it seems superfluous to show that the intersection of the two ages colors Paul's thinking about the kingdom of Messiah and God (cf. Isa. 40–66; Dan. 2:44; *1 Enoch* 6–36; 83–90; *Sib.Oracles III* 652–656; *2 Bar.* 39–40; *4 Ezra* 7). But in order to round out the discussion, we revisit the topic. As chapter 2 indicated, the establishment of the messianic kingdom at the resurrection of Christ reflects the already aspect of Pauline eschatology, while the kingdom of God proper represents the not yet aspect. The term "kingdom" (*basileia*) with reference to Christ and/or God occurs twelve times in Paul's writings. If the overlapping of the two ages is truly at work in this aspect of Paul's thought, then we should expect to find both present and future tenses attached to that reality. That, in fact, is the case, as the following chart indicates:

	Kingdom Of:	Tense:
Romans 14:17	God	Present
1 Corinthians 4:20	God	Present
1 Corinthians 6:9–10	God (twice)	Future
1 Corinthians 15:24	Christ/God	Present and future
1 Corinthians 15:50	God	Future
Galatians 5:21	God	Future
Ephesians 5:5	Christ/God	Future
Colossians 1:13	Christ	Present
Colossians 4:11	God	Present
1 Thessalonians 2:2	God	Future
2 Thessalonians 1:5	God	Future

Three observations emerge. (1) The kingdom of Christ/God is both present and future, already here and not yet complete. (2) Christ and God are, in at least two instances, interchanged, suggesting equality of deity between them. (3) First Corinthians 15:24, as we saw earlier in this work, gives the most precise description of the exact relationship between the kingdoms of Christ and God—the interim messianic kingdom begun at the resurrection will one day give way to the eternal kingdom of God.[29]

5. Resurrection of the Body by the Spirit

Judaism, as noted early on in this study, assigned the resurrection of the body and the coming of the Spirit to the end of time (see Ezek. 37; Dan. 12:1–3; 1 Enoch 62:15; 2 Enoch 22:8; 4 Ezra 2:39, 45). According to Paul, those realities are both present and future. A believer's spiritual resurrection will culminate in a physical resurrection—both based on the resurrection of Jesus Messiah. Three passages highlight these themes in Paul: Romans 8:9–11; Ephesians 1–2; 1 Corinthians 15.

Romans 8:9–11 juxtaposes spiritual and physical resurrections with reference to the believer. In verses 9–10, Paul asserts that a Christian by definition possesses the Spirit, who is the one who raised the believer from spiritual death to life. This is the already side of eschatology. According to verse 11, this will conclude one day with the Christian's resurrection body, the not yet aspect of eschatology. Both of these are based on the prior resurrection of Christ (v. 11).

Ephesians 1–2 says much the same thing. According to 2:1–6, the Christian has been spiritually raised up to the heavenly realms and is enthroned with Christ, thanks to Jesus' own resurrection, the already aspect of the age to come. But the age to come is not yet finished, for the presence of the Spirit within the believer is only the deposit or down payment of the resurrection body (1:13–14).

First Corinthians 15 repeats the pattern. In verse 45, Christ is characterized as the "life-giving Spirit" by virtue of his resurrection (v. 20). With 3:16 and 6:16, this must minimally refer to the dispensing of the Spirit to the believer at conversion, the reception of which constitutes a spiritual resurrection. But the age to

---

[29]For the debate over whether or not 1 Corinthians 15:20–28 envisions a temporary millennial kingdom on earth, see Kreitzer's handling of the issue, *Jesus and God in Paul's Eschatology*, chap. 3. It seems to us that Paul does not actually touch on the question anywhere in his writings, not that he did not subscribe to the belief. Revelation 20:1–6 seems relatively clear about the future existence of such an interval kingdom on earth.

come has not yet fully arrived (see 15:50–54, which predicts the believer's glorious resurrection body).

6. Judgment of the Righteous and the Wicked

Although Paul does not devote extended treatment to the theme of judgment in his writings, it is undeniably present (cf. Dan. 12:1–3; *1 Enoch* 10:8–9; *2 Enoch* 65:6; *4 Ezra* 12:33–34) under two categories: the justification of the saved and the wrath of God on the lost. Once again the overlapping of the two ages shapes his thinking. The saved have already been declared righteous in Christ and found to be not guilty (Rom. 3:21–26; 5:1; 8:1, 33, 34; 2 Cor. 5:21; 1 Thess. 1:10; 5:9). Yet they still must appear before the judgment seat of Christ/God to have their works evaluated for rewards or lack thereof (Rom. 14:10; 1 Cor. 3:12–15; 2 Cor. 5:10; Gal. 5:5; cf. Rom. 2:7, 10).

This combination of futurist and realized eschatology also impacts the lost. They will appear one day before God as recipients of divine eternal wrath (Rom. 2:5, 8, 19; 9:22), which has already begun to impinge upon their lives (Rom. 1:18; 4:15; 1 Thess. 2:16). They still have opportunity, however, to join the ranks of believers by faith in Christ (Eph. 2:3).

7. New Creation

The aspiration for a new creation runs deep in Judaism (Isa. 11:6–8; 65:17, 22; Ezek. 34:25–27; *Jub.* 1:29; *1 Enoch* 91:16; *Sib.Oracles III* 43, 431, 690; *4 Ezra* 6:1–6; *2 Bar.* 3:7; see also 2 Peter 3:10–13; cf. Rev. 21–22 with Gen. 1–3). Because we have dealt with this in chapter 2, we need only recall here that, for Paul, the new creation has already broken into this present age through Christ (2 Cor. 5:17), but its consummation awaits the *Parousia* (Rom. 8:19–23; cf. Eph. 1:10; Phil. 2:9–11; Col. 1:20).

8. New Temple

Another event associated with the end time in Jewish thinking is the heavenly, new temple descended to earth (Isa. 54:11–12; 60:1–22; Ezek. 40–48; Hag. 2:7; Zech. 2:6–13; *1 Enoch* 90; *2 Bar.* 4:3; 32:2–4; *4 Ezra* 7:26; 8:52, 53; 10:44–59; 13:36; see also

Gal. 4:26; Heb. 12:22; Rev. 3:12; 21:2, 10). For Paul, that temple has arrived in the form of the church of Jesus Messiah, whose stones are individual believers and whose makeup is the spiritual habitation of God (1 Cor. 3:16; 6:19; 2 Cor. 6:16–18; Eph. 2:19–22; cf. 1 Peter 2:5). Yet that temple is not yet complete; it is still growing (Eph. 2:21; cf. also 2 Cor. 5:1–2).

9. The Regathering of Israel

Another event associated with the signs of the times in Judaism was the regathering of Israel to final salvation (Isa. 51:5; 60:11; Dan. 7:27; Zech. 8:23; *Sib.Oracles III* 195; *T.Ben.* 9:2; 10:5; *T.Levi* 18:9). That Paul felt this day, distant though it might be, would happen is clear from Romans 11:12–32, a passage envisioning the future salvation of national Israel. But the present remnant of Israel, the Jews who respond faithfully to God by accepting Jesus Messiah, constitutes spiritual Israel, and as such is a foreshadowing of the future salvation of the nation (11:1–6).

10. Life After Death/Eternal Life

Life after death in the Old Testament is, at best, only intimated; it is not a well-defined concept. In the patriarchal period, the phrase that adumbrates the after-life is "he was gathered to his fathers," suggesting some sort of post-mortem existence. In 1 Samuel 28:3–14, Samuel's appearance after death as a shadowy figure gives rise to the notion that life in Sheol, the abode of the dead, was a mere shadow or shade of a person's earthly existence (cf. Ps. 139:8; Eccl. 9:5, 10; Isa. 7:11; Amos 8:2). It is only with Isaiah 24–27 and Daniel 12:1–3 that a fuller picture emerges—life beyond the grave will involve a future resurrection and judgment. In the intertestamental period, Judaism developed a concept of the intermediate state, a place where the souls of the departed await the resurrection and the final judgment. Sheol becomes a preliminary place of rewards and judgments, which is a foretaste of the final assize (*4 Ezra* 7:75, 78, 80, 87; *1 Enoch* 5:5–7; *T.Asher* 6:5–6; *2 Enoch* 23:4–5; 49:2; 58:5–6; *2 Bar.* 21:23; 23:5; 48:6; 52:2; 83:17). The intermediate state is divided up into two compartments: Hell or *Gehenna*, the abode of the wicked (*1 Enoch* 27:1; 48:9; *2 Bar.* 85:12, 13; *4 Ezra* 7:36)—

named after the Valley of Hinnom, the garbage dump outside Jerusalem that always smoldered with fire—and Paradise, the abode of the righteous (4 Ezra 4:36; 2 Enoch 42:3; Apoc.Moses 37:5; 1 Enoch 70:4; T.Ab. 20).

For the apostle Paul, the death and resurrection of Jesus Messiah greatly clarifies the idea of life beyond the grave (2 Tim. 1:10). Second Corinthians 5:1–10 is particularly helpful on the subject of the intermediate state. This text intertwines the already/not yet time frames of the two ages. Verses 1–5 highlight the not yet aspect; the age to come has not yet fully come. That will only happen at the Parousia, at which time the believer will be clothed with the glorious resurrection body. The presence of the Spirit in the believer is proof positive that this hope will be actualized. Verses 6–10 highlight the already aspect. Because of Christ's resurrection, the believer goes immediately into the presence of the Lord at the time of death to enjoy the bliss of heaven. But because even the intermediate state is still under the influence of this age, the Christian, before the Parousia,[30] will exist as a disembodied soul (cf. Phil. 1:21).

11. The Day of the Lord

The Day of the Lord is a standard feature in Jewish eschatological expectations, and it serves as an appropriate conclusion to this discussion of the signs of the times. In the Old Testament, the Day of the Lord designated, among other things, the final visitation of God to establish his kingdom, delivering the righteous and judging the wicked (Joel 3:1; Zeph. 1:14). In the New

---

[30]We should note here that premillennialists are divided in their understanding of the return of the Lord. Dispensationalists believe it will occur in two stages: a secret rapture of the church to heaven before the great tribulation period (1 Thess. 4:13–18) and, seven years later, the Second Coming of Christ to earth in glory (the Parousia). Post-tribulationists merge the two events together, holding that there will be only one return of Christ and that will be public, not secret. The biblical data is inconclusive on the matter and therefore should not occasion division in the body of Christ. Yet, we do find it interesting that in Jewish literature there are a number of reported instances of the righteous being caught up to heaven as a proleptic experience of the restoration of Paradise (cf. 2 Cor. 12:1–10; see Pate, The Glory of Adam, 112–27). This gives added weight to the dispensationalist perspective.

Testament as well as in Judaism, the term is an expression for the arrival of the age to come, which will terminate this present age. It will not be a single day, but a period of the climactic outworking of the divine plan (Acts 2:20; 1 Thess. 5:2; 2 Thess. 2:2; 2 Peter 3:10). Alongside the Day of the Lord in Paul's writings is "the day of Christ," referring to the same basic concept and elevating Jesus to the status of Yahweh (1 Cor. 1:8; Phil. 1:6, 10; 2:16; 2 Thess. 1:10; 2 Tim. 1:8); it signifies that in his ministry that day has already dawned. Related terms to these two are the "last days" (Acts 2:17; 2 Tim. 3:1; Heb. 1:2; James 5:3; 2 Peter 3:3; cf. 1 Tim. 4:1) and "the last hour" (1 John 2:18), both of which make clear that the end time has broken into this present age, beginning with the death and resurrection of Christ. All of the foregoing terms demonstrate that in early Christianity and in Paul, the age to come has already begun, though it is not yet complete. The Christian therefore lives in the intersection of the two. Or, as Paul put it so well in 1 Corinthians 10:11, Christians are the ones "on whom the ends of the ages have come" (pers. tr.).

CONCLUSION

Perhaps the most apt way to conclude this primer on Paul is to comment on some of the potential criticisms my Pauline colleagues might raise concerning the approach taken here. Three problems come to mind. (1) It can be argued that the dominance of the Jewish background championed in this work, especially the apocalyptic notion of the two ages, is debatable. In particular, many interpreters of Paul, past and present, prefer to root the apostle in Greco-Roman philosophical circles (e.g., Paul the Socratic, Paul the Platonist, Paul the Stoic). There is something to be said for this viewpoint, especially since Paul did not live in a vacuum. His world was undeniably influenced by Greek and Roman thinking. After all, he was a Roman citizen who spoke Greek. But the question is: Which of the two spheres of influence impacted the apostle's thought more, Hellenism or Judaism? Even after taking into account the interpenetration of these two movements in Paul's day, in our opinion, it is the Old Testament and the Jewish faith, albeit often expressed in Greek categories, that provide the strongest influence on his writings.

(2) Many contemporary interpreters of Paul will no doubt cast a suspicious eye at the purely theological tack followed in this study, arguing that such an approach is simplistic and passé. They would rather appeal to the social sciences as a new hermeneutic for uncovering the message of Paul. But this new avenue for investigating the apostle's writings must extricate itself from two countercriticisms. (a) How can the sociology of religion guard against anachronistically reading Paul in terms of modern theory? Which theory unlocks the meaning of Paul's letters anyway: cognitive dissonance? typologies of conflict? sectarian movement? Weberian leadership? Albert Schweitzer's masterful book on *The Quest for the Historical Jesus* demonstrated that throughout the years, one theologian after the next had projected his own views of Jesus onto the Gospels, rather than letting the Gospels announce their own perspective on Jesus. A book similar to "Jesus Through Many Eyes" could be written about our subject, "Paul Through Many Eyes" and, unfortunately, with similar results—especially if one follows the sociology of religion approach without question. (b) The application of the social sciences to Pauline literature runs the risk of being reductionistic. That is, one is too easily tempted to reduce theology to sociology, without leaving room for the work of the supernatural.

(3) The defense of Paul's authorship of these letters besides the ones commonly accepted as authentic offered in this work is refutable. While such an issue will probably not be solved in the near future, nor should it ever be a test of faith, this particular author has come to look suspiciously on the older criteria used for ascertaining Paul's authorship of this letter or that. Recent research on the subject, especially computer analysis, appears to be overturning some long-cherished conclusions in this regard. Moreover, this writer has become convinced that the eschatological tension resulting from the overlapping of the two ages is a constant in the Pauline *corpus* and speaks forcefully of his authorship or, at the very least, coauthorship of the disputable letters. In the final analysis, it will be the reader who must determine the accuracy, or lack thereof, of these three responses to possible criticisms of this work.

SELECTED BIBLIOGRAPHY

PRIMARY LITERATURE

Aland, K., C. Martini, B. Metzger, and A. Wikgren, eds. *The Greek New Testament*. 3d ed. New York: American Bible Society, 1975.

Charles, R. H. *The Apocrypha and Pseudepigrapha of the Old Testament in English*. 2 vols. Oxford: Clarendon, 1913.

Charlesworth, James H. *The Old Testament Pseudepigrapha*. 2 vols. New York: Doubleday, 1983.

Epstein, I., ed. *The Babylonian Talmud*. London: Soncino Press, 1948.

Etheridge, J. W., ed. *The Targumim of Onkelos and Jonathen Ben Uzziel on the Pentateuch Genesis and Exodus*. New York: KTAV, 1968. First published in 1862.

Freedman, H. and M. Simon, eds. and trans. *Midrash Rabbah*. London: Soncino Press, 1938.

Friedlander, Gerald, trans. *Pirke de Rabbi Eliezer*. New York: Hermon Press, 1970.

Hennecke, E. "Introduction to Apocalypses and Related Subjects." *New Testament Apocrypha*. Ed. W. Schneemelcher. Vol. 2. Philadelphia: Westminster, 1963–65.

Luther, Martin. *Luther's Works*. Vols. 26–27. Ed. J. Pelikan. St. Louis: Concordia, 1963, 1964.

_____. *Luther's Works*. Vol. 34. Ed. Lewis W. Spitz. Philadelphia: Muhlenberg Press, 1960.

Rahlf, Alfred. *Septuaginta*. Vols. 1–2. Worttenbergische Bibelaustalt Stuttgart, 1935.

Rouse, W. H. D. *Great Dialogues of Plato*. New York: Mentor Books, 1956.

Vermes, G. *The Dead Sea Scrolls in English*. Baltimore: Penguin, 1962 (rev. ed., 1987).

REFERENCE WORKS

Arndt, William F., and T. Wilbur Gingrich. *A Greek-English Lexicon of the New Testament and Other Early Christian Literature*. Chicago: University of Chicago Press, 1958.

Blass, F., and A. Debrunner. *A Greek Grammar of the New Testament and Other Early Christian Literature*. Trans. Robert W. Funk. Chicago: University of Chicago Press, 1961.

Brown, Colin, ed. *Dictionary of New Testament Theology*. 3 vols. Grand Rapids: Zondervan, 1980.

Kittel, Gerhard, ed. *Theological Dictionary of the New Testament*. Trans. G. W. Bromiley. Grand Rapids: Eerdmans, 1964.

SECONDARY LITERATURE

Alstrup, Nils. "The Neglected Factor in New Testament Theology." *Reflection* 73:1 (1975): 5–8.

Arnold, Clinton E. *Ephesians: Power and Magic: The Concept of Power in Ephesians in Light of Its Historical Setting*. SNTSMS 63. Cambridge: University Press, 1989.

Arrington, French L. *Paul's Aeon Theology in 1 Corinthians*. Washington, D.C.: University Press of America, 1978.

Aulén, Gustaf. *Christus Victor: A Historical Study of the Three Main Types of the Idea of the Atonement*. Trans. A. G. Hebert. New York: Macmillan, 1969.

Aune, David E. *The Cultic Setting of Realized Eschatology*. Supp.Nov.T 28. Leiden: E. J. Brill, 1972.

_____. *The New Testament in Its Literary Environment*. Philadelphia: Westminster, 1987.

Badenas, Robert. *Christ the End of the Law: Romans 10:4 in Pauline Perspective*. JSNT Supp.Ser. 10. Sheffield: JSOT, 1985.

Balch, David L. *Let Wives Be Submissive to Their Husbands*. SBLMS 26. Chico, Calif.: Scholars Press, 1981.

Barrett, C. K. *A Commentary on the Epistle to the Romans*. HNTC. New York: Harper, 1957.

_____. *A Commentary on the First Epistle to the Corinthians*. HNTC. New York: Harper & Row, 1968.

Bartchy, S. Scott. *First-Century Slavery and 1 Corinthians 7:21*. SBLDS 2. Missoula, Mont.: Scholars Press, 1971.

Barth, Karl. *Church Dogmatics*, II. Eds. G. W. Bromiley and T. F. Torrance. Edinburgh: T. & T. Clark, 1936.

Bassler, Jouette M. "Adam, Eve and the Pastor. The Use of Genesis 2, 2 in the Pastoral Epistles." *Genesis 1–3 in the History of Exegesis. Intrigue in the Garden*. Ed. Gregory Allen Robbins. Lewiston, N.Y.: Edwin Mellen, 1988.

Baur, F. C. *Paul, the Apostle of Jesus Christ. His Life and Work, His Epistles and His Doctrine*. London: Williams and Norgate, 1873.

_____. *The Church History of the First Three Centuries*. 3d ed. London: Williams and Norgate, 1878–79.

Beasley-Murray, George. *Baptism in the New Testament*. New York: Macmillan, 1962.

Bedale, S. "The Meaning of Kephalê in the Pauline Epistles." *JTS* 5 (1954): 211–15.

Beker, J. Christiaan. *Paul the Apostle: The Triumph of God in Life and Thought.* Philadelphia: Fortress, 1980.

Berkhof, Hendrik. "Israel as a Theological Problem in the Christian Church." *JES* 1 (1969): 329–47.

Berkouwer, G. C. *The Return of Christ.* Trans. James van Oosterom. Ed. Marlin J. Van Elderen. Grand Rapids: Eerdmans, 1972.

Best, Ernst. *One Body in Christ. A Study in the Relationship of the Church to Christ in the Epistles of the Apostle Paul.* London: SPCK, 1955.

Betz, Hans Dieter. *Der Apostel Paulus und die Sokratische Tradition. Beiträge zur Historischen Theologie.* Tübingen: J. C. B. Mohr (Paul Siebeck), 1972.

____. *Galatians. A Commentary on Paul's Letter to the Churches in Galatia.* Hermeneia. Philadelphia: Fortress, 1979.

Borkamm, Henrich. *Luther's Doctrine of the Two Kingdoms.* Trans. Karl H. Hertz. FBBS. Philadelphia: Fortress, 1966.

Bousset, Wilhelm. *Kyrios Christos.* Trans. John E. Steely. Nashville: Abingdon, 1970.

Brown, Raymond. *The Semitic Background of the Term "Mystery" in the New Testament.* FBBS 21. Philadelphia: Fortress, 1968.

Bruce, F. F. *The Epistle of Paul to the Romans: An Introduction and Commentary.* TNTC. Grand Rapids: Eerdmans, 1963.

____. *The Epistles to the Colossians, to Philemon and to Ephesians.* NIGNTC. Grand Rapids: Eerdmans, 1984.

____. *The Epistle to the Galatians.* NIGNTC. Grand Rapids: Eerdmans, 1982.

Bultman, Rudolf. "The Christian Hope and the Problem of Demythologizing." *ExpT* 65 (1953, 1954): 228–30.

Bultmann, Rudolf. *Der Stil der Paulinsichen Predigt und die Kynisch-Stoische Diatribe.* FRLANT 13. Göttingen: Vandenhoeck & Ruprecht, 1910.

____. *Theology of the New Testament.* Vol. 1. Trans. Kendrick Grobel. New York: Charles Scribner's, 1951.

____. *Primitive Christianity in Contemporary Setting.* Trans. R. H. Fuller. New York: World Publishing, 1956.

____. "The New Testament and Mythology." *Kêrygma and Myth: A Theological Debate.* Ed. H. E. Bartsh. Trans. R. H. Fuller. New York: Harper & Row, 1961.

____. "Prophecy and Fulfillment." *Essays on Old Testament Hermeneutics.* Ed. Claus Westermann. Richmond, Va.: John Knox, 1963.

Cadbury, H. J. "The Dilemma of Ephesians." *NTS* 5 (1958–59): 101.

Carr, Wesley. *Angels and Principalities. The Background, Meaning and Development of the Pauline Phrase Hai Archai Kai Hai Exousiai.* SNTSM 42. Cambridge: University Press, 1981.

Carson, D. A., Douglas J. Moo, and Leon Morris. *An Introduction to the New Testament.* Grand Rapids: Zondervan, 1992.

Cerfaux, L. *The Church in the Theology of St. Paul.* Trans. Geoffrey Webb and Adrian Walker. New York: Herder and Herder, 1959.

Clarke, Adam. *Commentary on the Whole Bible.* Grand Rapids: Baker, 1967.

Conzelmann, Hans. *1 Corinthians.* Hermeneia. Philadelphia: Fortress, 1975.

Cousar, Charles B. "A Theology of the Cross. The Death of Jesus in the Pauline Letters." *Overtures to Biblical Theology.* Minneapolis: Fortress, 1990.

Cranfield, C. E. B. "Paul and the Law." *SJT* 17 (1964): 43–68.

_____. *The Epistle to the Romans I–VIII.* ICC. Edinburgh: T. & T. Clark, 1975.

_____. *The Epistle to the Romans IX–XVI.* ICC. Edinburgh: T. & T. Clark, 1977.

Cullmann, Oscar. *Christ and Time. The Primitive Christian Conception of Time and History.* Trans. Floyd V. Filson. Philadelphia: Westminster, 1950.

Davies, W. D. *Paul and Rabbinic Judaism. Some Rabbinic Elements in Pauline Theology.* New York: Harper & Row, 1948.

_____. *Torah in the Messianic Age and/or the Age to Come.* SBLMS 7. Philadelphia: Society of Biblical Literature, 1952.

De Boer, Martinus C. *The Defeat of Death. Apocalyptic Eschatology in 1 Corinthians 15 and Romans 5.* JSNT Supp.Ser. 22. Sheffield: JSOT Press, 1988.

Deissmann, Adolf. "Prolegomena to the Biblical Letters and Epistles." *Bible Studies.* Edinburgh: T. & T. Clark, 1901.

_____. *Paul, A Study in Social and Religious History.* 2d ed. Trans. W. E. Wilson. Gloucester, Mass.: Peter Smith, 1972.

Dibelius, Martin, and Hans Conzelman. *The Pastoral Epistles.* Trans. P. Buttolph and A. Yarbro. Hermeneia. Philadelphia: Fortress, 1972.

Dodd, C. H. *The Parables of the Kingdom.* London: Nisbet, 1935.

_____. *The Apostolic Preaching and Its Developments.* New York: Harper, 1944.

_____. "The Mind of Paul II." *New Testament Studies.* Manchester: University Press, 1953.

Drane, John. *Paul: Libertine or Legalist?* London: SPCK, 1975.

Dunn, James D. G. "The Incident at Antioch (Gal 2:11–18)." *JSNT* 18 (1983): 2–57.

_____. *Romans 1–8.* WBC 38a. Waco, Tex.: Word, 1988.

_____. *Romans 9–16.* WBC 38b. Dallas: Word, 1988.

Eichholz, G. *Die Theologie des Paulus im Umriss.* Neukirchen-Vluyn: Neukirchener Verlag, 1972.

Ellis, E. Earle. *Paul and His Recent Interpreters.* Grand Rapids: Eerdmans, 1961.

____. *Pauline Theology. Ministry and Society.* Grand Rapids: Eerdmans, 1989.

Engel, G. "Let the Woman Learn in Silence." *ExpT* 16 (1904–5): 189–90.

Fee, Gordon. *The First Epistle to the Corinthians.* TNICNT. Grand Rapids: Eerdmans, 1987.

____. *1 and 2 Timothy, Titus.* Peabody, Mass.: Hendrickson, 1988.

Ferguson, Everett. *Backgrounds of Early Christianity.* Grand Rapids: Eerdmans, 1987.

Fiorenza, Elisabeth Schüssler. *In Memory of Her.* New York: Crossroad, 1983.

Fitzgerald, John T. *Cracks in an Earthen Vessel. An Examination of the Catalogues of Hardships in the Corinthian Correspondence.* SBLDS 99. Atlanta, Ga.: Scholars Press, 1988.

Fitzmyer, Joseph A. "Pauline Theology." *The Jerome Biblical Commentary.* Eds. Raymond E. Brown, Joseph A. Fitzmyer, Roland Murphy. Englewood Cliffs, N.J.: Prentice-Hall, 1963.

____. *Pauline Theology: A Brief Sketch.* 2d ed. Englewood Cliffs, N.J.: Prentice-Hall, 1989.

Francis, F. O. "Humility and Angelic Worship in Col 2:18." *Conflict at Colossae.* Eds. F. O. Francis and Wayne Meeks. SBLSBS 4. Missoula, Mont.: Scholars Press, 1975.

Gager, John G. "Religion and Social Class in the Early Roman Empire." *The Catacombs and the Colesseum. The Roman Empire as the Setting of Pauline Christianity.* Eds. Stephen Benko and John J. O'Rourke. Valley Forge, Pa.: Judson Press, 1971.

Gaston, Lloyd. *Paul and the Torah.* Vancouver: University of British Columbia Press, 1987.

Gritz, Sharon Hodgin. *Paul, Women Teachers, and the Mother Goddess at Ephesus. A Study of 1 Timothy 2:9–15 in Light of the Religious and Cultural Milieu of the First Century.* Lanham, Md.: University Press of America, 1991.

Grudem, Wayne. "Does *Kephalê* Mean 'Source' or 'Authority Over' in Greek Literature? A Survey of 2,336 Examples." *TJ* 6 (1985): 38–59.

Guthrie, Donald. *New Testament Introduction.* Downers Grove, Ill.: InterVarsity, 1970.

Hammerton-Kelly, R. G. *Pre-Existence, Wisdom, and the Son of Man. A Study of the Idea of Pre-Existence in the New Testament.* SNTSMS 21. Cambridge: University Press, 1973.

Harnack, Adolf. *The Mission and Expansion of Christianity in the First Three Centuries.* Trans. James Moffatt. Gloucester, Mass.: Peter Smith, 1972.

Hays, Richard B. *The Faith of Jesus Christ. An Investigation of the Narrative Substructure of Galatians 3:1–4:11.* SBLDS 56. Chico, Calif.: Scholars Press, 1983.

Hengel, Martin. *Judaism & Hellenism*. 2 vols. Philadelphia: Fortress, 1974.

Hock, Ronald. *The Social Context of Paul's Ministry. Tentmaking and Apostleship*. Philadelphia: Fortress, 1980.

Holmberg, Bengt. *Paul and Power: The Structure of Authority in the Primitive Church as Reflected in the Pauline Epistles*. Philadelphia: Fortress, 1980.

Hooker, Morna. "Adam in Romans 1." *NTS* 6 (1960): 297–306.

James, M. R. *The Apocryphal New Testament*. Oxford: Clarendon, 1926.

Jeremias, Joachim. *The Eucharistic Words of Jesus*. Philadelphia: Westminster, 1966.

Jewett, Robert. "The Agitators and the Galatian Congregation." *NTS* 17 (1970–71): 198–212.

Käsemann, Ernst. "Die Anfänge christlicher Theologie." Reprinted as "On the Subject of Primitive Christian Apocalyptic." *New Testament Questions of Today*. Trans. W. J. Montague. Philadelphia: Fortress, 1969.

_____. "The Righteousness of God in Paul." *New Testament Questions of Today*, 168–87.

_____. *Perspectives on Paul*. Trans. Margaret Kohl. Philadelphia: Fortress, 1971.

_____. *Commentary on Romans*. Trans. Geoffrey Bromiley. Grand Rapids: Eerdmans, 1980.

Kelly, J. N. D. *A Commentary on the Pastoral Epistles*. New York: Harper & Row, 1963.

Kennedy, H. A. A. *St. Paul's Conceptions of the Last Things*. London: Hodder and Stoughton, 1904.

_____. *St. Paul and the Mystery Religions*. London: Hodder and Stoughton, 1913.

Kidd, Reggie M. *Wealth and Beneficence in the Pastoral Epistles*. SBLDS 122. Atlanta, Ga.: Scholars Press, 1990.

Kim, Seyoon. *The Origin of Paul's Gospel*. WUNT 2, 10. Tübingen: J. C. B. Mohr (Paul Siebeck), 1981.

Klausner, Joseph. *The Idea of the Messiah in Israel, From Its Beginning to the Completion of the Mishnah*. Trans. W. F. Stipespring. New York: Macmillan, 1955.

Kline, William. *God's Chosen People: A Corporate View of Election*. Grand Rapids: Zondervan, 1990.

Kloppenborg, J. "Pre-Pauline Formula in 1 Corinthians 15:3–5." *CBQ* 40 (1978): 351–67.

Knox, Wilfred L. *St. Paul and the Church of the Gentiles*. Cambridge: University Press, 1939.

Koch, Klaus. *The Rediscovery of Apocalyptic. A Polemical Work on a Neglected Area of Biblical Studies and Its Damaging Effects on Theology and Philosophy*. Studies in Biblical Theology. London: SCM Press, 1972.

Kreitzer, L. Joseph. *Jesus and God in Paul's Eschatology*. JSNT Supp.Ser. 19. Sheffield: JSOT Press, 1987.

Kümmel, W. G. *Römer 7 und die Bekehrung des Paulus*. Leipzig, 1929.

_____. *Promise and Fulfillment. The Eschatological Message of Jesus*. Naperville, Ill.: A. R. Allenson, 1957.

_____. *Introduction to the New Testament*. Nashville: Abingdon, 1975.

Kung, Hans. *The Church*. New York: Sheed & Ward, 1968.

Ladd, George. *A Theology of the New Testament*. Grand Rapids: Eerdmans, 1974.

Lane, William L. "1 Tim iv. 1–3. An Early Instance of Over-Realized Eschatology?" *NTS* 11 (1965): 164–67.

Liefeld, Walter L. "Women, Submission and Ministry in 1 Corinthians." *Women, Authority and the Bible*. Ed. Alvera Mickelsen. Downers Grove, Ill.: InterVarsity, 1986.

Lincoln, Andrew. *Paradise Now and Not Yet*. SNTSMS 43. Cambridge: University Press, 1981.

_____. *Ephesians*. WBC 42. Waco, Tex.: Word, 1990.

Lohse, Eduard. *Colossians and Philemon*. Hermeneia, Philadelphia: Fortress, 1971.

Longenecker, Bruce W. "Different Answers to Different Issues: Israel, the Gentiles and Salvation History in Romans 9–11." *JSNT* 36 (1989): 95–123.

Longenecker, Richard N. *The Ministry and Message of Paul*. Grand Rapids: Eerdmans, 1971.

MacDonald, Dennis Ronald. *There Is No Male and Female*. HDS 10. Philadelphia: Fortress, 1987.

MacGregor, G. H. C. "Principalities and Powers: The Cosmic Background of Saint Paul's Thought." *NTS* 1 (1954): 17–28.

Machen, J. G. *The Origin of Paul's Religion*. Grand Rapids: Eerdmans, 1947.

Marshall, I. Howard. *Luke: Historian and Theologian*. Exeter: Paternoster Press, 1970.

Martin, Brice L. *Christ and the Law in Paul*. Supp.Nov.T 62. Leiden: E. J. Brill, 1989.

Martin, Ralph. *Carmen Christi Philippians ii.5–11 in Recent Interpretation and in the Setting of Early Christian Worship*. SNTMS 4. Cambridge: University Press, 1967.

Martyn, Louis. "Apocalyptic Antinomies in the Letter to the Galatians." *NTS* 31 (1985): 410–24.

McElewey, N. J. "Conversion, Circumcision and the Law." *NTS* 20 (1973): 319–41.

McKelvey, R. J. *The New Temple*. Oxford: University Press, 1969.

Mearns, C. L. "Early Eschatological Development in Paul: The Evidence of I and II Thessalonians." *NTS* 27 (1980–81): 137–58.

Meeks, Wayne A. "The Image of the Adrogyne. Some Uses of a Symbol in Earliest Christianity." *HR* 13 (1974): 165–208.

Minear, Paul S. *Images of the Church in the New Testament.* Philadelphia: Westminster Press, 1960.

Montefiore, C. G. *Judaism and St. Paul.* London: Max Goschen, 1914.

Moo, Douglas. "1 Timothy 2:11–15: Meaning and Significance." *TJ* 1 (1980): 62–83.

Morris, Leon. *The Apostolic Preaching of the Cross.* Grand Rapids: Eerdmans, 1955.

Munck, Johannes. *Paul and the Salvation of Mankind.* Trans. F. C. Clarke. Richmond, Va.: John Knox, 1959.

Murmelstein, B. "Adam, ein Beitrag zur Messiaslehre." *WZKM* 35 (1928): 242–75.

Neill, Stephen. *The Interpretation of the New Testament 1861–1901.* London: Oxford University Press, 1964.

Neumann, Kenneth J. *The Authenticity of the Pauline Epistles in Light of Stylostatistical Analysis.* SBLDS 120. Atlanta, Ga.: Scholars Press, 1990.

O'Brien, Peter T. *Colossians, Philemon.* WBC 44. Waco, Tex.: Word, 1982.

O'Rourke, John J. "Roman Law and the Early Church." *The Catacombs and the Colosseum. The Roman Empire as the Setting of Primitive Christianity.* Eds. Stephen Benko and John J. O'Rourke. Valley Forge, Pa.: Judson Press, 1971.

Pate, C. Marvin. *Adam Christology as the Exegetical and Theological Substructure of 2 Corinthians 4:7–5:21.* Lanham, Md.: University Press of America, 1991.

_____. *The Glory of Adam and the Afflictions of the Righteous: Pauline Suffering in Context.* New York: Edwin Mellen, 1993.

Polluck, John. *The Apostle.* Wheaton, Ill.: Victor Books, 1972.

Prior, Michael. *Paul the Letter-Writer and the Second Letter to Timothy.* JSNT Supp.Ser. 23. Sheffield: JSOT Press, 1989.

Räisänen, Heikki. *Paul and the Law.* Tübingen: J. C. B. Mohr (Paul Siebeck), 1983.

Ramsay, Sir William. *The Cities of St. Paul.* Grand Rapids: Baker Books, 1949.

_____. *St. Paul the Traveller and the Roman Citizen.* Grand Rapids: Baker Books, 1972.

Reitzenstein, Richard. *Hellenistic Mystery Religions.* Trans. John E. Steely. Pittsburgh: Pickwick Press, 1978.

Richard, E. Randolph. *The Secretary in the Letters of Paul.* WUNT 2, 42. Tübingen: J. C. B. Mohr (Paul Siebeck), 1991.

Ridderbos, H. N. *When the Time Had Fully Come.* Grand Rapids: Eerdmans, 1957.

Ridderbos, Herman. *Paul: An Outline of His Theology.* Trans. John Richard Dewitt. Grand Rapids: Eerdmans, 1975.

Rowley, H. H. *The Relevance of Apocalyptic, A Study of Jewish and Christian Apocalypses from Daniel to the Revelation.* London and Rodhill: Lutterworth, 1947.

Russel, D. S. *The Method and Message of Jewish Apocalyptic.* Philadelphia: Westminster, 1964.

Sanday, W. and A. C. Headlam. *The Epistle to the Romans.* ICC. Edinburgh: T. & T. Clark, 1895.

Sanders, E. P. *Paul and Palestinian Judaism. A Comparison of Religions.* Philadelphia: Fortress, 1977.

Schnabel, Eckhard J. *Law and Wisdom from Ben Sirato to Paul.* WUNT 2, 16. Tübingen: J. C. B. Mohr (Paul Siebeck), 1985.

Schnackenburg, Rudolf. *The Church in the New Testament.* New York: Herder and Herder, 1965.

Schoeps, H. J. *Paul: The Theology of the Apostle in the Light of Jewish Religious History.* Philadelphia: Westminster, 1961.

Scholer, David M. "1 Timothy 2:9–15 and the Place of Women in the Church's Ministry." *Women, Authority and the Bible.* Ed. Alvera Mickelsen. Downers Grove, Ill.: InterVarsity, 1986.

Schweitzer, Albert. *The Mysticism of Paul the Apostle.* Trans. William Montgomery. New York: Henry Holt, 1931.

Scroggs, Robin. *The Last Adam.* Philadelphia: Fortress, 1966.

_____. "Paul and the Eschatological Women." *JAAR* 40 (1972): 283–303.

Seeley, David. *The Noble Death: Graeco-Roman Martyrology and Paul's Concept of Salvation.* JSNT Supp.Ser. 28. Sheffield: Sheffield Press, 1990.

Sherwin-White, Adrian N. *Roman Society and Roman Law in the New Testament.* New York: Oxford University Press, 1963.

Smith, Jonathan Z. "The Garments of Shame." *HR* 5 (1966): 217–38.

Snodgrass, Klyne R. "Galatians 3:28—Conundrum or Solution?" *Women, Authority and the Bible.* Ed. Alvera Mickelsen. Downers Grove, Ill.: InterVarsity, 1986.

Stanley, Susie C. "Response to Snodgrass' Galatians 3:28: Conundrum or Solution?" *Women, Authority and the Bible.* Ed. Alvera Mickelsen. Downers Grove, Ill.: InterVarsity, 1986.

Stendahl, Kristen. "The Apostle Paul and the Introspective Conscience of the West." *HTR* 56 (1963): 199–215.

_____. *Paul Among Jews and Gentiles.* Philadelphia: Fortress, 1976.

Stone, Michael E. "Coherence and Inconsistency in the Apocalypses: The Case of 'The End' in 4 Ezra." *JBL* 102 (1983): 229–43.

Stowers, Stanley K. *The Diatribe and Paul's Letter to the Romans.* SBLDS 57. Chico, Calif.: Scholars Press, 1981.

Thielman, Frank. *From Plight to Solution. A Jewish Framework for Understanding Paul's View of the Law in Galatians and Romans.* Supp.Nov.T 61. Leiden: E. J. Brill, 1989.

Thiselton, A. C. "Realized Eschatology at Corinth." *NTS* 24 (1978): 519–26.

Tomson, Peter. *Paul and the Jewish Law: Halakha in the Letters of the Apostle to the Gentiles*. Minneapolis: Fortress, 1990.

Towner, Phillip H. *The Goal of Our Instruction. The Structure of Theology and Ethics in the Pastoral Epistles*. JSNT Supp.Ser. 34. Sheffield: JSOT Press, 1989.

VanRoon, A. *The Authenticity of Ephesians*. Supp.Nov.T 39. Leiden: E. J. Brill, 1974.

VanUnnik, W. C. *Tarsus or Jerusalem: The City of Paul's Youth*. London: Epworth, 1962.

Vielhauer, Philip. *Geschichte der urchristlicher Literatur: Einleitung im das Neue Testament, die Apokryphen und die apostolischer Väter*. Berlin/New York: Walter de Gruyter, 1975.

Volf, Judith M. Gundry. *Paul and Perseverance. Staying in and Falling Away*. Louisville, Ky.: Westminster/John Knox, 1990.

Von Campenhausen, H. *Ecclesiastical Authority and Spiritual Power*. Stanford, Calif.: Stanford University Press, 1969.

Vos, Gerhardus. *The Pauline Eschatology*. Grand Rapids: Eerdmans, 1952.

Wagner, Gunther. *Pauline Baptism and the Pagan Mysteries: The Problem of the Pauline Doctrine of Baptism in Romans VI.1–11, in the Light of Its Religio-Historical Parallels*. Trans. J. P. Smith. Edinburgh and London: Oliver & Boyd, 1967.

Wanamaker, Charles A. *The Epistles to the Thessalonians*. NIGTC. Grand Rapids: Eerdmans, 1990.

Wedderburn, A. J. M. *Baptism & Resurrection. Studies in Pauline Theology Against Its Graeco-Roman Background*. WUNT 44. Tübingen: J. C. B. Mohr (Paul Siebeck), 1987.

Westerholm, Stephen. *Israel's Law and the Church's Faith: Paul and His Recent Interpreters*. Grand Rapids: Eerdmans, 1988.

White, John Lee. *The Form and Function of the Body of the Greek Letter*. SBLDS 2. Missoula, Mont.: Scholars Press, 1972.

Wrede, William. *Paul*. Lexington, Ky.: American Library Association Committee on Reprinting, 1962.

Yamauchi, Edwin, *Pre-Christian Gnosticism*. Grand Rapids: Eerdmans, 1973.

Zahn, Theodore. *Die Apostelgeschichte des Lukas*. KNT 5. Leipzig and Erlangen: Deichert, 1921.

SUBJECT INDEX

SCRIPTURE INDEX